Adam Shand is a leading Australian author and journalist. A Walkley Award–winning reporter with experience in television, print, radio and on-line, Shand is the author of three other non-fiction titles: *BIG SHOTS: Carl Williams & the Gangland Murders*, *The Skull: Informers, Hitmen and Australia's Toughest Cop* and *King of Thieves: The Adventures of Arthur Delaney and The Kangaroo Gang*.

Over a 25-year career, Shand has reported on high finance, African affairs and crime and justice. He is currently a freelance journalist and screenwriter.

OUTLAWS

THE TRUTH ABOUT AUSTRALIAN BIKERS

ADAM SHAND

ALLEN&UNWIN

SYDNEY · MELBOURNE · AUCKLAND · LONDON

First published in 2011
This edition published in 2013

Allen & Unwin
Sydney, Melbourne, Auckland, London

83 Alexander Street
Crows Nest NSW 2065
Australia
Phone: (61 2) 8425 0100
Fax: (61 2) 9906 2218
Email: info@allenandunwin.com
Web: www.allenandunwin.com

Cataloguing-in-Publication details are available
from the National Library of Australia
www.trove.nla.gov.au

ISBN 978 1 74331 196 7

Set in 11.5/16 pt Bembo by Post Pre-press Group, Australia
Printed and bound in Australia by the SOS Print + Media Group

10 9 8 7 6 5 4 3 2

For my children, Jack and Noliwe.
Popular wisdom isn't always so wise.

CONTENTS

CONTENTS

SUBURBAN MAN AND THE 1 PER CENT

The driver hears the threat long before the infernal rumble takes ghastly form in his mirrors.

A biker is snaking his way through the cars at the traffic lights. The handlebars of his chopped Harley all but graze the paintwork of the cars as he glides to the front of the queue.

He stops, the bike straddling the pedestrian crossing.

Behind reflective sunglasses, the biker's expression is impassive, but the mouth, amid a thick ginger beard, is set in an expression of grim belligerent assertiveness. He plants his heavy steel-capped boots on the road and crosses his thick tattooed arms across his chest. He is a massive, implacable force.

A man driving a large GM Suburban is displeased at losing his pole position at the lights. He throws a poisonous glare at the biker's back. While everyone else is following the rules, the biker is making his own, doing what he likes.

It's an opportunity to see the beast up close, like viewing a lion

1

at a safari park. He's dressed in familiar biker garb: faded grimy jeans, a plaid shirt and a leather vest.

There's no club insignia on the vest, no rocker on the back explaining which 'gang' he is from. Bikers say that's how it is now—if you ride in your club 'colours' you're going to be stopped by cops every five minutes. A day on the bike with a patch on your back becomes a procession of questions, warrant checks and defect notices. So mostly the patch is reserved for massed club runs, quick escapes to the country, or days when you feel defiant enough to take it all on.

But even without the patch, there's no mistaking what he represents—this is the bikie menace. This is the 1 per cent of bikers that no-one else will claim. He lives beyond the pale.

Suburban Man knows all this from shows he has watched on pay TV. Amid the peace and tranquillity of a Sunday morning, it's proof the bogeyman still lives. The outlaw has blown in from the wastelands of his worst nightmares.

Suburban Man edges his car forward till the bumper is almost touching the back wheel of the Harley. He's letting his wife know he won't be intimidated. She wants none of this.

The biker is now aware of the vast chrome grille looming over him. He's used to this, and to people's belligerent attitude towards him.

His reputation sparks fear and loathing and he enjoys that. It reminds him that the world is divided into Us and Them. The hatred validates his choice to become an outlaw. There's no justice; there's just us.

The biker suddenly throws his Harley into gear and, after a cursory check for oncoming traffic, he breaks the red light. But rather than just blast through the intersection, he drops his hip and takes the machine sideways onto the pedestrian crossing. It's the same cheap, irritating manoeuvre that cyclists use every day, but if you pull it on a Harley, it looks infinitely more heinous.

As the back wheel smokes and fishtails, the biker looks at Suburban Man from over his shoulder. *C'mon, he seems to be saying, no-one will know and no-one will be hurt—even if the cop station is just 50 metres away. Just make a decision.*

Then the rider snaps the back wheel under him and opens the throttle. As he guns the bike up the hill, there's a great thunderous roar that echoes off the walls of the concrete canyon.

You can read the disgust on the face of Suburban Man. This is a clear statement, a hideous wet fart in his face: *Part of you wants to be me. You would run me off into those parked cars, if you could. But you can't because, in your heart, you are a sheep.*

For all his badness, there are moments when the biker feels free, or what he believes it to be. And freedom, even to be bad, is a rare thing indeed.

1

MEDIA MIKE AND THE MORAL PANIC

In 1996 the then South Australian Opposition Leader, Mike Rann, became the herald of a new dark age. He warned of a looming bikie war that state governments up to that point had ignored at their peril.

Rann told parliament that an investigation by New Zealand police into trans-Tasman gang activity had revealed that by the year 2000 there would be just six Australian clubs remaining: the Hells Angels, the Outlaws, the Bandidos, the Rebels, the Black Uhlans and the Nomads. The balance, up to fifty clubs, would be consumed by force or agreement into the Top Six.

It was a powerful and enduring notion, demonstrating that bikers posed a new threat to the social order. A once disorganised rabble, the bikies could apparently form a parallel government, just as US mobster Charles 'Lucky' Luciano had done in creating the National Crime Syndicate for the Mafia back in the 1930s.

The 'Australia 2000' pact would apparently centralise the

control of crime worth hundreds of millions of dollars a year into the hands of the six foundation clubs. Outbreaks of inter-club violence could be tracked back to a 'fight for supremacy', with the six clubs pushing for exclusive control of turf. Rann said he had been warned of the potential for bikie violence when he visited the FBI that year and at the time had passed those warnings on to the South Australian Police (SAPOL), the National Crime Authority 'and even in person to the Prime Minister' (then—Liberal leader John Howard). But his earnest advice had fallen on deaf ears.

In 2002 Mike Rann became the Premier of South Australia in a minority government. With his background first as a political journalist with the New Zealand Broadcasting Corporation and later as a speechwriter for the legendary Don Dunstan, he was media savvy and inevitably came to be dubbed 'Media Mike'. According to Flinders University lecturer Haydon Manning, Rann was a 'self-consciously constructed' leader who 'assiduously appealed to popular prejudices for his tough and almost perpetual campaign on law and order'. Successful leaders 'command attention and make it look as though they have discovered the neglected concerns of the general public. Rann was a champion of such politics', Manning concluded.

For a time Rann was one of the most successful state politicians in Australia. His attempts to take on the bikies resonated right around the country and were mimicked by many of his fellow premiers. In one sense, he was a founding father of the 1% Nation. Adelaide had long been regarded as the bikie capital of Australia, setting the tone for how the clubs were organised and run around the country. To defeat them here would have national implications, the theory ran.

But his campaign to eliminate this scourge would ultimately only serve to unite the bikies. And a large group of sympathisers and friends would in time discover they had a common cause with them.

In such matters, of course, inevitably what goes around comes around. And in Australian state politics what comes around has often been around the circuit at least once before. Rann's master plan was, in effect, to revive the old consorting laws, which police had used to restrict the interaction of the criminal classes until they fell into disuse in the 1980s.

South Australia had in fact been the first state to introduce consorting laws, in 1928, giving police the power to prevent the mingling of habitual criminals, drunkards, thieves, prostitutes, fortune tellers and vagrants. The other states soon followed: New South Wales in 1929, Queensland and Victoria in 1931, Tasmania 1935 and Western Australia in 1955.

Yet, while revolted by the bikers' wild and unkempt appearance, the South Australian community had never held any burning objection to them until the mid-1970s.

The roots of the biker subculture that emerged in Adelaide from the late 1960s had been purely social. Every Saturday afternoon, they had gathered out the front of Burnie's Bar on Rundle Street, long before it became a pedestrian mall. They would hang out all afternoon, talking motorcycles and swapping recent war stories about life on the road. All bikers were welcome, even as they formed into clubs under various patches. The early clubs had included the Undertakers, who were mostly the sons of European migrants, and the Iroquois, who were Anglo boys from Elizabeth. The Filthy Few became the Mandamas (Latin for 'We Command') after the Hells Angels had objected to them using Filthy Few, which they regarded as the property of their club. There were Reapers, Barbarians and a grab bag of other clubs, making up a total population of about 200 bikers in 1974.

Sometimes up to a hundred bikers, plus their women and machines, would line the footpath on Rundle Street without attracting any grief from the cops. They would drink and loll about, talking shit and planning their next debauch before heading off into the night. There was always a party to go to, or one to crash, where they were happy to flog a few footballers or other bikers if the chance arose.

Today's old-timers still remember fondly those days. The occasional serious dispute between clubs was settled in time-honoured fashion—a punch-on at a discreet location beyond public view.

But on 4 June 1974, everything changed after what the press called 'a wild beach brawl' at Port Gawler, an hour north of Adelaide. It started as a disagreement between the Iroquois and the Undertakers, but soon affiliated clubs and friends lined up behind the two clubs.

As eyewitnesses remember it, the fight was over ethnicity. The Iroquois believed the Undertakers were getting out hand and failing to show respect to the established order, which mirrored chauvinistic attitudes in the broader society. The Iroquois were going to put 'the wogs' in their place. But it seemed the wogs had plenty of mates prepared to show the Aussies that the world was changing.

After dark two mobs, totalling more than a hundred bikers, gathered on the edge of a highway above a deserted beach. They left their bikes and walked down through the scrubby coastal dunes ready for battle, carrying hockey sticks, cricket bats and motorcycle chains. All this would have stayed below the radar if one biker had not turned up with a shotgun.

In the melee that followed four shots were fired and one biker was wounded in the chest, a few others less seriously. Police made eighty-five arrests and as the *Advertiser* newspaper later noted, South Australia had a 'new breed of bad guys': 'Port Gawler is recognised among the biker fraternity as being the end of an old era of biker, and the beginning of a new one,' the paper solemnly opined.

Out of the public outrage that followed Port Gawler, a new police squad emerged, which would become infamous. The leader of the Bikie Squad, Rodney Piers (Sam) Bass, was a very unusual policeman by today's standards. In fact, some bikers said if Bass hadn't been a cop he would have made a fearsome biker. A former champion speedway rider, Bass understood the mentality of the motorcyclist—how his machine symbolised a spirit of rebellion. He knew that this was a genuine sub-culture like the hippies, not a dedicated crime group.

I found Sam Bass in 2011 living in a quiet coastal town six hours' drive from Adelaide on the road to Port Lincoln. A Google search revealed he was now a volunteer ambulance officer and had recently helped deliver a baby on the highway, a far cry from his rollicking days as head of the Bikie Squad. He had fond memories of tangling with the Rundle Street biker crowd: 'There was the odd druggie and rapist among them, a few thieves as well, but the overwhelming majority were actually decent sort of blokes,' he told me.

Bass believed that by mingling with the bikers, he would gain some respect and a huge amount of information. So he encouraged his squad of eight members to grow beards and wear their hair long. He himself sported a denim cut-off jacket with a patch, just like the rest of the bikers, and topped off the ensemble with a belt inscribed 'Fat Sam'.

Bass's squad were big, bluff types normally found in pubs and they roared around town on 750cc Suzukis and Yamahas. They were hardly undercover, because news of the 'bikie cops' quickly spread through the clubs. Initially, the bikies warmed to Bass, who drank and played pool alongside them. He seemed to be one of them. When things got out of hand, he was prepared to put aside the badge and duke it out with them, just as the bikers had at Port Gawler.

'I didn't lose too many fights with the bikies, because I was big and strong, but win or lose these were incidents that were never reported,' Bass recalled. 'One night on Hindley Street, Pete [a colleague] and I took on four bikies. We dealt with the first three quite easily, but the fourth one was a huge bloke and he and Pete had a huge stoush that went on for nearly twenty minutes, right there in the street. When he finally got the better of him, Pete turned to me and asked: "Why the hell didn't you back me up?" I said it was too much fun watching him, it was like a boxing match.'

In the early days, there was little confrontation. Bass had used his friendly relations with the clubs to quietly gather intelligence for other squads to act on, compiling dossiers on key targets in the clubs. After the Port Gawler incident, the state government had in fact directed the police to drive the bikies out of South Australia using the consorting laws.

From 1976 to 1981, conflict between Bass and the bikers progressively escalated. The arbitrary power the Consorting Act offered the police, plus Bass's own flexible approach to the law, made him a dangerous and ruthless foe. 'Sometimes you had to break the rules, if you were going to get the job done,' says Bass now, still unrepentant at seventy.

Tom Mackie liked to say that he had never won a fight until he got to Australia.

Growing up on the tough turf of north Auckland in the early 1970s, Mackie and his brother Perry were used to conflict, but taking on the Maori gangs had been a recipe for a weekly flogging. Every Saturday night, the Maori heavies from the south side of town would pile into their old Ford Zephyrs and come looking for a blue at the north-side dances frequented by the Mackie boys and their mates. There were no guns or knives back then, so the worst they would take home was a black eye or a split lip. But as long as they inflicted something similar on the enemy, they would call it a good night out.

But once they got settled in Adelaide in the early 1970s, Tom and Perry didn't lose too many fights and the outlaw motorcycle club they founded in 1974, the Descendants MC, has stood the test of time.

Around Australia, literally hundreds of independent clubs like the Descendants have disappeared over the last thirty-five years. They have been patched over by choice, or by force, as the big US clubs have transformed and dominated the local scene. Others have just disappeared, harassed into non-existence by the police or wives and families anxious that their wayward sons might finally grow up.

Today the Descendants' colours, featuring the mythical griffin with the head of an eagle and body of a lion, still fly over the clubhouse. An inscription over the club reads: 'OF GRIFFINS; So doth it well make out the properties of a Guardian, or any person entrusted; the ears implying attention, the wings celerity of execution, the Lion-like shape, courage and audacity, the hooked bill, reservance and tenacity, also an Embleme of valour and magnanimity, as being compounded of the Eagle and Lion, the noblest Animals in their kinds'. The bikie professor, Arthur Veno, once wrote that the Descendants 'contained some of the hardest bastards you'll ever meet'. To remain viable and independent, they had no other choice than to stand their ground. They had never expanded from a single chapter, but they had never retreated.

A mutual friend took me to meet Tom Mackie at the Descendants' clubhouse in 2008. He was still every inch the outlaw bikie with his long flowing grey hair and goatee beard. His face bore the scars of old battles and he had the almost obligatory limp of the veteran rider, courtesy of a serious motorcycle accident in the 1990s. Ironically, the club had the police to thank for their longevity, he said.

He recalled those far-off times in the 1970s, when the bikers had made matters worse by ridiculing and taunting Bass: 'We'd say, "Thanks Sam—all the pressure you're putting on helps test the mettle of our members and friends." If they didn't fold to him, we knew they were the right kind of blokes for the club.'

Those who failed to cooperate with Fat Sam could expect plenty of attention. After one of the Bikie Squad's motorcycles turned up at the bottom of a dam, it was the Descendants' turn to feel the heat.

In 2010, the club gained access to a slew of old court records through Freedom of Information applications. Included was a report by Mackie's probation officer, Lew D Vincent, which captured the action as Bass unleashed his wrath on the club in the summer of 1977.

'*18/1/77* I have received information to the extent that the Police are "out to get" Tom Mackie and his brother Perry. My contact [a Police Officer] indicates that Sam Bass wants to send Tom "down" for a long time. According to my contact Tom will be arrested for consorting very soon.'

'*18/1/77* Phone call from Tom. I suggested he come and see me this P.M. as wished to discuss the above with him and his forthcoming court appearances.'

But Mackie failed to turn up for the meeting.

'*20/1/77* Phone call from Tom—apology for not keeping appointment. Had been arrested and charged with Consorting as he stepped from the phone box after calling yesterday.'

At the time, Mackie was on bail for two cases of minor assault. He was hardly an accomplished criminal—his entire record consisted of a few fines for summary offences, including theft and forgery, totalling a few hundred dollars—but Bass had set out to crush him. Mackie had racked up more than thirty bookings for consorting with other club members. In December 1976, Bass and his squad had made a seven-hour round trip to Minlaton on the remote Yorke Peninsula simply to catch the Descendants hanging out together in contravention of the Consorting Act. He could add another black mark to the Descendants' files, which would allow him to lay charges against the whole club.

With Mackie on remand in Adelaide Gaol, police poured on the pressure. They charged Tom and brother Perry with the theft of a safe in the northern suburbs. There were more assault charges and threats of more legal action against him.

His probation officer could hardly follow the myriad dramas Tom was living through. 'Somehow so much appears to be going on with Tom I am losing track of what charges are still pending,' Vincent noted in July 1977.

Tom's father had been a sailor and later a customs officer. He had a strong affinity with authority and order. His attitude was that if Tom and Perry's wild ways caused them grief with the police, then so be it. But he thought Bass was going too far in what seemed to be a campaign against his sons. The probation officer wrote: '9/5/77 Visited Tom's parents. Brother Perry was there too. Discussed at some length—Police confirmed Tom's views. Both Mr and Mrs Mackie extremely resentful and bitter toward them.'

Lew Vincent noted he would investigate the views of other parents of 'lads involved in consorting', and would see what action they could muster, 'e.g. Civil Liberties'. But public opinion, of course, was firmly behind the Bikie Squad. Dramatic stories of Bass's derring-do had appeared on the front page of the *Advertiser* while ABC TV's *Weekend Magazine* program had run a national story on 'The Bikie Cop'. Only a good lawyer could help Mackie now.

By September 1977, many members of the Descendants had been sentenced to jail terms of up to three months on consorting charges. Some sentences were suspended on condition that the members did not continue to associate. But of course, they continued to associate regardless, whether in or out of jail. Their bonds of friendship were now strengthened by their defiance of what they believed was an unjust law.

In jail Mackie and his club mates resolved to 'do the time on their ear'. If threatened with discipline or punishment, they would fiercely insist authorities carry it out. They would demand to work seven days a week in the hell of the jail's boiler room or laundry. While other lags feared a transfer to the maximum security jail at Yatala, they would insist upon it.

For the next year Mackie fought the charges. An eighteen-month sentence for assault was reduced on appeal to nine months. The state withdrew a larceny charge relating to the stolen safe and then dropped a lesser charge of illegal use.

Through it all, the club's resolve to remain together had only hardened. Bass had failed to break them. 'He couldn't whip, flog or hang us, so, having put us in jail, he could not punish us any-more,' Mackie now recalls.

But their jail experiences had pushed the Descendants to the margins. While in jail for petty crimes and consorting, some had learnt to be real criminals. The club leaders subsequently turned the focus of recruiting from the Saturday afternoon crowd on Rundle Street to the habitual criminals they had met in the boob. The Descendants rejected any notions of social conformity and embraced their bad boy status with gusto. Hard drugs like heroin began to dominate the recreational menu, where beer and can-nabis had previously been the norm. Soon some of the lads were using or dealing heroin and LSD.

Their experiences with Sam Bass had taught them to be clever and cunning. No-one kept their stashes at home or anywhere else that could be linked to them. So, according to Mackie, police began loading them up. The heat just continued to ratchet up.

One night in early July 1979, the climax of this conflict was reached.

A Descendant nominee, 19-year-old Antonio 'Morelli' Esposito, and two club associates, Mick Carey and Dave De Angelis, arrived at the Arkaba Hotel in downtown Adelaide to do a drug deal. They had agreed to sell heroin to two customers from Melbourne staying in the hotel. But there was no heroin: this was a robbery. Armed with a shotgun and a knife they slipped on balaclavas and prepared to burst into the buyers' room. But the men inside weren't buyers; they were undercover cops.

From the next room Sam Bass and another officer were watching events unfold. As soon as Bass saw the guns and balaclavas, he sprang into action. Esposito allegedly got off two shots, but Bass, from less than six feet away, fired five rounds from his Winchester pump-action shotgun. Esposito took a mortal wound under his left armpit, which blew out the side of his heart. He died there in the breezeway, but Bass kept firing as a warning to any other lurking bikers that he meant business. 'I put one into the doorknob. One in the air conditioner and one into the back window of the room, just in case anybody else wanted to put their heads up,' he recalls today.

It's club folklore that Bass had murdered Esposito in cold blood. According to Carey and De Angelis' version, Morelli had dropped his gun and was putting his hands up when Bass opened fire. How else could you shoot a bloke under the armpit, they asked. But Bass is as adamant today as he ever has been that Esposito opened up first; he says his conscience is blemish-free. 'I could give my evidence just as clearly today as I did back then,' he states with great self-confidence.

Carey and De Angelis both received eight-year sentences for the attempted robbery, but Morelli's death did nothing to dissuade some of his brother bikies from the heroin trade. In 1979, police found a small quantity of heroin in Tom Mackie's garden shed. It wasn't his, he tells me. He claims the police had planted the package with the smaller deal bags inside to build a case for trafficking. Mackie says that when he told his lawyer during a post-arrest telephone call that he had been 'loaded up', the call was interrupted by police. He says he repeated the claim during his four-day trial a year later but it was ignored. No-one, it seemed, would back the word of a bikie over that of a police officer.

In the end, he copped the four-year sentence on the chin. This wasn't his dope, but he had plenty over the past years. This was the square-up.

Getting loaded was a moral victory of sorts for Tom. The police had brought their own dope because they could never catch him with any of his own. The pressure that Bass had brought down had turned Tom into a very good crook. He would do his stretch easy and he would be back flat out with his mates. It was only a matter of time. You couldn't destroy the Descendants with laws, any more than you could kill the mythical griffin. In fact, the more you attacked them, the stronger they became in the minds of the believers.

Earlier in May 1977, a prison psychologist, Warwick Lloyd, had not been optimistic for Mackie's future. His report was among the documents Mackie obtained through FOI. As if club membership was a mental affliction rather than a rational life choice, he wrote:

MACKIE is a leader in the Descendents [sic] Motor Cycle Club and this involvement seems to be the pivot around which he has arranged his life. That Mackie passed three out of 5 Matric subjects and became a foreman at Eastern Projects before he was laid off after a fire forced the business to fold attests to his capabilities. Nevertheless he seems unable to find his niche in life, disinterested in continued study but unhappy with labouring as a vocation. Due to consorting charges laid on the whole club its continual existence, in which Mackie places some store, is in doubt. MACKIE has given little thought to his role in a post-Descendents [sic] world.'

Three decades on, talking to me in 2011 over a beer in the Descendants' clubhouse, Mackie could reflect that it hadn't been such a victory for the police after all. While Mackie was in jail, the Bikie Squad was disbanded soon after and the careers of its members had not prospered. In 1981, the South Australian government held an inquiry into media allegations of police corruption arising from the Bikie Squad era, which largely cleared the force. However, a former Supreme Court judge, Sir Charles Bright, in reviewing the inquiry findings, said he had 'residual suspicions' about one of the eight police officers mentioned. In the end, the South Australian Director of Public Prosecutions did not prosecute the one case that was referred for consideration. In 1981 Sam Bass left active service to become the boss of the Police Union, before quitting the force formally in 1984. His rugged style of 'ways and means' policing had fallen out of favour. In 1993, Bass was elected as the state Liberal member for the seat of Florey but lasted just one term, losing office in 1997.

A couple of the squad members had later committed suicide. In less charitable moments, Mackie had often hoped their deeds of unpunished evil had pressed down on them at the end.

2

THE 99 PER CENT SOLUTION

On 2 January 2001, 120 Gypsy Jokers from around Australia descended on the quiet South Australian seaside town of Beachport for their national run.

A small posse of officers from the STAR Group (the Special Tasks and Rescue tactical group in the SA Police) also made the 383-kilometre journey south down the coast to Beachport to keep an eye on the bikers. Other Adelaide-based police were also around, having attended a siege in the Robe area in the afternoon. When the siege ended peacefully, these police had reportedly gone drinking at the Robe Hotel. According to locals, when it became known that the Jokers were down the road in Beachport, some of the cops started saying they were going to teach the bikies a lesson. Local police had paid little attention to the Jokers as they filled the Beachport Hotel, playing pool and drinking, largely keeping to themselves.

The commander of the STAR Group, Superintendent Thomas

Reiniets, told a different story in a later witness statement. The bikies were 'taking over the hotel', 'getting boozed' and 'committing numerous traffic and behavioural offences', he claimed. However, the only complaint police received about the bikies was that some had allegedly jumped the fence into the Beachport Caravan Park. A tourist was also asked not to take photographs of the members without permission.

The Jokers would later claim Group, Superintendent Rieniets, came looking for a fight. The elite force, acting more like commandos than police, took it upon themselves to do a walk-through of the pub just before closing time at midnight. There had been no complaints from the public or the hotel: guidelines had been agreed upon with the local commanders during liaison. Earlier in the day, the bikers had even happily extinguished a campfire they had lit in contravention of a total fire ban. Patrons in the hotel later described the mood in the pub that night as 'noisy and relaxed'.

But the arrival of these soldier cops changed the game entirely. The most highly trained and best-equipped police in the state had been flown to Beachport to enforce the midnight closing of a pub, a task that a local sergeant on a pushbike had performed for years.

By overriding the local authority, the visiting storm-troopers risked losing theirs. It was now personal—one gang versus another. Not much different from rumbling with another MC, except this gang wouldn't shoot you unless you shot first. There had been rising tension between the Jokers and the STAR Group for years.

At best, it was a poor tactical move by the police. They were heavily outnumbered, increasing the chances of violence. There was no way that a pub full of Jokers was going to buckle before the STAR Group patch. Although it was later portrayed in the media as a melee, the Battle of Beachport was over in less than a minute—a short sharp exchange that put two cops in hospital, followed by several minutes of posturing and threats.

Superintendent Reiniets walked into the front bar of the hotel where up to twenty Jokers were drinking. When senior constables Ben Hodge and Andrew Thiele tried to follow him in, a Joker blocked their path and elbowed both cops in the chest, they later claimed. When they tried to arrest him, another member, Steve Williams, king hit Hodge, breaking his jaw. However, the Jokers claim the cops had already started the fight outside. In 2011, one member told me that a nominee had been walking out of the pub carrying two drinks when a STAR Group officer elbowed him under the chin. This had been the first blow, he claimed.

When Williams hit Hodge, Rieniets put him in a headlock as other Jokers attacked the STAR Group contingent. Williams was throwing his arms around wildly trying to break Rieniets' hold while shouting he was going to kill all the police, until someone broke a bottle over the cop's head. Williams put on the commander's hat and got a slap from one of his own clubmates, such was the anger they felt towards police. As they took a kicking on the ground, the STAR Group members feared they might be killed. Reinforcements poured in from the police station less than 100 metres away and with batons and capsicum spray order was soon restored. The bikers retreated to their camp, some threatening to return with weapons to finish the fight. However, cooler heads prevailed and there was no further incident that night.

Rieniets stood in the street, the back of his uniform shirt drenched in blood to the waist from a head wound. If he rued his tactical error, he gave nothing away. The cops succeeded in clearing the bar, but in every other way they had been routed.

Two days later, the tension began to rise again as the club began its ride into Adelaide. The outlaws had stayed overnight in Robe, just a few kilometres from Beachport. The club alleges that a member was giving a local woman a ride on the back of his motorbike when a carload of detectives forced him off the road. The member broke his back and was permanently confined to a wheelchair. (The woman received facial injuries and, according to club sources, was secretly compensated by the State Government. In 2011, the member was still awaiting receipt of police files relating to the case so he could sue for compensation.)

The Jokers then ran a gauntlet of roadblocks teeming with hundreds of police all the way back to town. The 'blue gang' was out to vent its spleen for the flogging its members had taken in Beachport.

Two hours down the road at Salt Creek, a Joker named 'Duff' bore the brunt of that anger. Duff alleged in a later statement that, after being accused of refusing to remove his helmet, he was dragged behind the cover of a booze bus and viciously assaulted by numerous police. 'I was getting hit with fists, batons. One particular man was talking in my ear: "You can thank Steve Williams for this." One would hold my head up from the ground so they could kick me in the face, then shove my face back into the dirt.'

But then Duff suffered the ultimate indignity. He claimed the cops cut his colours from his back with a knife, shredding the Gypsy Joker club symbols and souveniring his badges and club belt buckle. This was something a rival bikie club might do, not members of the police force. In fact, this arrest had now become robbery with violence in common parlance.

'The one that cut my colours off was asking me, "Where are your mates now? They are not here, are they? That's where we differ. We care for our own. This is for last night; Williams got one of ours, so we are getting even".'

Duff and another member were taken to Murray Bridge police station, an hour away. Meanwhile, the rest of the Jokers were herded through another half a dozen roadblocks with TV camera crews on hand and media helicopters hovering overhead. In 2011 a Gypsy Joker named Rob told me it was a hellish ride. 'Between the stops, they were diving between our bikes with their cars trying to run us off the road. They were letting capsicum spray off out of their windows so we're riding through clouds of the shit,' said Rob.

Finally, the bikers could take no more and they broke away

from the police convoy and made a high-speed dash for Murray Bridge. The police could only follow.

The first stop was the local shopping strip, where members bought every baseball bat, axe handle and star picket they could lay their hands on. The Jokers as a club had decided they would not leave town without Duff's badges and belt buckle. As the two battle groups faced off across the street in the blazing sun, there was a deadly resolve among the Jokers. 'We decided that we would die rather than leave our club insignia behind,' said Rob. 'It was worth dying for,' he said emphatically.

Some members had been ambivalent about taking on the cops in Beachport but now the entire club stood as one. Fearing a very public bloodbath, the cops blinked first. A senior commander ordered that Duff's gear, which was now in Adelaide, be returned immediately to the club. After nearly an hour, the stand-off ended with a handover in the middle of the street.

As if to underscore the embarrassment of this fiasco, Williams was the only Joker punished over the Beachport incident, later pleading guilty to a charge of assault occasioning actual bodily harm, common assault and resisting police. Eight other Jokers were charged with various offences, but the Crown did not proceed.

Horrible Williams received an 18-month sentence, later reduced to a $100 fine and a two-year good behaviour bond. The three officers injured on the night launched civil action against Williams in early 2003, claiming damages; these included broken bones, damaged teeth, neck injuries, soft-tissue injuries and psychological injuries.

Though the Gypsy Jokers was the only club involved, the Battle of Beachport was a turning point in relations between all of South Australia's outlaws and the state police. The club's small victory over the police could not be allowed to stand. There were explicit orders for police to strike back hard, to re-establish dominion over the bikers.

Outlaw clubs differentiate themselves from other motorcycle groups by a small diamond-shaped patch on their vests bearing the legend '1%'. It proclaims the outlaw's pride in being an outcast. The symbol was adopted after the seminal event in biker history. In 1947, a horde of motorcyclists, many fresh from military service, ran amok in the small town of Hollister, California during a Gypsy Tour race meeting sanctioned by the American Motorcyclist Association (AMA). An AMA spokesperson is said to have told the media that the trouble was caused by 'the one per cent deviant that tarnishes the public image of both motorcycles and motorcyclists'. The AMA later denied making this statement, but the two clubs who had been at Hollister began wearing the 1% patch soon after.

After Beachport, members of the STAR Group began wearing patches or badges on their uniforms proclaiming their membership of 'The 99 per cent'. The idea that the STAR Group spoke for the other 99 per cent was just as unlikely as the notion that only 1 per cent of all bikers were evildoers.

After Beachport, the argument between the cops and the bikers became very personal. Soon after, the Gypsy Jokers elected Williams to the Adelaide presidency as a further arse kick to the system. Some members of the club were advocating reprisal attacks against police, but they were in the minority.

However, Horrible Williams was elected not to wage war, but to help restore the peace. Ironically, he would have some success as a public advocate, but completely lose the respect of his own club.

Steve Williams had needed someone to help him engage with and interpret the unfamiliar world outside the Jokers' fortress. His fellow members reluctantly allowed him to seek that person but later regretted the decision.

Professor Arthur Veno was a veteran of moral panics. He had

been on a beach in Monterey, California during the Labor Day weekend of 1964 when two teenage girls had stumbled out of the darkness—one naked, one half-naked—claiming to have been raped by a pack of Hells Angels. It sparked national outrage. It didn't matter that charges against three Angels were dropped: the incident put the club on the map and stained the reputation of every biker in America. A year later, Veno was on the Berkeley campus of the University of California when eight Hells Angels waded into an eight thousand–strong anti-Vietnam demonstration to teach them a thing or two about patriotism.

And he had been on Mount Panorama at Bathurst, New South Wales to see the 1981 Australian Motorcycle Grand Prix dissolve into a battle royale between police and bikies. If he had learned one thing, it was that bikies always lose these confrontations with society. Even if they can explain themselves, no-one cares to listen. It's only the violence and the barbarism that people remember.

But Veno saw the biker movement as a true counterculture, not a subset of the crime world. Like the hippies he had seen in his youth in California, the bikers were rejecting traditional values but were not hell-bent on conflict, at least not with mainstream society. Veno had forged a career explaining this phenomenon.

In 2001 Veno came to Adelaide to write a book on the clubs entitled *The Brotherhoods*. It was the very moment when the latest moral panic was beginning and he ended up right in the middle of the action.

Williams realised that Veno was the man he needed. The professor had been hanging around motorcycle clubs since the mid-1960s, establishing an international reputation through academic research, but here was an opportunity for Veno to see a motorcycle club through the eyes of a president. Few reporters or academics had ever mingled with outlaw bikers, much less enjoyed the kind of access that the Jokers afforded Veno.

There had been no serious analysis of the nature of crime amongst bikers in South Australia, or anywhere else in Australia for that matter. It had become a fact established in the public mind that the bikie clubs ran crime in that state, even if people were hard-pressed to explain just how they did it. People instinctively recognised this strange, secret society as a threat to their way of life. Misinformation, recycled endlessly in the media, stood unchallenged.

The Australia 2000 pact that Rann had warned of, for example, was later proven to be a furphy. It was eventually discredited as the work of a single detective in New Zealand and never taken seriously by law enforcement. The pact was certainly a failure—every state in Australia hosted at least a dozen clubs and new patches continued to emerge without incident.

It was true that bikers were killing each other from time to time; in Adelaide's streets there were murders, arson attacks, mail bombs and running battles. However, there was little evidence that the violence was centrally coordinated, either by a local or international cabal.

In motorcycle clubs around the world, Veno had observed: a disorganised, anarchic crime model. Clubs tolerated criminals in their ranks, so it was easy to believe the club hierarchy was the criminal enterprise. From time to time, individuals had committed crime working with elements *outside* the club. The club itself was not the unit of crime, but could provide back-up muscle and an image to intimidate rivals. It was a personal choice for members as to whether they involved themselves in crime. It was not a condition of membership as many believed.

This was a hard sell to the public given that the top clubs had been founded on fear and misinformation. Fear was useful to them because it allowed their clubs to establish turf. This footprint was desirable to create a space where members and their families could prosper legitimately.

A chapter of an outlaw motorcycle club shared some of the characteristics of a franchise system. As with a McDonald's or a KFC, there had to be sufficient territory to avoid self-destructive competition with other brands, unless the club believed it could drive out rivals. There must be room to grow without continual conflict. The Bandidos, one of the world's strongest outlaw clubs, had tried to set up in Adelaide in the early 1990s and met such resistance that they abandoned the plan.

Clubs needed to exercise de facto ownership of 'their' pubs and clubs, and the strip bars and brothels they liked to frequent. They tried to establish local monopolies in their pet industries: tattooing, debt collection, nightclub security, event management, transport and motorcycle shops. This created legitimate employment for members, club associates and friends, creating a micro-economy around the club, much of it picked up by the radar of the Australian Taxation Office.

The list of service providers to the outlaw nation included strippers, prostitutes, personal trainers, builders, motorcycle mechanics, assorted tradesmen, lawyers and accountants. These local community links made the bikers a largely benign presence in the suburbs. There was rarely conflict at the clubhouse: neighbours were more likely to read about it in the newspaper than witness it firsthand.

South Australian Premier Mike Rann had long maintained that the clubhouses were citadels of evil, even though police had failed to find the methamphetamine factories and firearms caches alleged to be there. 'If you believe the bikies, then you believe they run *knitting circles* inside the fortresses. I don't believe that and neither do the public,' 'Media Mike' told anyone who would listen.

So, at Veno's suggestion, the Gypsy Jokers threw open the gates and gave guided tours of their clubhouse in the industrial northern suburb of Wingfield. Keys for the clubhouse were sent to the Premier and Police Commissioner with an invitation to the

Premier to come see what went on behind the walls. Not surprisingly, these were never taken up.

ABC Television's *Stateline* program detailed what police had apparently been unable to reveal: 'The site contains bars, a gym, a memorial to departed members, workshops and storage rooms for members' bikes. And the club says it was to protect those bikes that it built the huge sleeper fence around the site that the government wants demolished.'

For a while, Premier Rann appeared genuinely flummoxed by the return media fire. Among bikers, Rann became known derisively as 'the knitwit' for his crack about knitting circles in clubhouses.

'Out there in the real world, no-one believes these bikie gangs—maybe there's a few people around town. Look, there's a PR campaign going on,' Rann told the ABC. 'It won't work, because there has been murder after murder, drug deal after drug deal, associated with bikie gangs.'

But it *was* working. The average South Australian had nothing to fear from the bikers, unless they went out of their way to antagonise them. There could even be a pro-social function for the clubs. Men who would recognise no conventional authority would submit to the control of their peers inside a club.

Select journalists were reporting on the inner workings of the Gypsy Jokers for the first time, much to the discomfort of the police. One New Year's Eve, a female reporter from the *Advertiser*, accompanied the Jokers on a run to Mount Gambier, riding pillion on a senior member's bike. As the clock wound down to midnight, she was drinking with the bikies in a hotel when she was called outside by a senior policeman. She was told in no uncertain terms to stay away from the Jokers. Not because the cop feared for her safety, but because she was choosing a side—the wrong side.

Once inside the bikies' clubland, reporters found it difficult to maintain their preconceived ideas. Williams was prepared to answer everything, including questions that might have previously brought stony silence or a smack in the mouth. 'We're not a criminal organisation; we run wholly and solely on the dues, the fees charged weekly by membership. Our books have been gone through and checked. The club hasn't got any major assets—we're not millionaires here. I'd don't know where the evidence is that we are into organised crime,' he told the ABC.

Veno and Williams also turned the spotlight on police involvement in crime, setting up a telephone hotline for people with complaints about the cops. They took hundreds of calls from people alleging offences by police that had either been ignored or covered up.

Horrible Williams found the public acclaim intoxicating. The charismatic biker was irresistibly good copy. But Veno wanted to take this campaign much further. He saw an opportunity to leverage Steve's growing profile to help the clubs create a confederation that could resolve inter-club disputes and present a united front against government efforts to ban them. A similar body had been set up in the US under the auspices of the Hells Angels and it had met with some success. This would be the culmination of a life's work for Veno.

But a confederation was ahead of its time, given the deepseated rivalries between key clubs in Adelaide. However, what did unite the clubs was a visceral loathing of child abuse.

To Williams and his outlaw brothers, fighting to out paedophiles was the ultimate battleground, even if it was not a club sanctioned crusade. It crystallised their contempt for the system and confirmed their outcast status. A government that deemed them outlaws, while failing to protect children, even covering up the rape and murder of children, was corrupt. It had no authority over them. To create a hue and cry over bikies, while failing to root out the monsters abusing children, demonstrated a bizarre double standard.

Every year, famously, bikies all over the world would put on their Christmas toy runs, raising money for children's charities. It was a rare moment of engagement with society. Bikies dressed as Santa riding through town presented a different, if slightly incongruous, image. It was too easy to claim that these toy runs were intended simply to throw the public off the scent of crime in the clubs. There was more than cheap PR going on as these great hairy thugs dinked kids on bikes decorated with teddy bears and reindeer horns. At a deeper level, the bikies used these runs to demonstrate their contempt for the neglect of children generally. Whatever heinous things some of them had done, they all fiercely protected their children.

And make no mistake, the bikies on these toy runs did not want to be regarded as warm and fuzzy. If the police and courts would not cut out the cancer of child abuse, they were prepared to do it—if need be, with the rusty switchblade of rough justice.

Among the most potent mythologies in Adelaide was the existence of 'The Family', an elite group of citizens who had allegedly operated a paedophile ring in Adelaide for the past quarter of a century, during which time they had kidnapped boys and young men and then killed them in a particularly sadistic fashion. With one exception, these men—alleged to be prominent members of the legal and business community—had never been brought to justice. Bevan Spencer von Einem was convicted of the murder of 15-year-old Richard Kelvin in 1984, but a great number of people from all kinds of backgrounds have always held firmly to the belief that von Einem had about a dozen accomplices—the so-called Family—and that they were responsible for at least another four murders.

For the bikies, The Family represented the monstrous hypocrisy that lay beneath the conservative, morally upright image of Adelaide. In their view The Family was everywhere: watching the bikies, assessing them, plotting their demise. The undercover coppers who had followed the outlaws for years were easy to spot, but The Family were like mist.

In Horrible's drug fuelled revenge fantasies, the high-society paedophiles of Adelaide would be paraded down leafy North Terrace past the State Parliament and Government House, to be jeered and spat upon by the people before being ritually beaten, chain-whipped and then drowned in the Torrens River.

Now, Williams said, Rann and his cronies were trying to get rid of the bikies, the only ones with the courage to stand up against the paedophiles. Williams at this time joined forces with an anti–child abuse campaigner, Wendy Utting, who was working inside the office of the South Australia Speaker, Independent MP Peter Lewis.

For two years, Lewis had been running an increasingly strident campaign. Utting and a colleague, Barry Standfield, took statements from a wide range of people alleging sexual misconduct in the state. Three years earlier, Lewis's vote had given Rann the numbers to form a minority government and he had been rewarded with the South Australian Speaker's post. Now he had declared under parliamentary privilege that a serving government minister had engaged in sex with two under-aged boys at a local gay beat. The minister was also linked to the deaths of two anti–child abuse campaigners, he said. Two senior police officers were also accused of being paedophiles, while Lewis threw into the melting pot allegations that a former Liberal MP had sex with under-age boys in the 1980s.

Williams became eager to help Lewis expose the monsters he believed lurked in polite society. But as he descended into the half-light of this new crusade, Arthur Veno decided it was time to get the hell out of Stormy's.

The membership who had elected Williams looked on with growing anger at the increasingly crazy antics of their president. He was a loose cannon who was no longer following club rules.

His rampant drug use was pushing him over the edge. They hardly recognised their member, who was turning himself into a media celebrity, and that was the very last kind of person they wanted in their midst.

Even people closest to him, like the senior member who had brought him into the club, were despairing of him. In 2011, when I asked the club to sum up their former president, the Gypsy Jokers settled on the quote: 'With all due respect to his family, he became a fucking selfish cockhead on a massive fucking ego trip. We couldn't wait to see the back of him!'

3

THE PUNISHER

In the aftermath of Beachport, with the cops swarming all over them, the Gypsy Jokers needed their leaders to stand up. However, their president, Steve Williams, was missing in action.

It's understood that sometime in 2001 or 2002, the largest ever shipment of crystal methamphetamine into South Australia hit the streets of Adelaide. This new drug, known as ice, took everyone by surprise in much the same way as heroin had in the 1970s. And suddenly the place was awash with the stuff.

Clubs had banned all needle drugs but because ice was generally smoked through a glass pipe, it seemed less of a threat at first. The bikies soon decided ice was a very bad drug indeed, the kind of substance that would destroy club unity. An addict would choose his ice pipe before anything or anyone, whether they were family, friends or clubmates. And Horrible Williams had taken it up with gusto, boasting of a prodigious consumption that would have killed any normal person.

He would go three or four days at a time without sleep when he was 'on the pipe'. Then he would crash, disappearing for up to a week. He would retreat to his flat and get on the pipe, behind a thick steel plate that shielded his bed from the street. Horrible saw enemies everywhere. Some were real.

At the same time, bizarrely, he was still running his public campaign with Arthur Veno. Most of the time he was aggressive, irrational, unpredictable and deeply paranoid. His clubmates felt he was on another planet when he expounded his conspiracy theories, raving about draconian new laws the police would use to ban the clubs. He would speak of meetings he had held with senior police and politicians who had warned him of what the Rann Government was planning. At a certain point, his brothers stopped listening, believing Williams had become psychotic from drug use. He certainly acted like it.

In January 2004, the members did not re-elect Horrible as president but through his ice haze he apparently had not seen it coming. Three months later Williams quit the club in disgust.

Williams had become increasingly autocratic and unpopular. Arthur Veno had introduced him to the world outside the club and Steve now craved acceptance there. He no longer wanted to be feared by polite society. His campaign to portray bikers in a better light was in fact very personal on one level, selfish even. This was a way out for him, to a bigger stage. Veno and Williams had become mates, but, if truth be told, they were using each other. The charismatic bikie could grab the public's attention through the media in a way the civilian academic could never hope to. And Veno had drafted a plan to create a confederation of Australian outlaw clubs, working together to become a political lobby in the halls of power. In Williams, Veno saw a chance to achieve his most cherished career ambition.

But the Jokers wanted nothing to do with Veno and Horrible's plans and schemes anymore.

They had joined the Jokers to be part of a 1 per cent motorcycle club. They were the 1 per cent of bikers who gave the 99 per cent of law-abiding motorcyclists a bad name. They were not members of some social movement. They just wanted to assert their right to be left alone by the cops and the media.

The club still wanted peace in Adelaide, but it would be achieved with quiet diplomacy behind closed doors with other clubs, not under the public spotlight. It had been a mistake to let an egocentric ice addict run a public campaign on their behalf. The club had other staunch men who could step up to the plate next time and keep their shit together. They didn't know it yet, but there were bikers in other clubs across Australia of a similar bent who were destined to connect with them. But for now, internal business took priority. Over the next seven years, the Jokers would kick out several members for being on the pipe, contrary to club rules. They would save a few more by enforcing a regime of drug testing. Ice would be a much bigger threat than any law the government could dream up.

Williams' name would hardly be spoken of around the clubhouse. Though he had done some good early on, he had ended up ruining his own standing in the club. There was no sympathy. He had made his own bed, complete with bullet-proof shield. Now he could lie in it, as far as the Jokers were concerned. They were done with him.

Stormy Summers, an ageless buxom platinum blonde, ran the best-known bordello in Adelaide, a multi-storey menagerie on Waymouth Street overlooking Light Square, near the city centre.

Stormy had been outraging Adelaide's decency at regular intervals over the past three decades. Every so often there would be public denunciations, police raids, the chirruping of the media, followed by a court appearance, a fine and then back to business. Everyone would return to ignoring her or enjoying her wares.

Behind the glass facade, a shadowy network of thugs and bikers was said to operate a wide range of criminal enterprises. That little evidence was ever found only deepened the concern. It showed these crooks were smart and hard to catch. If they were hiding in brothels, then the bordellos would have to go too, said the city elders. But no-one ever put much effort into it. This was a social institution, if not a moral one.

The closed-circuit TV monitor in Stormy's penthouse showed the clientele stepping furtively off the street into the mirrored foyer below. Doctors, lawyers, businessmen, cops, AFL football-ers, crooks and bikers; they all shared Stormy's girls.

The moral tide could rise and fall, but good men (as well as the bad) had always kept her in business. As far as she could see, there was no crime in paying for sex. Or for that matter in the wider world, getting high, drinking sly grog or having an SP bet, as long as no-one got hurt. The authorities could make these things ille-gal, but not unpopular.

Stormy had found a way to exist between the letter and the spirit of the law. Prostitution was not illegal in South Australia per se; girls used sex to get what they wanted from men all the time, she said. 'It's only illegal to live off the earnings of a prostitute and they've got to catch you doing that, lovey,' she would laugh, flash-ing a pearly grille of gold-inlaid teeth.

Stormy's Adelaide was not the City of Churches but the home of assorted misfits, thugs, fetishists, occultists, psychopaths and sex addicts. In 2003, Adelaide University's Dr Allan Perry, when discussing local crime with a reporter, referred to 'a culture of degeneracy in South Australia'. There was 'an increasingly sig-nificant subculture of people' whose lives were 'totally amoral and parasitic upon society'. And they were all welcome at Stormy's, if they obeyed the house rules. Adelaide's 250-strong biker community had long been enthusiastic customers and Stormy had made sure that rivals did not bump into each other.

That's where Steve Williams came in handy. In return for his security services, Stormy had given him the apartment on the first floor where her 26-year-old son Jason had died in 2000 from an adverse reaction to painkillers. Few people would play up if they knew Horrible was in the building.

Stormy had encouraged Steve in his public campaign to project a more realistic image for the bikies. It was little more than a PR campaign, but he seemed to be growing into the role. She had herself once run for the Lord Mayoralty of Adelaide so, if a brothel madam could do that, why couldn't a biker take on the Premier?

Horrible had felt at home in Stormy's. He had called it his 'underworld sanctuary'. But cheap perfume and disinfectant could not mask entirely the ever-present whiff of conflict in the place. He suspected that people outside the walls were plotting his demise. Drug use had made him paranoid, but he also had many real enemies.

By June 2005 the walls of his grimy little flat at Stormy's had closed in on him.

On speed-ravaged sleepless nights he imagined he was 'The Punisher', an antihero from a Marvel comic. A vigilante in a sick and corrupt society, the fictional Punisher justified murder, torture, kidnapping and extortion in his one-man war against crime.

Earlier that year he had written a poem called *Rider on the Storm*, after his mother asked him to explain to her why there was so much darkness and unhappiness in his life. Veno later forwarded me a copy of the tortured work, on which Williams had spent several months:

Sometimes I look in the mirror at night and I see the Punisher—wild
eyed and losing focus.

In a sense, I'm homicidal in this thug's life, staying locked up in this
drug life.

I'm binging [sic] on Juice [speed] and using Green [cannabis] to try and
numb the pain that lives in my heart.

Juice and Green dreams makes the nights seem hopeless.

The Punisher had done his best work on Williams himself, but this ruthless alter ego lent him courage to face the forces, some real, some imagined, that were circling him. From the 'underworld sanctuary' of Stormy Summers' bordello, Williams and The Punisher were on the move. First he would have his day in court, facing the civil charges brought by the police officers he had bashed at Beachport. Then he would take down the filthy monsters of The Family.

Steve was now a citizen, as the 1 per centers call the rest of society. His Harley was up for sale. His ride was now a family sedan, an old white Falcon. His mode of transport was no longer a symbol of rebellion, but instead a conveyance for the journey from A to B in his job as a debt collector.

His priorities were also different now. He was trying to put his family first, as unconventional as it was. His daughter Blayze was thirteen years old now and the centre of his universe. He was no longer with Blayze's mother, Kim Asling, but he had always made sure that Blayze was provided for, sometimes generating friction with his current girlfriend. There were other women in Steve's life too. 'He would sleep with them once and then make friends of them,' according to Veno.

He was always busy looking after the problems of one or another of them. Keeping this all going, while maintaining a raging ice habit, was no mean feat. New intrigues and dramas seemed to pop up almost daily then.

On the morning of 14 June 2005 he had smoothed his long brown hair into a ponytail and prepared for the day ahead. It was nearly fourteen months since he had quit the club, but Williams was still the biker from Central Casting. At 191 centimetres and 100 kilos, with a barrel chest and muscular arms the size of many ordinary men's thighs, he was an imposing figure.

The story of his life was scored into his torso and forearms: club tattoos, the names of lovers, emblems and mottos coloured and half-concealed scarring from a bike accident. This was all out of view under the sleeves of the work-day shirt he wore now.

He had promised Blayze he would leave the Jokers before she was in her teens and now he had done so. His thirty-ninth birthday next week would not be celebrated with his bikie brothers in the clubrooms or some sleazy strip joint. He and Blayze would be together in this one-room apartment inside Stormy's brothel, opening his presents, talking and listening to the thump of music from the nightclub below.

On that chilly winter's morning, like millions of normal South Australians, he went to work, meeting a colleague in the debt collection business to sort through the latest issues. He then visited his mother, Jan. They were much closer now that he was out of the club.

Jan had recently lifted a burden her son had been carrying for years. Most of his life he had believed he'd accidentally killed a school mate in a playground accident when he was eight years old. This dark secret had always stalked him. He had convinced himself that he was evil and unworthy, and he had acted this out in his life. There could be 'no peace for this killer', so he 'became a Rider, Thug and Gladiator', he wrote in his poem, *Rider in the Storm*:

My mind was broken, split and confused by this shit.
The Punisher emerged to protect me with true grit.
The bigger they were, the harder they fell.

Steve had come from a conventional suburban family. His
father had been a teacher. He was a stern but loving man; he had
encouraged his children to work hard and speak up for what they
believed in. Steve's elder brother, Les, had become a firefighter; his
sister, Marion, whom Steve most closely resembled, had become
a lawyer. His family could never quite understand the reasons for
Steve's rebellion and it was a source of great angst for his parents.

The bikies had accepted him into their ranks despite this stain
of guilt that Williams felt. They had demons of their own so there
was no judgement upon him. All that mattered was that he was
loyal and staunch to the club, 'a righteous biker'. The rage that
lived within him was useful to the club in times of conflict. Little
by little, Steve's father had lost him to clubland.

When Jan finally unearthed the truth, it turned out that there
had been an accident in the playground—a boy had been hurt and
taken to hospital by ambulance. But the boy had not died. For
thirty years, Steve had been beating himself up (and many around
him) for nothing. The guilt had become The Punisher and had
exacted full toll from Steve.

A huge emotional outpouring followed this discovery for
mother and son. Jan was distraught that a self-created myth had
determined so much in Steve's life. Many things he could not
change: the convictions for assault and possession of marijuana and
amphetamines. But Jan was proud of her son; who at thirty-eight
finally seemed to be growing up. He had become a public advocate for the outlaw nation. He was making a contribution.

Hit the media, became a star, went the distance
I'm accepted now as the icon of resistance.

Now, strangers, passer bys [sic], politicians, straights and riff raff
Come right up and say 'Onya mate, give the bastards the shaft'
Public acceptance has started to heal me well.
The Punisher inside me started to chill.

But on this day in June, when Steve caught up with her, Jan thought he seemed distracted and distant. She knew he was pursuing this shadowy group of paedophiles that he believed had operated in Adelaide city for decades. His crusade against The Family had given him new purpose in life after leaving the Jokers, but it was taking him to some dark places. She had gotten used to the roughneck bikies in Steve's life, but this was another dimension.

Jan was worried when she learned he was close to dropping the bombshell, revealing the identities of the high-profile people who were 'fucking our kids'.

A work colleague drove him to the Gepps Cross Hotel on the city's northern fringe, where he was due to meet an anti-paedophile crusader. He had apparently left his car there earlier. At 2.30 p.m. his colleague left him outside the hotel. Williams had planned to go alone to his next meeting later in the day, with a member of the South Australian police in the city.

He had arranged to hand over goods stolen from the house of an alleged member of the paedophile ring, Peter Michael Liddy. Liddy, a former magistrate, had been jailed in 2001 for twenty-five years, with an 18-year non-parole period. Williams had bought the goods, including a Samurai sword, a rare coin collection and a cache of documents, from a 'whizzer', a street speed dealer, according to Arthur Veno. Williams was convinced there was ample evidence in the documents to implicate others in more heinous crimes against children. The sword and the coins he planned to sell to raise money to compensate the victims of child abuse.

This would be a kind of redemption for his wayward life, he believed. 'The legacy gives meaning for my struggle and an example for others resisting the system and its abuses,' he wrote in his poem. He would 'bring down these state terrorist bastards known as The Family spreading fear and hopelessness to the vulnerable in the community, with immunity from laws, rules and morality'.

To many in Adelaide, such words rang with irony. For a long time, right-thinking folk had believed that it was bikies like Horrible Williams who had ruled the town 'with immunity from laws, rules and morality'. They had spread fear and violence in the streets while peddling drugs to kids, so the story went.

But that day, when he went to the Gepps Cross Hotel, Steve felt he was working with the system, not against it. He had a righteous cause.

Williams was due to meet the senior police officer later that afternoon, but he never turned up for that meeting. Police believe that he left the hotel with someone who was known to him, perhaps someone he trusted. He was too paranoid to have gone quietly if there had been even a hint of danger.

His Falcon was later found in the car park of the hotel. He had occasionally dropped off the map for short periods on other occasions, but never without maintaining contact with Blayze.

The fringe dwellers, the poor white trash who hung around biker clubs, were certain that The Family had got Steve Williams. The ruling-class conspiracy that in different ways kept them all down, that trampled on their aspirations, had silenced him. It was quite possible the police had been in on it too, ran the theory. It was one thing to flout the law, to live with impunity on the outskirts, but quite another to take on the institutions of a city. You would be isolated and reviled as a crank and a lunatic, then hunted down by the police and handed over to The Family.

Then it would run like a bad slasher movie. They would take you to the dungeons and the catacombs to show you it was much worse than you ever imagined. Then they would kill you slowly, slicing bits off you while you were still alive, to eat with a top-shelf South Australian red.

Bikers are not generally avid readers, but they have a lot of interest in the world around them. Stories pass by word of mouth quickly through their circles and once a conspiracy gets going it's virtually impossible to stop. Official denials usually have no effect. The bikers view the relationship between the media and government as being part and parcel of the bigger conspiracy. A cryptic hint from a drunk in an outback pub will have more force in a biker's mind than stone-cold gazetted fact from 'The System'.

Reporters heed the adage that when faced with a choice between conspiracy and a stuff-up, you always choose the latter. In Steve Williams's world the opposite was true and there was enough evidence in Adelaide to suggest that this was more than just paranoia. Perhaps there *were* serial killers and their associates parading themselves as model citizens up and down Rundle Mall in the city. There were enough unsolved murders on SAPOL's books to suggest that could be so.

But the investigators had a more mundane explanation. Williams' disappearance was probably the result of a falling-out over some nefarious business with rivals.

If police had evidence, they were giving nothing away. 'Given his history, police are clearly concerned for his welfare and safety,' a police spokesman, Chief Inspector Peter Graham, said four days after his disappearance. It seemed clear to police that he was probably dead.

Without a body, there would be no biker funeral, no cortege of outlaws rolling through the city as a mark of respect. Within a few months, his name would rarely be spoken outside his family circle.

To ordinary folk, Steve's disappearance was a stark reminder of the vile treacherous world he inhabited. He had been the spokesman for the outlaws. Horrible Williams had tried to tell people they had nothing to fear from bikies and look what had happened.

Four months after Steve's disappearance, Stormy opened the dark and dank apartment on the first floor where he had lived so I could see it for myself. It was no more than a bed-sit, hardly the home of a powerful organised crime figure, as the government rhetoric had tagged him. It was empty, but the signs of his anarchic habitation were evident. The mirror was cracked and there were a couple of holes punched out of the wall, apparently during fits of anger. He had written notes and snippets of verse on the walls. There were mysterious stains on the carpet, and burns where he had indulged his new hobby of glass-blowing. The room still smelt faintly of bong water, old cigar smoke and cologne.

Flashing lights and loud music from the neighbouring nightclub down below pumped into the apartment. The place reeked of failure and disappointment. It felt like something had happened here at Stormy's, but it was over now. We were too late. Everything was coming apart at the seams.

Arthur Veno, 'The Bikie Professor', who had come from Melbourne with me, seemed uneasy to be back in the heart of darkness, even if the media was paying him to take us there. I was in town to write a cover story for the *Bulletin* magazine on the outlaw club scene. If a club opened up to us, we would also produce a television story for the Nine Network's *Sunday* program.

Veno was engaged to help us meet the bikies, but so far the TV crew and I had sat around Stormy's for three nights drinking and watching on the closed-circuit television as the clientele walked in off the street. There was time for Veno to explain how his relationship with Steve had developed into a full-blown PR campaign against the government.

Veno and Steve had lost this fight, though for a while they had been winning. By the end, they had alienated almost everyone: the police, the State Government and even sections of the media. Steve had fallen out with his own club. It was profoundly depressing to Veno to see how things had fallen apart in just a few months.

Stormy's brothel had always been chaotic, but it was disintegrating fast now. The lady herself had put the title of the building in the name of her manager who turned out to be a drug-dealing fraudster. Unbeknown to Stormy, her manager had mortgaged the building and now the brothel was in default.

Stormy was drinking heavily and blowing much of the takings on the pokies. She had locked out her husband, 'Marky G'; in a rage he had tried to scale the outside of the building and then smashed his leg after falling from the second storey to the street below. Now Marky, a former nightclub bouncer, was installed in a double bed in the lounge room.

The only living creatures that seemed to be keeping order were a brooding Hells Angel and Stormy's hulking crossbred mastiff, Ned. The dog kept a baleful eye on newcomers at all times, chewing ruefully on his teddy bear. Occasionally, for no particular reason, he would leap up growling and slavering. You would have to shoot Ned if you bothered him enough for him to drop the bear. Stormy's had left a mark on that dog, like everyone else, Veno thought.

4

AVATAR RISING

When Rebels and Hells Angels members clashed at the South Australian Dance Music Awards inside a local stadium in May 2005, it became abundantly clear that the South Australian police had lost any semblance of control over the bikers.

The Hells Angels, in particular, had form and this was not their first violent run-in with the Rebels. In 1999, three Rebels had died in an ambush with individuals aligned to the Hells Angels on Wright Street, a few blocks from Stormy's. Three men had later been charged with murder, but the case collapsed when the Rebels refused to testify against them.

The Hells Angels had been fighting occasional battles with other clubs in pubs and nightclubs in Adelaide (and across Australia) for years. The Angels' contingent in Adelaide was divided into three chapters, the Adelaide, North and Hell End crews. In 2004 the North Crew were believed to be behind efforts to control security in nightclubs, causing friction with other clubs. It was reported that only a peace summit involving local and inter-state clubs had averted another bloody confrontation. Meanwhile, proxy battles were still being fought between street gangs that were said to be feeder groups to the outlaw clubs.

At the 2005 Dance Music Awards, seven Rebels had stormed the venue and attacked a table of Hells Angels. Chairs and tables flew, and then shots were fired. No-one was seriously hurt but the melee was seared into the public consciousness. As the Adelaide *Advertiser* newspaper noted: 'The unexpected violence in front of more than 600 guests brought unsuspecting members of the public into the middle of a violent gang war.'

This melee followed a spate of bombings, incidents of arson and brawls between Hells Angels and Rebels, which police linked to a turf war over drugs. However, senior officers conceded they did not know the Hells Angels and Rebels were feuding until the bullets began to fly at the awards night.

It was common practice for police to suggest that every conflict between clubs was over drugs. Yet crime statistics suggested quite a different picture. There were individual bikers involved in the trade but there was no proof to date that the clubs themselves were organised to traffic narcotics. The majority of disputes between clubs could be sheeted home to personal disputes or matters of honour and ego. It often just came down to a public disrespect for another's club colours. This made the public violence no less terrifying, but it was strange that police knowledge of the essence and organisation of the 1 per cent world seemed to be so weak and unreliable. Bikers believed the cops just ignored what should have been painfully obvious in their own intelligence.

A police task force code-named Avatar had been working on the bikies since 1999. Avatar is a Sanskrit word meaning the incarnation of a god on earth, usually Vishnu, the preserver of the Hindu universe. Maybe they just liked the name.

More than twenty officers were assigned to Avatar, including members of the elite Drug and Organised Crime Investigation Crime Branch. The task force had been producing a torrent of figures to prove it was all over the bikers like a cheap suit. The Premier boasted that Avatar had made 264 arrests in the four years to April 2004, seizing 294 firearms and a small mountain of drugs and other contraband, and yet they hadn't had an inkling of a serious conflict between the two most prominent clubs in town.

Curiously, their statistics did not provide a breakdown of indictable and non-indictable offences. Serious offences like rape, kidnapping and murder were lumped in with lesser infractions like unpaid parking fines or traffic warrants. The list of seized firearms did not record whether the owner had a permit for the weapon or whether it was ultimately returned. Avatar was also coy on whether its arrests and seizures involved fully patched members of clubs or a mixture of members, associates and friends. If you hang around the magistrate's court in a small town like Adelaide, it soon becomes obvious that everyone knows everyone, but that doesn't make them criminal associates, until the web gets drawn up on a whiteboard at police HQ.

In November 2005, I raised these concerns with the government PR spinners, who referred me to the police PR spinners, who sent me back to the government flacks. So I asked the editor of the *Advertiser* newspaper, Melvin Mansell, who had been running detailed accounts of Avatar's exploits. He didn't seem to know either. It was a curiosity to Mansell that the number of arrests and seizures trumpeted in press releases did not tally with convictions achieved in court, or even the number of cases that made it to court.

Mansell would have loved to run endless columns of bikie mayhem and destruction, but he could not explain where all these villains had ended up. Bikies had been known to intimidate witnesses until they withdrew their testimony, but this couldn't fully explain the statistical gap. Exactly how much the police knew of the bikies' involvement in serious criminal activities seemed a fair question to ask. The Dance Music Awards punch-up seemed to hint they didn't know much.

Then Avatar boss Detective Inspector Graham Goodwin conceded to the media there had been a failing of Avatar's 'intelligence holdings and gatherings' over the Rebels–Hells Angels tete-a-tete.

To many fearful citizens, it seemed the bikies were on the verge of taking over. 'What it goes to show is that these people are so confident that they will do that sort of thing in public. They've got an attitude, a boldness that says we can do anything and we've got control of the city, and this has got to be stopped,' a 'bikie industry insider' told the *Advertiser*.

In the wake of the Dance Music Awards, South Australian Attorney-General Michael Atkinson claimed that eight out of ten licensed premises had crowd controllers supplied by companies associated with outlaw motorcycle clubs. Police alleged that, by controlling the doors of nightclubs, the 'gangs' could dictate who could sell drugs inside. The answer was to remove the licence of any bouncer who police could demonstrate had links with clubs, which, in this small city, was almost everyone.

The South Australian Government rushed through parliament amendments to the Security and Investigation Agents Act, which legislated that crowd controllers could be fingerprinted and subjected to random drug and alcohol tests, and could have their licence revoked if they were known associates of criminals or bikies. Atkinson believed that these new provisions would help the government remove up to two thousand undesirables from the industry so that the flower of South Australia's youth would be safe from their corrupting influence.

Moral panic refers to a phenomenon in which society experiences deep fear and uncertainty fuelled by the perception that a particular moral institution is under threat. The threat often takes the form of a socially excluded, alien group of people, like bikies. The incitement of moral panic requires the rapid and efficient exchange of misinformation by the mass media.

As a serious drought deepened in South Australia in late 2005, the state was literally running out of water. If anything should have caused panic in Adelaide, it was the dwindling supply of water. Yet it was only a ripple in the public's mind. Industry, investment and employment were already in long-term decline and, if the big dry continued, economic catastrophe loomed. Premier Mike Rann and his strategists must have been pleased that recent polling showed that voters in marginal electorates were more concerned about law and order than water, the essence of life. As the Murray River, the state's very lifeline, plumbed record lows, attention was instead focused on crime statistics.

Crime at this time was falling steadily across Australia as economic prosperity cut unemployment, but South Australia was lagging behind. Since 2001, crime had fallen only 7.3 per cent in that state, compared with a 12.4 per cent nationwide average. More alarmingly, the State Opposition claimed that SAPOL had a clearance rate (the number of crimes solved) of only 11.4 per cent. Each week, there were 4000 new offences being committed that would never be solved, according to the Opposition. The cops were losing the battle for the streets.

Meanwhile Rann was suggesting a horde of stinking, arrogant thugs on motorcycles was parading its contempt for the law while bashing, shooting and stabbing each other. It had been such an easy political connection for Rann to make. Rid the streets of bikies, and law and order would be restored.

Lower-income earners living in the suburbs always bear the brunt of street crime. Voters in this Labor heartland were most susceptible to politicians promising to get tough on crime. The water crisis would be an esoteric issue until the taps ran dry in

Adelaide, but crime was real and terrifying. The Premier could not make it rain before the next state election, which was due in March 2006; instead he would seek re-election by speaking to people's fears about crime.

The law and order horse had originally helped carry Rann to a very narrow victory and minority government in 2002, but since then he had vaulted to record approval ratings. On this issue, his most effective opposition had not been in Parliament House but in an outlaw clubhouse. In the beginning, Steve Williams's campaign had cut through.

Horrible had challenged the Premier to provide evidence backing his claims that motorcycle clubs were the root of all evil in Adelaide. He had begun to persuade influential minds in other clubs that it was time to stand together against the Premier's attacks. For a moment, this had threatened to become a popular movement. Williams had been pure novelty at first but the press, fascinated by the articulate, forthright biker, had begun to listen to his arguments.

But with Williams's disappearance, all had returned to normal again. Rann could dismiss the entire campaign as 'a bizarre PR stunt'.

The bikies were generating enough bad PR of their own to suggest that Rann was right. Where once the clubs had coexisted easily, mingling at bike shows, swap meets and rock concerts and in clubs and pubs, the city and suburbs were now carved up into club territories. A chance meeting on a booze-fuelled night out was enough to set off weeks or months of hostilities. The sergeants-at-arms of the clubs were kept busy fielding late-night calls from members in trouble in downtown fleshpots. A spilt drink could end up with a call-out of all members for battle at any hour. It was important to win these skirmishes decisively and quickly to prevent a poisonous escalation of violence—at least that was the theory.

Firearms were having the last word in a number of these exchanges. Guns always up the ante. Police suggested at that time something north of 10 per cent were carrying all the time. It was a matter of self-preservation, as Steve Williams had told the ABC a month before he vanished: 'There have been times in the past where we've felt we needed protection,' he said.

He had been asked whether he and other members had guns. 'Ah, I don't, I don't at all. [But] I wouldn't be telling you honestly if I said I knew exactly what was going on in every member's house.'

There were enough cases of cops catching bikies and their associates with handguns, both legal and illegal, to suggest a good number were tooled up.

In 2003, with much fanfare, South Australia had passed the Statutes Amendment (Anti-Fortification) Act, which sought 'to prevent the construction of outlaw motorcycle gang headquarters in South Australia and also to allow police to demolish the existing fortifications when they are excessive'.

Behind the fortified walls of the clubhouses, Rann had said, the evil empire was to be found: the drug labs, the weapons caches, the piles of cash from extortion, prostitution and stand-over tactics. If police could breach the barbed wire, security systems, man traps, thugs, dogs and guns, they would find the black box for Bikie Inc.'s criminal enterprise.

But now, two years on, the bikie walls were still standing. Police had so far made only a single application under the new legislation: they had removed the battlements from the private residence of a Hells Angel in the Adelaide Hills.

Radio shock jocks, like 5AA's Bob Francis, were flaying Rann alive for his failure to deliver on his promise to eradicate the bikie scourge: 'Mike Rann is great at coming out with rhetoric: We are doing great things, we are going to get rid of bikies. Bullshit!' said Francis in an interview with me. 'There is no way in a million years they will get rid of bikies in this state, but it seems to be that Mike loves to get the good news out, get his headlines, but nothing ever happens. Nothing ever happens.'

But heading into an election, Mike Rann could be sure there were no votes to be lost in going after the 'pond scum', as he called the bikies. They were the visible face of the state's law and order crisis. Someone had to do something before it was too late.

Rann's strident sense of moral duty was to prove so dramatically successful in South Australia that it soon caught on with state politicians all over the country. In the next six years, bringing down the bikie bogeyman proved far more newsworthy than the tedious business of building roads, dams, hospitals and schools.

The most striking aspect of the new provisions of Rann's amended Security and Investigation Agents Act was that the onus of proof was now reversed. To keep a licence, a bouncer needed to prove he was not working for the bikies, whom the government claimed controlled 80 per cent of nightclub security.

The Law Society of South Australia wrote to the government complaining that the Security and Investigation Agents Act risked undermining a fundamental tenet of the law: the presumption of innocence. But that was a minor detail. Attorney-General Atkinson, like his Premier, knew public opinion was behind him: 'We're going to crack down through this legislation and bring in a law that, on its face, could be quite unjust in its operation. Many of these people we're targeting are cleanskins—they don't have any convictions—but nevertheless, they need to be removed from the trade because of their association with the gangs,' he argued.

The beefed-up Security and Investigation Agents Act was a crucial test of the public's appetite for laws that curtailed the right of free association. Not since the consorting laws had fallen into disuse in the 1980s had police attempted to regulate social interaction.

Meanwhile, many bikies seemed unable to accept their role in bringing heat down on their clubs. They were simply doing what they had always done, to a lesser or greater degree; they were confident that the public had nothing to fear from their feuding, even if it was becoming increasingly deadly. But the bikies failed to grasp the shadow play in which they had been cast as central characters.

5

KILLER DAYS

In late October 2005, Tom Mackie caught wind of a letter I had written to the Adelaide clubs, inviting them to take part in a novel exercise. Stormy Summers had distributed the letter on my behalf through her contacts and soon almost every club had a copy. I proposed that the clubs provide spokespeople for a series of interviews that would form the basis of a cover story for the *Bulletin* magazine and the *Sunday* program on the Nine network. This was an opportunity for the clubs to put forward their side of the story, to show how Premier Rann and his police were unfairly targeting them with dubious tactics.

It was a worthy ambition, but there was fat chance that the clubs would step up, thought Mackie. There hadn't been too many reporters poking their noses around the clubs since Steve Williams had vanished. And nobody seemed to miss them.

The last time a reporter had come knocking on the Descendants' door was after a police raid that had taken place years earlier.

The local media had been tipped off about the raid and a reporter and a photographer came along to record the crime busters at work. One of the lads had turned the garden hose on them over the clubhouse fence. To watch the media pair running away was so amusing that it almost made getting raided worthwhile.

The irony was that they had plenty of damaging material on the cops that they could have shared with the media. There were so many cases of bikers being loaded up with evidence, bashed, illegally searched and harassed at their homes and workplaces. Yet none of that would ever see the light of day. The bikers never complained or explained; that was the way things had always been done. There was a feeling that whatever they said to the media would be twisted and misrepresented, so it was better not to say anything.

Mackie thought that about the only thing going for this new approach was that we had come from out of town. The local media was in the pocket of the State Government and enthusiastically printed all the lies and exaggerations. Every so often, the government would dump a load of new material on one of its lackeys in the press and a double-page spread would appear condemning bikies as terrorists or child-eating monsters. These reporters weren't very interested in comments from the bikies. That might risk spoiling a good story, Mackie thought.

Adelaide, a city of 1.4 million people, now effectively had only one newspaper, the *Advertiser*, owned by Rupert Murdoch's News Corporation. The city had been the cradle of Murdoch's global expansion from the 1950s. Young Rupert originally inherited ownership of the *News*, an afternoon tabloid that over many decades had competed hard with the *'Tiser*, but by 2005, the *News* had been gone a dozen years and Murdoch now owned the *'Tiser*.

While investigative journalism had flourished in the pluralistic media markets of Sydney and Melbourne, Adelaide's media clique remained a stodgy defender of the status quo. Any journalist of an independent bent risked losing patronage and access to government and the big end of town. If you wanted that kind of career, there was always Melbourne and Sydney. So most of the media pack toed the party line, and even the most egregious beat-ups went unchallenged.

The previous year, the local media had reported as fact comments in parliament by Attorney-General Michael Atkinson that bikies had cooked a cat on a new coin-operated barbecue in a park and then devoured it in front of horrified families. Capitalising on this outrage, Atkinson had planned to introduce legislation banning the consumption of cats. It was hardly the moral challenge of the age, but the link to bikies gave it relevance and a guaranteed headline.

Atkinson's later retraction in parliament was less widely reported. He told the house he had been mistaken. The cat had in fact been a fox, the episode had occurred thirteen years ago and no bikie had been involved. He gave a somewhat flippant apology to the bikers but the damage was done—the story had gone global. If these filthy barbarians would eat cats, there was no limit to their depravity. The story had followed them ever since, like so many myths and legends about them. Curiously, at the same time the government had alleged the bikers were living in luxury, earning millions from organised crime.

The contradiction in the political rhetoric had given the cat-eating episode a bizarre, ritualistic edge. Perhaps this was part of some disgusting initiation process in outlaw clubs, the media speculated—anything was possible if the family cat could be consumed in front of shrieking, traumatised children. Mackie had seen bikers eat most things, he said, but they had drawn the line at road kill, at least if it wasn't fresh.

The interaction with media was restricted to occasional sightings at roadblocks put together by SAPOL, eager to show the public they were on top of the bikie menace. These were big dramatic set pieces, guaranteed to gain prominent coverage in TV news bulletins and newspapers.

There would usually be hundreds of police, helicopters hovering overhead, the STAR Group armed to the teeth and even sniffer dogs. The rigmarole would go on for hours with licence and rego tests, outstanding warrant checks, breath tests and endless questions about destinations and plans, and who was who in the group. That would be followed by a battery of tests for noisy exhaust pipes and non-standard modifications to frames, wheels and handlebars. Almost all the riders failed one or more of the tests. If they looked like passing the noise test, the cops would just hold the meter closer to the pipes until the needle went into the red.

What had traditionally been a 'killer' day, riding through the countryside, would be reduced to an arse-kicking waste of time. The media would get a handy headline or two, but the effect on law and order was hard to gauge. The next week the bikers would troop off to the Motor Registry at Regency Park to appeal the defect or pay the fines after showing they had rectified the issues. This game would be played out almost every time the clubs appeared on the streets in numbers. It was getting so bad that just riding in colours was an act of defiance.

But there was another reason for the clubs to consider breaking their code of silence. Media coverage had led the public to believe the membership of clubs to be riven with criminals. Mackie had read over and over in the media that supposedly a man could not join a 1 per cent club without being a criminal. This was patently false. Mackie knew the majority of members in most clubs paid their club dues from their weekly wages, not the proceeds of crime. There were some criminals in the clubs, but they were in the minority. Mackie could sense that the State Government was planning to use this bikie stereotype to make membership of the club a criminal offence. Then all bikers would be lumped in the same category. That was what the consorting laws had done to the club in the 1970s; whether they were workers, businesspeople, servicemen, layabouts or drunks, they were all criminals by virtue of the patch on their backs.

SAPOL had made no secret of the fact that it was on a mission to 'disrupt and dismantle' the clubs. They were hell-bent on driving the clubs out of existence, or at least out of town, on the pretext that that the outlaws congregated for one purpose only: organising crime.

SAPOL believed it could beat them 'by dismantling the criminal circles in which they operate, dissuading the professional relationships upon which they depend'. And destroying club runs with roadblocks and highway escorts was a central plank of the strategy. It would also include regular raids on the club headquarters, and impromptu visits to members at their homes and workplaces. Every time an outlaw took to the streets, he could expect plenty of attention. Life would get too hot for the average caveman biker, who would then quit the club or even leave the state, disavowing his misspent years with the outlaws. Or so the theory went.

Mackie often joked that the case against the bikers had become like former US President George W Bush's hunt for weapons of mass destruction in Iraq after the toppling of the dictator Saddam Hussein. There was a sense that Avatar was on the brink of discovering the mother lode: methamphetamine labs, caches of guns, shallow graves, bank accounts and warehouses full of cash.

South Australian police had better investigative tools than most cops in the country. The general search warrant (GSW) allowed police to raid any premises day or night for a period of six months, where they had 'reasonable cause' to suspect 'an offence [had] been recently committed: or [was] about to be committed; there [were] stolen goods; anything that may afford evidence as to the commission of an offence or anything that may be used for the purpose of committing an offence'. No other state gave the police such wide discretion. And the GSW did not have to be endorsed by a court. South Australian cops could just carry around blank forms to be signed when needed.

Even though there were specific warrants under other laws like the Controlled Substances Act, the GSW was more convenient—the Swiss Army knife of warrants. According to defence lawyers, the GSW effectively allowed police to enter any premises and then make up whatever they needed later as a reason for doing so. And yet still they hadn't breached the walls of Bikie Inc. in South Australia.

There were enough police busts in South Australia each year to keep the media interested: hydroponic cannabis factories in underground bunkers, speed labs, pill presses and vacuum-sealed bricks of money for display on television. But police had rarely linked patch members to the evidence, or caught them in the act. Occasionally a raid picked up members with small amounts of drugs, not much above personal-use quantities or low-level trafficking. Friends, club associates, hangers-on and the occasional nominee were regularly caught in the net with a blaze of publicity, yet, when the cases came to court, the outlaw links had often vanished or been discredited.

Avatar had put some outlaws in jail, but they had still not proved that the club hierarchy controlled and directed criminal enterprises. There was no doubt the clubs were organised, but to what end remained to be proved. Crime had to be the unifying theme, the orthodoxy dictated. But fortunately, finding evidence of this was unnecessary as convictions were no longer the measure of SAPOL's campaign.

The results of these 'disrupt and dismantle' operations were now judged in arrests, not convictions. Locking up bikers was less important than harassing them into quitting clubs, or into not joining in the first place. The bikies had abused their right of free association by committing crime. The motorcycle was now just a prop, police told the media. Today's bikie was more readily found in a car or, worse, in a suit, mingling with the state's worst criminal elements.

There were links to prostitution, extortion and every heinous act imaginable; the clubs acted as a gateway for hoods and gangsters moving back and forth freely between the criminal underworld and their brothers, according to police.

Clearly the police were now a tool of social policy, not just law enforcement. Despite regular announcements heralding Avatar's success in rooting out the villains, Premier Rann had been ramping up his anti-biker rhetoric, promising extra resources and new powers. And not to be outdone, the conservative Opposition had been piping up too, slamming the government for not doing enough to rid the state of the scourge. The Rann Government had promised to bring down the walls of the outlaw bikie clubhouses, but they had done nothing. A Liberal premier would run a fleet of bulldozers through the biker compounds, like General George S Patton commanding a tank division in World War II.

Earlier in October, a confidential SAPOL report on the bike clubs compiled in 2001 had been leaked to the *Sunday Mail* newspaper. The Opposition police spokesman Robert Brokenshire took the opportunity to lay down a challenge. '. . . In light of the new information brought to our attention by the *Sunday Mail*, we plan to introduce the toughest possible comprehensive package to stamp out crimes committed by bikie gangs,' he told the paper. In an accompanying story, titled 'Terror on Two Wheels', the *Sunday Mail* breathlessly warned that SAPOL believed 'the operation of bikie gangs on a national and international basis, together with tactics and activities used, would, by any other definition, classify them as terrorist organisations'.

In 2001, Mr Brokenshire had actually been the Police Minister in the Liberal government of former premier John Olsen. Yet somehow, four years later, this police report came as a revelation to him. A media event ensued. According to the report, police intelligence suggested that up to 200,000 people were believed to be 'sympathetic or deliberately supportive of these groups'. Just how they had identified this huge group of collaborators was not explained. It concluded that bikers en masse were frightening: 'One of the most intimidating aspects of their behaviour is their sheer presence in large numbers, adorned by their colours.' Despite the official-sounding language, the SAPOL report's most compelling conclusions were pure harum-scarum.

Brokenshire said that, despite the tough talk, Rann was actually soft on bikers. If only police had more powers, they could smash the bikers' wall of silence, he thundered. A Liberal government would give police those powers and the community would be safe once again.

Mackie reasoned that all this public debate, however misinformed, was a tremendous windfall to SAPOL. A state election was due within five months and the police were prepared to get involved in this pissing contest between the politicians. Who could blame them? After years of morale-sapping budget cuts, the politicians were jostling to offer them millions of dollars in new resources. And all they had to do was produce lots of lovely, opaque crime statistics that could never be properly analysed. Whichever party won, the biker panic would be a bonanza for the department.

Police are never the standard bearers for civil liberty in a society. In a totalitarian regime, the police officer is always the instrument of oppression, but in a democracy they work within parameters set by the parliament, following its orders. And if police are asked whether they need bigger guns and more powers to do their job, they would be fools to argue. They want to get home to their kids like anybody else.

But now police were getting the chance to set the parameters of their power themselves. They would have laws tailored to order, which would supposedly end the bikie scourge once and for all. The cops said that the Premier and the Attorney-General had asked SAPOL to research laws that would make membership of a club a criminal offence.

If there was ever a time to speak, it was now. For years they had been known as outlaw clubs, but soon they would be *outlawed* clubs. That wouldn't mean people would be rushing at the opportunity, though, Mackie thought. In fact, if certain clubs called for volunteers to give the media a flogging, the queue might stretch around the block. Certainly, the Descendants wouldn't be responding. There would be a time in the future, but not now. The most likely candidates would come from clubs that had been in the headlines for all the wrong reasons. They would be the first to feel the heat of new laws. The campaign would eventually be extended to smaller independent clubs like his as Rann sought to tighten the noose around all their necks. Mackie had no doubt about that. But for now he would wait for the battle to arrive on his doorstep rather than put his club on the media chopping block. These things had an unhappy knack of turning sour.

And besides, he could not be sure how other clubs might react if anyone were to purport to speak on their behalf. He had mates in other clubs, but he was lucky to meet them once every five years.

Any club letting the media in was taking a risk. If it all turned sour, there was prestige at stake and possible dramas with other clubs. Not every member in a club got their way, but they were always guaranteed a say. Internally, such a move would provoke spirited debate before any kind of consensus could be arrived at. It might take weeks in the big national clubs.

The Hells Angels had a no-talk policy with Australian media, so they couldn't speak. The Gypsy Jokers had backed away from making public comments after Steve Williams quit the club. The

Rebels were the fastest-growing outfit but their public comments were tightly controlled from their Sydney headquarters. That left the Finks MC.

As I later wrote in *The Bulletin*, this opportunity had also arisen at a strategic moment. That week, as my letter circulated, the Finks were setting off on a national run for Mildura in Victoria. Members from all over were converging on the Murray River town and riding together back into Adelaide for a party.

The previous night, six interstate members had been stopped at a roadblock on the border and each had been hit with a 'canary'. A canary is the slang term for the yellow defect sticker police place on vehicles that don't meet noise or other Australian standard design rules. A defected bike must be off the road within seventy-two hours or the owner faces arrest and fines. It was the ultimate tactic to thwart a biker run, the new millennial equivalent of US regulations forbidding 'parading without a permit' that were used against bikers and other rebels in the 1960s. The cops had told the visiting members that all the interstate Finks could expect the same treatment. The run would be harassed into non-existence.

If this run was ruined, interstate members might be reluctant to come to South Australia next time, which is of course what the police wanted to hear.

Still, how much could be achieved by doing media remained to be seen. People wanted to believe whatever matched their fears, Mackie thought. And motorcycle clubs had put a lot of effort into making themselves institutions of fear. They had adorned themselves with swastikas and satanic images, hunkered down behind forbidding fortresses and followed secret rituals and rules. They had all-too-eagerly embraced the public's view of them as bogeymen. Maybe it was too late to even try anything else. In the end, it was only the Finks who stepped up to the plate.

In their 36-year history, the Finks MC had given just one interview. In 1973, while at film school, director Phillip Noyce made a documentary, *Castor and Pollux*, which juxtaposed the stories of two counterculture leaders: one a Fink sergeant-at-arms leading a club run and the other the hippy leader of a commune. The film depicted the hippies partaking in free love sessions, chanting and enjoying cleansing enemas, while the bikers fought, drank and spread their arse cheeks for the camera.

At the climax of the film, the Finks divided into two teams and fired cement-filled beer cans at each other from makeshift cannons. This apparently had been a much-loved feature of club runs for years. Amazingly, no-one had ever been hurt. It was the road that had claimed the lives of most members. Phillip Noyce helped the club make a sequel, *Finks Make Movies*, a scriptless free-form production that featured the members taking on a gang of country rednecks.

Until now, the club had been prepared to rest on these images. In a minor concession to public order, the artillery sessions had ceased sometime ago.

6

IN THE BELLY OF THE BEAST

Every bikie stereotype I knew was flashing through my mind. I was on the back of a speeding Harley-Davidson, wedged between the sissy bar and the broad back of an outlaw bikie.

I was riding with the Finks on a national run from Adelaide to Mildura. Members from the Northern Territory, New South Wales and Queensland would join the parade later in the day, swelling the numbers for three days of riding, drinking and carousing.

As Adelaide quickly disappeared in the west behind us, we were in the middle of a pack of riders moving in unison. I was trying to find a way to stay on without clutching the rider. His face was obscured by a bandanna emblazoned with a grisly skull that had staring demonic eyes. He didn't seem the type to appreciate being hugged round the middle by a perfect stranger. On the back of his grimy vest was the club patch, a comic-strip court jester: Bung, from 'The Wizard of Id'. As in the strip, he was drunk, extending a pie-eyed toast to the world, but the other hand was tucked behind his back, coyly concealing something.

Police said that behind the facade of the biker brotherhood, almost all the outlaw clubs were hardcore organised-crime groups involved in every facet of villainy. And from the back of this bike I had seen nothing so far to contradict that view. It was Day One of my education.

That morning we had arrived at the Finks' North clubhouse to a breathtaking sight: dozens of outlaw bikers in full colours standing by their bikes ready for the road. There were four crash wagons driven by nominees and associates in black T-shirts promising 'Attitude with Violence'. These would carry the outlaws' personal gear and transport bikes that broke down or were slapped with canaries by the cops. And every steely eye had been trained on us. What an incongruous sight we must have been to the bikies—a TV reporter from the *Sunday* program with a producer, cameraman and sound recordist, all jammed into a white minivan overflowing with gear. Until now the media had been a distant, but hated, adversary. We were under their microscope as much as they were under ours.

Affecting a jaunty casualness, I leapt out of the van and greeted the massed marauders. 'G'day! How are you fellas this morning?'

There was deathly silence. It was immediately apparent that not all members were on board for this episode of 'Meet the Press'. Everything about us must have screamed *cop*. 'Nice day for it, eh?' I followed up weakly.

More silence, except for the faint sound of blood pounding in my ears. The *Sunday Mail* had been right. Their 'sheer presence in large numbers adorned by their colours' was indeed intimidating, like confronting a line of medieval knights ready to mount up for combat.

I really could have just driven away right there and then, but a loud voice cut the tension. *'Members! Members only!* Come on in here, fellas,' the voice said from behind the cyclone fence. The sergeant-at-arms of the North chapter sauntered into view, instantly gaining the attention of all the troops, who followed him inside the gates, leaving the associates to keep watch over us. 'North' was hosting the run and therefore the sarge of the chapter was responsible for every detail.

We had met him the day before, at the North headquarters. The sarges of the two other Adelaide chapters had also been on hand for this final interview. But it was the North sarge who was clearly running the show. A natural leader, he was charismatic and friendly, but his massive physical presence left one in no doubt that he took no shit.

North chapter was remarkably low key for the locus of evil it was supposed to be. Set on a half-acre block in an industrial area, the new clubhouse was a cheap and cheery affair, two or three breeze block sheds tacked together. But the boys had done some landscaping at the front with a lawn and some palm trees. Inside was a pool table, a bar and kitchen, a little private space with a bed and an en suite bathroom.

As bikie fortresses go, it was about as forbidding as a jumping castle for kids. The only 'fortifications' were a Colorbond steel gate and some security screens. A berm of earth had been created at the edge of the lawn, blocking the line of sight from the street to the clubhouse. It was either for seclusion or to provide a barrier against anyone trying for a pot shot at the clubhouse. A mural alerted anyone foolish enough to break in that the premises were part of the Finks' 'Invincible Empire'.

On the morning of the run, we stood baking in the heat while the bikies performed the rituals of their democracy.

The sarges had taken a risk by proposing the idea that we join the run. Members didn't always get their way, but they were guaranteed a say. I learnt later that there was spirited debate about our presence before a grudging consensus was reached.

When they re-emerged, the North sarge said that everything was cool, but we had to remember one thing: 'Not too hard, too fast.' National runs were big events for the club. They didn't want outsiders stuffing things up, or making themselves a nuisance.

'I can't order the members to talk to you; it's up to them. But if they want to, they'll make their views clear to you, don't worry about that,' he laughed. That was hardly reassuring. There had been no appreciable change in attitude to us. The same frosty expressions blanked any attempt at friendliness.

So just be cool, said the North sarge. I was tempted to confess that I had already been deeply and totally uncool, a fact I had been trying to block out for the past half-hour. On the way there, I had tried to call the North sarge, to check the address of the clubhouse, but somehow I dialled the boss of Avatar, Inspector Graham Goodwin, instead: 'Hey, sorry mate . . . just trying to find the clubhouse, we'll be there in a few minutes, sorry to hold you guys up, but I've just got the address stuffed up,' I had sputtered.

'Adam, this is Graham Goodwin . . .' said a man who was definitely not a Fink.

'Sorry, wrong number . . . Shit.'

After all the secret planning and subterfuge that had gone into the run, the reporter had rung the cops and pretty much told them what Public Enemy Number One was up to. I could explain this and cop the wrath of the Finks—that was the manly way. Or I could choose the craven coward's way and just hope that, if we ran into a monster roadblock, no-one would connect it to me.

It was a very inauspicious start to the day, but there wasn't time to dwell on it. The members were keen to get on the road before the morning heat and humidity turned into a thunderstorm right in their path. With a cyclonic roar, the Harleys came to life.

I was offered a full-face helmet which I accepted. At least if I was on the back of a motorbike when the massed heat of SAPOL came down, I'd be close enough to hear my name mentioned. Then the helmet would come in handy.

The rider with the skull bandanna motioned me behind him without a word. Then like a great fat gleaming serpent emerging from its lair, the tangle of riders and bikes uncoiled, forming two orderly lines that stretched for more than a block.

A motorbike, no matter how big and powerful, is the most vulnerable vehicle on the road. Invisible to many motorists, it just takes one mistake for the rider to be under the wheels of a truck or skittering along the highway using his skin for brakes. But put a pack of Harleys together running in close formation and it becomes the biggest thing on the road, a solid mass that must be respected by other road users.

Traffic signals mean little. If the lead rider runs the amber signal, then everyone does. If anyone were to pull up, the result would be catastrophic: a chain reaction of squealing tyres and blue sparks as chrome hits the tarmac. That's why police have traditionally given outlaws escorts through towns, overriding the traffic signals and deploying cops to keep other motorists from mingling in with the bikes. It infuriates other drivers and radio shock jocks, but it's better than risking confrontation between the outcast travelling circus and the citizenry.

This was more like an armoured division on the move through the suburbs than normal traffic. Even without the escort, the group moved smoothly through the morning peak hour, communicating its intentions clearly and efficiently.

As the bikers rumbled their way towards the outskirts of the city I was expecting a fleet of Avatar cruisers to pick up our tail, but nothing happened. My sense of relief was exquisite. As we hit the dual carriageway, the same feeling seemed to pass through the riders. The tight defensive formation was easing a little now. Soon the bikers were spread over nearly a kilometre and the grimness of their body language was giving way.

Getting out of town is usually the hardest part of a run. The run leader knows that over the course of a few days there are bound to be at least a couple of roadblocks. The stops are part of the drama of the event, unifying the group. But being waylaid for three or four hours just five minutes into the first morning is bound to put everyone in a fractious mood, and the run leader knows that. He is the one who will have to deal with the poisonous effects of bad temper somewhere down the track—in a pub or a police station, but hopefully not in a hospital.

There was a lot riding on this journey. Already, some of the interstaters had their doubts about coming to South Australia, because of Avatar's overzealous attitude. There had been talk amongst the leading clubs of scrapping runs to South Australia, or just shipping the bikes to and from Adelaide, rather than put up all with all the heat. But that would only be a last resort. To the old guard, submitting to the pressure would be a humiliating surrender. Pressure had forged the spirit of outlaw clubs and riding in unison was an expression of the bonds of brotherhood. On the road there were no factions, no power struggles, no differences of opinion, just one entity with a single purpose.

There was a hard core of members who would never put their bikes on a train or a semi-trailer. The road, with all its vagaries and challenges, was the reward. You couldn't be a bikie without it.

Membership of an outlaw club comes with onerous rules and responsibilities. On the road, much of that is left behind. The freedom seems to be free once more; all the pressure seems worthwhile. Canadian biker academic Daniel Wolf had seen the 'harassment' of club runs while riding with the Rebels MC as part of a social anthropology research. 'For these outlaw bikers, riding in the wind with their brothers goes beyond being a theatre of togetherness. It becomes an act of defiance,' he wrote in an anthology, *The Mammoth Book of Bikers*.

These notions, common to all outlaw clubs, were quickly discernible on the road that morning.

The popular perception of bikies in Australia had been formed from a handful of violent incidents over the decades. There was the Father's Day Massacre between the Bandidos and the Comancheros at the Viking Tavern in Milperra in September 1984, which left seven people dead, including a 14-year old bystander. In 2001, the Gypsy Jokers were accused of blowing up former Western Australian policeman Don Hancock and his mate Lou Lewis with a car bomb in retaliation for a sniper attack that killed one of the Jokers. Interspersed were snippets from police files: bashings, shootings, bar fights, melees, drug dealing, motorcycle thefts and a tableau of other unsavoury incidents. They had been typecast as amoral psychopaths battling for control of the wasteland with Mel Gibson's Mad Max.

There were periods of years where nothing of significance took place in clubland. To fill those gaps in the narrative, researchers needed to include the United States or Canada, where the Rock Machine had battled the Hells Angels in a bloody no-holds-barred battle. In Europe, the Angels had fought the Bandidos in the Great Nordic Wars for three years.

As we roared past gawping citizens, I wondered why I hadn't met these denizens of the underworld before, given my line of work. Mike Rann had assured the public these fellows were not 'meatheads on motorbikes' but 'the foot soldiers of organised crime'. If so, whose army were they fighting for?

At this time I was still enmeshed in research into Melbourne's gangland war, which had claimed more than thirty lives between 1998 and 2005, revealing the slimy entrails of Australia's multibillion-dollar drug trade. The public killings had been very bad for business, providing a unique insight into how the Victorian underworld worked. The baby-faced crime lord Carl Williams had tried to snuff anybody who posed the slightest threat to him, working his way through many of the best crooks in town. In my conversations with him, Williams liked to say his crew was 'the new generation'. The old generation, represented by the Moran family, was a mixture of former waterside crooks from the Painters and Dockers Union, wannabe Italian gangsters and some unspeakably violent Eastern Europeans.

The bikies had been almost invisible bit players in the drama. Individuals had popped up as muscle in a couple of scenes, but the bikies were never a serious faction in the power struggle. If they were foot soldiers for organised crime, they had missed out on a huge pay day in Melbourne. Williams had been shelling out $100,000 per hit to assassins as he worked his way through his kill-list. Outlaw bikers had acted as security at funerals and popped up at the occasional party, but these were cameo appearances.

In *Underbelly*, the highly successful TV drama series on the gangland war, the Moran brothers were depicted buying a pill press from a gang of bikies dressed in full colours in every scene. The club, the Iron Bloods, was as fictitious as the transactions with the Morans. One of the few Morans to escape Williams's murder spree told me the bikies were regarded as 'scroungers' in the underworld. 'There were always a few bikers looking for an earner, popping up from time to time wanting to cook speed for you or collect some debts,' he said. They were damn good at bashing people but crime was more than violence, he said. 'To be a real success at organised crime, a bloke has to be likeable. He's got to have a certain charisma about him. Bikies don't play well with others as a rule, that's why they end up in clubs together, where they don't mind getting clobbered by each other from time to time.'

All this contributed to a dissonance in my mind about the bikers. Nowhere in any official source could I find proof that bikies were the new Mafia. And it wasn't as if they were hiding—they were riding around on loud motorcycles with bad-assed names plastered across their backs. And their so-called 'hideouts' were known to everyone.

We cleared the city limits and the bikers opened up the throttle. Looking over the rider's shoulder I could see the speed steadily increasing to 140 kilometres per hour. We blew past a frowning cop on a billboard holding a radar gun and posing a redundant question: 'Speeding: What's your excuse?'

Wheat fields and citrus groves gave way to the monochrome plains of the riverlands. Spinifex and twisted grey gums flashed past. Storms were forecast and through my full-face helmet I could smell the air, rich and earthy, full of rain. We narrowly skirted a couple of towering squalls, grey-black thunderheads trailing shrouds of icy moisture, but then one caught us smack in the face. Visibility dropped to a few metres; the raindrops were like needles on my exposed skin.

Few of my fellow travellers were dressed for such weather. This trip was not about comfort or safety; it was about flying the flag, defying the danger. Not for them the head-to-toe coverage of leather and Gore-Tex favoured by the weekend Harley hero. If they made a mistake and dropped their bike, they would wear the excruciating consequences. Some riders were wearing leather jackets under their colours, but most just had windcheaters or T-shirts on and soon many were wet through.

After half an hour of beating into the wind and rain, the run leader signalled a stop at a lonely country service station. His hand signal was relayed almost instantaneously to the back of the pack, a kilometre behind him, with a flash of red tail-lights.

As we pulled in, it was time for me to meet the outlaw whose colours I had been pressed against all morning. Communication is impossible on a speeding bike with the wind howling in your ears, so our interaction had been limited—a gesture towards the storm clouds, or a subtle shove to get me off his back when he braked. When we stopped, he whipped off his helmet and the fearsome skull bandanna and gave me a huge gap-toothed smile. 'How did you like that?' he inquired, slapping me on the shoulder.

'You hang in all right? I tried to lose you on a coupla bends. Nah, just joking, I wouldn't do that,' he said, laughing hard. He was about my age and came from an eastern European background. Whenever I saw him in the coming years, he always had the same cheerful demeanour. He took nothing seriously, except for three things: his colours, his bike and the family.

The solid wall of hostility I had seen at the clubhouse was now falling away. The successful escape from 'Rann-istan' (as bikies called Adelaide) had lifted spirits enormously, making them far more approachable. The Finks, far from being an Anglo-Saxon clique, were in fact highly multicultural with just about every race represented. They were all unified under the banner of Bung, the drunken court jester.

'Look, he's walking two foot taller already,' I heard a rasping voice say, as I was going into the service-station shop. The voice belonged to a man in a white helmet with a bright blue bandanna tied round his throat. With his Western shirt, faded jeans and dirty old cowboy boots, he looked like he should have been on a horse rather than a motorcycle. He had a rugged sun-burnished face and eyes as blue as an outback sky. 'The Drover' introduced himself as one of the old-timers of the club. He had been there in the late 1960s, when the whole thing began, and proceeded to tell me a little of his story.

Growing up, The Drover never had the chance to fit in anywhere. His mother had been a singing cowgirl in the style of Annie Oakley and the family had travelled the rodeo and country show circuit right through his youth. When he was old enough, he had become a drover and a professional roo shooter and had been moving ever since. He had a bolthole in western Queensland, but he was often away for months. Sometimes, he would just wake up and jump on his Harley and days later pitch up in Adelaide, Sydney or the Gold Coast, wherever he could find a club mate. He had learned more from travelling Australia on the back of this 1988 Harley than he ever had from books, or listening to the hateful media.

'Some people never get off their own dung hills. You know what I mean?' he said, offering me some beef jerky.

The Drover said he used to change bikes regularly, but he had become attached to this one. 'I used to say, never get sentimental about women, dogs, horses or machines, but this one's special—lost my leg on it in 1990,' he said matter-of-factly. He pulled up his jeans to show his prosthetic limb and the stump of his leg.

He had been pushing a mob of cattle on his Harley when a 16-year-old kid driving the Toyota alongside him didn't see him for the dust and turned across him. The tow bar had taken his leg below the knee in a most unsurgical manner. He had flown in the Royal Flying Doctor aircraft to the nearest hospital, an hour away, watching as the toes of his severed leg on its bed of ice slowly turned a horrid shade of blue. He had saved the boot, but that was all.

'I knew it was gone. I promised the doc I would stop riding if he could keep my knee, and he did. But the first time I couldn't get a park for the truck in town, I got the bike out of the shed. It's my wheelchair now,' he said.

Disabled though he was, he had more mobility than the most able-bodied person because his mind was unrestrained, he reckoned. But then he broke off and was suddenly restless to get back on the road. A stiff breeze was blowing the storm clouds away to the north and the best riding of the day was just ahead.

'With a tailwind like this up our bum, we'd be in Mildura in five hours,' he said, watching his brothers fill up on petrol, nicotine and cholesterol. 'But these young blokes like their smokes and sausage rolls too much.'

My perception of the club was changing with each conversation. Perhaps the club was a different thing to each and every member. Fortunately, a common enemy was close at hand.

There had been no sign of Avatar thus far, a rare event for an outlaw run these days. The pack had met no resistance as it passed through small towns. Kids had run out to the roadside waving like the circus had arrived. Young women had stopped and stared openly, thrilled at the idea of something new in town. Their boyfriends had thrown edgy sidelong glances at the barbarians and pulled their girls closer. But before too long the cop network had swung into action and country patrol cars were waiting behind billboards as we rode into small towns, sitting at a safe distance at fuel stops.

At Waikerie, a grey Commodore sedan, so nondescript it could only be an undercover police car, pulled up. A paunchy middle-aged detective sergeant from Avatar got out and sauntered over. Two young clean-cut officers stayed in the car, one with a video camera carefully capturing every outlaw on tape like a tourist in a safari park. They must have been going like the clappers of hell to catch up with the pack after giving us an hour's head-start.

There were twenty officers assigned full time to Avatar at that time, shadowing a group of no more than four hundred outlaw bikers and close associates in Adelaide, probably less. Do the numbers. It couldn't have been good for a senior officer to let his personal quota of suspects in full colours get out of town without a tail. Especially when a reporter in their midst had inadvertently tipped off the boss that bikers were on the move. That nugget of intel seemed to have been overlooked. Standing among them, helmet in hand, I must have looked to the detective like part of the crew.

'Gurrr-day mate!' said the detective to one biker he recognised, with exaggerated friendliness, like he had happened on an old friend in the middle of nowhere.

The biker immediately adopted the cop's mock friendly tone. 'Gurrr-day officer,' he said.

'So where are you off to today?' the cops asked hopefully.

'Dunno,' came the reply.

'Come on, you know this is all a game. You tell us where you're going and when you'll be back home, we let 'em know back in Adelaide and everybody's sweet. Okay?'

'Sure,' said the biker.

'So where you blokes headed?'

'Dunno. We'll know when we get there.'

The detective's face reddened and he shook his head. He didn't need this shit. While crooks were hard at work back in Adelaide, he and his team would be providing an escort to a bunch of hooligans. If he put in a hard day's work on them, he would write out a few tickets, maybe arrest someone for outstanding warrants or slap a few canaries on these motorcycles.

The detective changed tack. This was just like going to the dentist, painful yet brief, he said. It was so much better to cooperate, but either way he was going to do his job. The biker was not the least bit interested. He chewed loudly on his beef jerky, with his mouth flapping open so little fragments flew in the cop's direction.

And then he just turned his back on the officer. Further communication was rendered impossible as the outlaws started their bikes. The pack mounted up and rode away again, now with the grey Commodore in tow.

Meanwhile, the film crew from *Sunday* was waiting a kilometre ahead to capture the cavalcade on a long straightaway, rather like the opening shot of *The Wild One*. As the pack zoomed past, the men from Avatar spotted the camera and swung around. They pulled up with their camera still rolling to ask tersely where the crew was from. Then they asked them if *they* knew where the outlaws were headed.

'Dunno,' said Les the cameraman as he filmed the Avatar cameraman filming him. The detective glared down the lens and sped away to rejoin the column.

Our presence was something different. These were normally tediously unpleasant operations for the police, but at least out on the highway there was no public scrutiny of proceedings. If the press was on hand, it was usually organised and orderly: set pieces at roadblocks, where the SAPOL spin doctors could control the message. A pissed-off outlaw with a fistful of fines and a canary on his bike was unlikely to give interviews. In those situations the media and the cops were serving the same master.

The cops could get away with a lot unless they charged an outlaw. Then a high-priced lawyer would pick over the entrails of the affair to find ways to get evidence kicked out of court. But short of that, what happened on the road stayed on the road. It came with the patch. You had to take some heat, even the occasional kicking, without running squealing to the media. If you couldn't, you weren't outlaw material. But the rules of the game had suddenly changed. Adelaide bikers had rarely complained to the media about police treatment before. This new tactic must have been puzzling to Avatar.

And I figured that, soon enough, the cop from Avatar would review the tape and recognise the reporter that he had recently dined with. I would be officially included in the 200,000 people that SAPOL believed were sympathetic or aligned with the bikers.

7

DICKHEAD MAGNET

We rode another couple of hours to Berri by the Murray River, the Avatar cruiser always 50 metres off the back of the pack.

The police presence was not totally reassuring. It was hard to shake the feeling there were two opposing points of view facing off on that road, rather than a simple struggle between good and evil. This scene had more to do with politics than law and order, although the police escort did keep the bikers' highway brio in check—the front-runners kept the column within the speed limit and eschewed any provocative passing manoeuvres. Now the pack had become tightly bunched again. With the rest of the club converging on Mildura, the Adelaide members needed to make it to there without dramas.

The politics of this roadhouse theatre was reinforced when I found an opportunity to check my messages. I discovered that Robert Brokenshire, as the Opposition police spokesman, had issued a press release claiming he had information that the Finks were on a run and Avatar was acting as free chaperone, fixing traffic lights for the outlaws and standing back while they consumed copious amounts of beer in country hotels en route. It's an outrage, he said; they should never have got past the city limits.

He clearly had well-placed sources of information, even if it was completely false. I shared this with one biker, who shook with laughter. 'They're great stories these politicians come up with about us. The problem is sometimes we just don't recognise ourselves in 'em.' The police on the road might have agreed.

There was nothing left for Avatar but to trail the pack for the next hour through Renmark and Paringa until we crossed the border into Victoria. I had been off-loaded by now. Nothing personal, the rider said, but with both our weight on board, his fuel consumption was shot to pieces. I was shifted to a big yellow Triumph 1000 owned by a nominee.

The nominee didn't look particularly happy about it, but as a 'nom' he didn't argue. The nominee took orders from any or all of the patch members. That could include cleaning toilets, serving drinks at the club bar, running errands or any menial shit a member could think of, including dinking the reporter. As a nom, he had to ride at the rear of the column, just ahead of the police car.

We were half-expecting to find a new posse at the Victorian border, but there was nothing other than an empty highway bathed in sunshine. We were crossing into the grain belt of western Victoria and on both sides of the road freshly ploughed fields stretched out to the horizon. Once out of South Australia, the speed limits were forgotten and riders let their bikes wind out to a comfortable cruising speed, about 140–150 kilometres per hour.

Up ahead, the leaders were engulfed in orange-pink dust churned up by a farmer on his tractor. It was about an hour's run dead straight into Mildura, where cold beer and a warm welcome from the interstate brothers awaited. This was an experience to savour, a reward for all the drama that came with the patch.

Here on this remote highway they could really live the romantic image they had of themselves, a travelling brotherhood sharing the intense emotions that came with the risks they were sharing. No-one could understand what this was about if they hadn't experienced it.

For no particular reason, one senior member peeled off and let the column pass until he was alongside us. The member had brought the nominee into the club after getting to know him in the gym and they were very close. It's said that you don't join an outlaw club, you join your mate in a club. As an outsider, if you have a friendship with a patch member, it can only go so far. The member cannot share his club life with you, unless you take the next step and become a nominee, as this man had.

The senior member smiled at him and gave him a gentle pat on the shoulder, as if to say: 'This is the pay-off; enjoy it, my brother.' If only life could be like this all the time: a straight road with plenty of mates, and more at the journey's end.

A column of bikers riding two by two in close wheel formation at over 140 kilometres per hour is a unique test of cooperation and discipline. At that speed, one mistake, or a pothole or a tyre blown off a semi, and the highway would be scattered with metal, blood and body parts. The leader must communicate the road conditions; to avoid a truly horrific pile-up, his hand signals must reach back through the pack right to the last rider.

The road captain was responsible for the route. 'If you're lost, it's not cool to pull out a map, or ask directions,' the road captain told me at one of our stops. 'You just keep riding round and round town till you work out the track!' But that's a luxury. At high speed, an error at the front, even the slightest misjudgement, works its way from bad to worse through a column.

About twenty minutes out of Mildura the column was passing a B-double semi-trailer on a long straight incline with just one lane either way. It was a simple pass for the frontrunners, but at the back all we could see, when it came to our turn, was blue sky beyond that rise. The nominee had to trust there was nothing looming up on the other side and wait our turn to pass, steadily accelerating. There was no thought of breaking ranks, which might have caused mayhem and destruction. Rather than putting the nominee in a bear hug, I grabbed two handfuls of the sports bag tied over the back mudguard of the Triumph.

Over the nominee's shoulder I could see the speedometer was nudging 150 kilometres an hour. We were still 50 metres behind the truck on the wrong side of the road. Another B-double loomed up from the opposite direction. There was no pulling back, despite the blaring air horns of the truck bearing down us. The nominee just dropped the machine down a gear and ripped the throttle. The yellow beast leapt forward so violently I was nearly pitched off the back. If I hadn't caught a finger in the webbing of the rider's colours I could have been rolling under the truck.

When the two trucks passed, no more than two metres apart, we were right between them and the speedo was hitting 180. They were so close I could have reached out and touched either one. At the same time I could feel the heavy suction as the air folded around the trucks, each one trying to pull us under its trailer. I could smell the hot stink of the tyres rolling by. I could hear the roar of the rubber on the asphalt.

The nominee was leaning forward, almost flattened on the gas tank, focusing only on the shaft of light ahead. And then we shot back into the sunshine, like a pip squeezed between giant fingertips. 'Now I understand,' I thought. 'There could be criminals among us today, but surely there are easier ways to earn a dishonest dollar than this.'

If the motorcycle was a prop, then this was reality theatre. My fear and dread gave way to pure exhilaration; the dull thud of adrenalin in my brain was replaced by a rush of endorphins. As we cruised into Mildura I felt like I had just taken my first skydive.

As afternoon shadows lengthened, we rolled into Mildura and pulled up out front of the Grand Hotel where a long silver rank of Harleys had formed. The tailwind had made the first day's ride a pleasure and spirits were high among the Adelaide crew.

Other members had already arrived from the eastern states cursing the heavy conditions they had encountered on the hot arid plains of western NSW. The lovely breeze at our backs had been a desiccating headwind for them.

But none of that mattered now they were here. There was a relaxed and friendly atmosphere as the men greeted each other with hearty embraces. The profile of the interstate contingent was so similar to the South Australians the two groups just blended seamlessly. Soon I couldn't tell them apart, the only distinguishing feature was in the patch. Bung's pants were a different colour for each state.

There was a wide range of ages and looks in the group from classic old ragtag bikers like the Drover through to clean-shaven and gym-toned young members with vivid new tattoos and gold jewellery. But there was no division in their ranks. They were all Finks, together on the road again.

As the first cold beer washed away the grit of the road, they were picking up conversations that had been paused months earlier at the end of the last run. They exuded a proud self-confidence. There was a solidarity that most drinking men would find appealing but also quite intimidating. You could easily see how that could have led to trouble on occasion.

Only a fool would tangle with a pack of outlaw bikers fresh from the road, but hotels are the natural habitat of the fool. 'We're dickhead magnets,' one member said. 'Drunks in bars like to test themselves against a so-called outlaw.'

But that night in Mildura, no blood was spilt. After a few drinks out the front of the bar in the setting sun, they broke up into smaller groups to sample the town's wide range of cuisines. A few went on to nightclubs but by eleven the core of the club was back at the Hotel in the groove of a long session of drinking.

Testosterone hung heavy in the air. Only a fool would tangle with a pack of outlaw bikers fresh from the road, but hotels are the natural habitat of the fool. 'We're dickhead magnets,' one member said. 'Drunks in bars like to test themselves against a so-called outlaw.'

The police were called to the Grand Hotel, but only to eject a drunken obstreperous local who wouldn't leave the outlaws alone. However, late in the evening a curious scene was played out. Two drunken young women came into the bar and were conspicuously trying to mingle with the outlaws. There was something phony about them, but in the beginning the bikers welcomed them. The girls claimed to be tourists heading from Melbourne to Adelaide but, when asked why anyone would make that trip via Mildura, they seemed lost for an answer.

They began to ask questions, keen to discover who was who. The bikie hackles really started to rise. Then one pulled a video camera from her handbag and began to film the crowd, giggling and laughing as if this were a great joke. At this there was a heavy ponderous silence, like a wall had been instantly built around the bikers. Then one old member drew the girl close and spoke to her softly, but with unmistakable conviction: 'If you don't put that away and fuck off, I'm going to stick it fair up you, okay love?'

She didn't need to be asked twice. Rapidly recovering their sobriety, the girls beat a hasty retreat to their car and made off into the night.

After years of being filmed and followed, it was easy for the bikers to conclude that these were undercover cops. In their minds, Avatar was everywhere and anywhere. There had been sillier attempts at infiltration than this one before. And the fact that the Victorian cops had been invisible on the road into Mildura didn't mean they weren't watching.

I was quick to knock down the idea. What kind of police boss would send his subordinates into such obvious danger with a silly plan like that? And what police constable on her miserable salary would be prepared to go along with it?

At the time, the bikies seemed to me to be paranoid. However, I later brought this up with the bar manager and he said the women had spent ten minutes earnestly quizzing him about the bikers before making their appearance in the bar. They had been driving a South Australian–registered vehicle and they were not drunk when they arrived.

By the morning, Mildura was well and truly aware of the club's presence. A local radio jock told listeners that 'the Finks had landed in town like a fleet of 747s last night' and encouraged callers to ring in with stories of depravity and debauchery. The segment fell flat when no-one could come up with anything salacious or exciting enough.

I felt sorry for the local radio shock jocks. Nothing much ever happened in a town like Mildura, so when a horde of bikers arrived, it was like some kind of devil cult had landed. They were like rock stars that had to live up to the reputation or people would be disappointed. It was the riding season across Australia and there were thousands of bikers making their national runs. The club runs would invariably pass without incident but if there was just one altercation it would be front page news across the country.

Statistics showed that bikers, despite their reputation for depravity, posed a much lower risk to families than footballers. Yet, at the sound of a Harley in their quiet streets, people jumped to the conclusion the bikies were in town to defile their daughters.

That day, when the procession began rolling back into South Australia, Avatar was ready for them. Three unmarked cruisers and a black Toyota LandCruiser from the STAR Group resumed the pursuit. The cops, now in polo shirts and jeans, stood at a safe distance watching and eating their burgers while the bikers ate counter meals in the Waikerie pub, halfway home.

Many of the Finks weren't drinking and just sat out in the street yarning and smoking, watching the cops watching them. 'Bunch of wusses!' sniffed the Drover. 'They're afraid. In the old days, one old sergeant on a bicycle could have sorted this lot out. I got that many floggings back then. Even with me own guns. And now look at this. Funny thing is, it's our taxes paying for it too.'

It's hard to see what role Avatar was playing. Not a single biker was breath-tested, no bikes were defected, no warrants were checked. Three days of pursuit and planning, and then nothing. The parade moved on, eager to get back to Adelaide to christen the new North chapter with a memorable party.

The highway home seemed to be full of police and at the next fuel stop word filtered back from advance scouts that there was a major roadblock further ahead. The sight of the STAR Group vehicle screaming past with full lights and sirens reinforced this notion. The outlaws prepared themselves for the confrontation. As much as they disliked the attention, a full-scale police contingent was a back-handed compliment to the bikers, publicly validating their claim to outcast status.

Yet the tension proved anticlimactic. The great roadblock vanished into thin air. We expected to run into it over every rise, but Avatar had slipped back to Adelaide. The only outlaws booked that day were some tourists in a campervan who crossed double yellow lines.

By nightfall the Finks were back at North chapter, drinking beer and eating steaks. The crowd was quiet and contained. There were several circles, consisting of older members and men they had brought into the club who had now transferred to other chapters interstate. This was a rare chance to catch up and renew their fraternal bonds.

Discussions mostly centred on mundane family and work issues. Many seemed to be juggling a couple of families—there were plenty of demands from wives, girlfriends and children. To get out on the road was a welcome respite. There were few women present tonight—no partners, just two topless barmaids and a troupe of Adelaide's finest strippers. In fact, the strippers seemed to be having difficulty in keeping the attention of the men. Certainly, they were in no danger of unwanted molestation.

In a corner, three smiling half-drunk bikers were contentedly pawing the huge pendulous bosoms of one of the topless barmaids. She was not fazed in the slightest. 'I'd much rather work the biker parties than the football clubs. At least here, if any of the blokes gets out of hand, one of the older men will step in and make sure you are okay,' she said.

One of the bikers offered me a feel of her boobs. When I hesitated, he just plopped one in my hand, saying it was rude to refuse. The barmaid and bikers brayed with laughter, but the sexual charge in the air was just about zero.

The strippers were de rigueur, but the members had come here to be with each other, to renew fraternal bonds.

Wonder Woman, the star stripper for the night, was now disrobing inside the club house; but a number of the members were outside talking to me about their loyalty to the club and their motivations for joining.

Many it seemed had previously sought brotherhood in other avenues of life: in the military, sporting clubs in business or even down at the local pub but nothing matched the camaraderie they had found in the Finks MC. Being accepted into its ranks had been the making of his life, at least one said. Some believed they would have been long dead if they hadn't been inside a club. Their peer group had kept them from going off-track and acted as a sounding board and support mechanism. Outside they were confronted by all the contradictions of modern life. Australia was an affluent society that would not protect the well-being of its children. Materialism had corrupted everything. Governments enacted laws to protect the rich at the expense of the poor. Their rules and by-laws held no moral authority. The outlaw world was the last bastion of freedom.

One NSW member said he had been awarded an Order of Australia the year before. Looking at him, with his much broken nose and his club tattoos, I found it hard to believe but sure enough, when I checked, this man had indeed been gonged for services to charity and youth work.

Later *The Australian* newspaper reported that this man had given up a prosperous business to manage a tattoo parlour for the club, while throwing himself into charity work. Previously he had donated money to surf life saving clubs, but now he helped young offenders find work. He had also set up a foundation to support young accident victims who lacked insurance or financial backing. The contrasts could not have been sharper. Here was an organisation which its critics vehemently insisted was responsible for selling drugs to kids. Yet some members were working hard to save them. If I had an image of a typical bikie, it was no longer so clear-cut now. There was no way you could generalise about this group or the entire biker scene for that matter. Each man had his own story and it would require me to speak to a wide range of them to come up with any sensible conclusions. Three days on the road with this group was just an introduction.

All night the police cars had been cruising up and down the street, stopping cars going in and out. If Premier Mike Rann and the cops had their way, gatherings like this one would become illegal. 'I've paid my debt to society and why should my kids believe that I am a criminal, just for riding with my brothers,' said one member.

'If being a 1% club is the problem, why not just take it off the jacket?' I asked, pointing to the diamond-shaped badge on his colours.

'It's not that simple,' he said, opening his shirt to reveal the livid red 1% symbol inked into his chest. 'And it goes much deeper than that too.'

Long after Wonder Woman had stowed her magic rope and cape, I was still talking with the members in the moonlight of death, philosophy and justice

About midnight, I left the party. One of the members had sauntered over and told me the bare-knuckle fighting was due to start soon. Which weight division would I like to fight in, he asked. Paperweight, I said, taking this as my cue to leave.

Leaving them to their bonding, I caught a cab back to town, passing through the police cordon, which now consisted of more than a dozen vehicles. They might have missed us leaving town but they weren't going to miss the party. Who knows how many crime stats were on offer for the taking there that night? It narrowly beat swallowing flies on a roadblock in the middle of nowhere.

I found I couldn't sleep, so I decided to take a walk. On a warm spring night every species of nightlife was on the move: drunken wedding parties, kids from the suburbs, soldiers on leave, streetwalkers and whizzers. A mad man in circus tights was twirling hula hoops.

I ended up in a greasy burger joint on Hindley Street and, as I waited for my meal, there was a loud rap at the window. A dozen Finks wearing windcheaters in club colours were standing there grinning, their faces glowing with sunburn. By Christmas, Finks clubhouses and many homes would be raided; there would be more arrests and reams of bad publicity. But tonight, the Finks would feel like an invincible empire, enjoying their freedom, right or wrong. For as long as it lasted, the Fink was a king.

Perhaps even being up close to this thing, whatever it was—be it fraternity of rough heads or an organised-crime gang—was not enough, I thought to myself. It was no guarantee that one could draw a clear and accurate picture. I wondered how an organisation like this could ever survive in a time of political fear and terror-mongering. People saw in it what they wanted to see. Maybe I had fallen for the romance.

I was very grateful the club had given me this opportunity to make up my own mind. The fact that the material published from this short sojourn was perceived as fair and balanced by the biker community would also be a crucial reference in my favour when approaching other groups both in Australia and the United States. Word travelled fast in this sub-culture. If this trip had gone badly wrong, it was doubtful this book could have been written. No other clubs would have been prepared to take the risk on me. So courtesy of the Finks, this run became the start of a much longer journey into the outlaw world.

Weeks later, I interviewed then Prime Minister John Howard about his new anti-terrorism laws, which had been passed in the wake of the London Underground bombings of 7 July that claimed the lives of fifty-six and injured more than 700. Under this legislation, the Commonwealth had awarded itself the right to arrest and detain people for being members of organisations suspected of terrorist links or sympathies. A new form of legal sanction was born. The control order did not confer guilt, just a suspicion that you were up to no good. The government didn't like the people you were hanging out with. This verdict was unchallengeable and based on secret evidence.

'There are people in this country who are hostile and antagonistic to our interests. There are people who in certain circumstances would be not only of interest but of danger, and they are the people that we clearly target. We're not trying to target a section of the community,' Howard said.

The rules of the game were changing in Australia. It wasn't enough to drop out of society. It was no longer tolerable to be on the fringe, to have your own internal values and ethics. In the struggle to come, if you didn't stand up for your right to remain undefined you would be overwhelmed. You would be compelled to forsake your friendships or pay the consequences.

The Finks would later be recognised amongst their peers as having played a crucial role in the fight against such notions. They would inspire others to join the resistance to the draconian anti-biker laws that were coming around the country. As awkward as it had been to have our crew on the run, putting themselves in the public spotlight was a step in that process on behalf of all the clubs.

8

A PRIVATE ARMY

When 15-year-old Ralph Hubert Barger Junior saw *The Wild One* at his local cinema in 1954, he decided a biker's life was his destiny. He had flirted with becoming a beatnik, but he had loved the motorcycle from the moment he straddled a $20 motor scooter.

That movie, which inflamed America, helped Barger and many other juvenile delinquents understand the anarchic possibilities of life on two wheels. At eighteen years old, fresh out of the army, he bought his first Harley, a 1936 Knucklehead. Yet unlike most of his generation, Barger did not idolise the hero Johnny Strabler, played by Marlon Brando, but rather the antihero Chino, portrayed by Lee Marvin. Johnny and Chino had once been part of the same club, which had split in two after a dispute that was never fully explained. Angry young men like Barger took Chino's image and turned it into a 1960s counterculture that roared across the concrete highways of California.

In his 1966 gonzo classic, *Hell's Angels*, Hunter S Thompson introduced Ralph 'Sonny' Barger to the world as the 'Maximum Leader': 'There is a steely thoughtful quality about Barger, an instinctive restraint that leads outsiders to feel they can reason with him. But there is also a quiet menace, an egocentric fanaticism tempered by eight years at the helm of a legion of outcasts.'

In December 2005 it had been a long, tortuous process for me to get permission to interview Barger for the *Bulletin* magazine and the Nine Network's *Sunday* program. Letters had originally been sent to the Australian presidents of various Hells Angels chapters and correspondence had gone back and forth as credentials and bona fides were checked. A San Francisco–based lawyer Fritz Clapp had contacted us when we arrived in Los Angeles and further discussions were held. Clapp acted for the Angels and as a personal adviser to Barger. While not a patch member of the MC (that might have made legal practice difficult), he was the next best thing.

A lifetime biker, Clapp sported a bright red mohawk, like the fin of a tropical fish, and a patch on his vest that read 'Lawyer from Hell'. He divided his time between Hawaii, San Francisco and numerous courtrooms around the nation. On behalf of the Angels, he had successfully sued numerous companies that had infringed the club's copyright and intellectual property by daring to steal its insignia, including its trademark grinning winged death's head logo. These intellectual property thieves had been trying to flog everything from haute couture in Saks 5th Avenue in New York to T-shirts and coffee mugs in Wal-Mart. The Hells Angels MC was now a corporation, something no other so-called 'crime gang' had ever achieved.

The Angels had created an impressive defensive infrastructure to ensure their survival. I visited the club's number-one lobbyist, Jeff Rabe, the president of the Sacramento Angels chapter in northern California. From a cluttered office in the state capitol, Rabe dealt with everything from managing the media and petitioning

Congress on road safety and gang laws to arranging bail bonds and legal defence for accused bikers. Rabe, a burly gravel-voiced man, was also the lobbyist for the US Modified Motorcycle Association and the Collation of Clubs, which spoke for many of America's outlaw clubs.

Rabe dismissed the popular wisdom that the clubs existed to perpetuate crime. On his salary, he wasn't about to work this hard to help criminals operate unfettered, he said. This was about preserving fundamental rights, such as freedom of association and the right to bear arms. 'Freedoms we use each and every day,' he added. Some Angels still enforced extralegal solutions to problems with baseball bats and motorcycle chains but life had become much more civilised, he said. He was wearing a tie and business suit these days almost as often as he did his patch. Bikers were no longer outlaws, but taxpayers and voters, who were entitled to a say in how they were governed.

But still the notion persisted that bikers wanted only to rip at the fabric of Western society, I said.

'I don't know if *rip* is the correct term. I think maybe just brush against it, because it's exciting and it breaks up the monotony of the day,' replied Rabe, with a huge grin.

The Lawyer from Hell had finally managed to fit us into Sonny's schedule, which was hectic with book signings, personal appearances and media interviews across America. As I flew with a cameraman over the desert from Los Angeles to Barger's home in Arizona, I couldn't decide whether I was meeting a gang boss or an American icon of freedom.

Today, *The Wild One* seems embarrassingly dated with cringeworthy lines that Brando must have struggled to deliver with a straight face.

> *Kathie Bleeker*: Do you just ride around or do you go on some
> sort of a picnic or something?
> *Johnny*: A picnic? Man, you are too square. I'm . . . I . . . I'll
> have to straighten you out. Now, listen, you don't go any one
> special place. That's cornball style. You just go. [*snaps fingers*]

But the film and its source material, drawn from true life and
fiction, are still valid today in understanding 'the biker menace'
and how bikers perceive themselves. Despite its appalling dialogue
and costumes later parodied by the gay community, *The Wild One*
set the opposing archetypes of the movement for decades to come,
the fraternity of equals versus the criminal hierarchy, the brotherhood versus the gang.

In the film, Johnny's Black Rebels all appear to be in uniform. Each has a leather jacket with BRMC over-crossed pistons
stencilled on the back. Each member's name is embroidered on
the front as in a military unit. Their bikes are remarkably similar too—equal numbers of well-kept BSAs and Triumphs, which
they ride in a tight orderly formation. By contrast, Chino's Beetles
ride a ramshackle collection of beat-up Harleys and Indians.
Beyond the grimy Levis, each Beetle sports his own look, from
Chino's striped sweatshirt to other members' tasselled cowboy
jackets, flight-deck hats, skunk-skin caps, engineers and logger's
boots. Chino's gang embraces an almost organic diversity and
individuality, while Johnny's group seems to glory in uniformity
and discipline.

This battle has continued in different ways inside clubs (and
between clubs) ever since. It's a struggle between those who join
to enjoy a conditional freedom and those prepared to fall into line
behind a charismatic leader.

Today the public image of bikies suggests that Johnny's Black
Rebels have won that argument, just as Brando beat Marvin in
their punch-up in the film. To cinemagoers, the Black Rebels

represented the frightening potential of a bunch of hoodlums welded into one disciplined, cohesive unit. Critics say the Hells Angels MC and its clones today are the bastard children of that fear: franchised criminal organisations that hold the values of mainstream society in sneering contempt.

In part, *The Wild One* was inspired by that legendary 1947 incident in Hollister, California, when several hundred bikers ran amok in the small town during the American Motorcyclist Association–sanctioned race meeting. On the 4th of July holiday weekend, four thousand motorcyclists had descended on Hollister for the popular Gypsy Tour, overwhelming the town of just 4500 citizens.

The *San Francisco Chronicle* described what followed as an 'outburst of terrorism—wrecking of bars, bottle barrages into the streets from upper story windows and roofs and high speed racing of motorcycles though the streets': 'Riders, both men and women, steered their machines into bars, crashing fixtures and bottles and mirrors. They defied all traffic regulations racing full speed through the streets and intersections. Hundreds loosed bottle barrages,' the paper thundered.

Sixty people were injured, three seriously, including one rider who had his foot nearly severed. Bartenders in Hollister's twenty-one saloons halted the sale of beer, mistakenly believing the group could not afford whisky. Riotous activities continued as the seven-man Hollister police contingent looked on, helpless. The bars closed two hours early, but still pandemonium reigned.

At dusk on the second day of the outrage, forty state highway patrol officers arrived with an ingenious plan. They 'forced a lull in the terrorism' by putting on a concert. According to the *Chronicle*:

> Armed with tear gas guns, the officers herded the cyclists into
> a block on San Benito street, between Fifth and Sixth streets,

parked a dance band on a truck and ordered the musicians to play. Hundreds of individuals who invaded the town yesterday for the motorcycle show, about 10 per cent of them women, halted their riotous 'play' to dance.

The formal ball at the American Legion Hall was cancelled, presumably because there was no band.

Members of early outlaw clubs, the Boozefighters and the Pissed off Bastards of Bloomington, were among fifty of the riotous 'gypsycycles' to be arrested and fined a total of $2000 over the incident. Days later, when all had dispersed, *Time* magazine staged a famous photograph of a drunk sprawled over a motorcycle in a Hollister street surrounded by broken bottles. The story caused a nationwide sensation, America's first motorcycle-inspired moral panic.

The following year on the 4th of July weekend, the bikers descended on Riverside, California, and a tradition of motorcycle gangs taking over terrified communities was well established. The undersheriff of Riverside County captured the hysteria in an open letter to news media: 'Just what is the extent of damage caused by these hoodlums and tramps, these uncivilised demons, who ride exploding and fire-belching machines of destruction, hell-bent on destroying the property and persons of Riverside citizens . . .' Just as Americans were getting used to peace, here was another threat to the social fabric. But in the Hollister and Riverside 'riots' there was no evidence of leadership or organisation; this was a spontaneous reaction from too much beer and high spirits.

But when Hollywood got hold of the story the drunken rabble was transformed into a dark, paramilitary-style force—Johnny's Black Rebels MC, moving from town to town on the whim of its resentful, sociopathic leader. America had seen outlaws like Chino riding the roads ever since motorcycles had come on the scene, but the brooding Johnny Strabler was something new and darker.

The model for the regimented Black Rebels had been sketched by Frank Rooney in an article called 'Cyclists' Raid', published in *Harper's Magazine* in 1951. 'Troop B of the Angelenos Motorcycle Club' roars into the small town of Pendleton. All the riders are on red bikes, except for the leader, Simpson, whose cycle is white. They intend to 'bivouac' outside of town, but plan to spend the evening at a hotel run by former army veteran Joel Bleeker, for whom distasteful memories of war service are still fresh. He takes an instant dislike to what he calls Simpson's 'private army'.

The Angelenos, in Rooney's story, look more like Adolf Hitler's storm troopers, the brownshirts, rather than outlaw bikers:

> Like all the others, [Simpson] was dressed in a brown wind-breaker, khaki shirt, khaki pants, and as Bleeker had already observed, wore dark calf length boots. A cloth and leather helmet lay on the table beside Simpson's drink, but he hadn't removed his flat green goggles, an accouterment [sic] giving him and the men in his troop the appearance of some tropical tribe with enormous semi-precious eyes, lidless and immovable.

From the rollicking, pleasure-seeking chaos of Hollister, Rooney had created a sinister alien force. Simpson's twenty men were really only 'variations of the one, the variations with few exceptions being too subtle for him to recognise'; his troop of clones was just one unit of a growing army fanning out across the nation.

'You say you're from Troop B? Is that right?'

'Correct. We're forming Troop G now. Someday . . .'

'You'll be up to Z,' Bleeker said.

'And not only in California.'

To his horror Bleeker discovers that, in return for their loyalty, the leaders of the wealthy Angelenos MC give members carte blanche for destruction and mayhem. 'In an organisation as large and selective as ours it's absolutely necessary to insist on a measure of discipline. And it's equally necessary to allow a certain amount of relaxation,' Simpson says.

When the drunken mob begins ripping up Bleeker's hotel, Simpson merely hands over a wad of bills to cover the damage. When, in the climax of the story, Bleeker's daughter is killed in the hotel lobby by one of the cyclists, the leader is a mere spectator.

> He saw Simpson—or rather a figure on the white motorcycle, helmeted and goggled—stationed calmly in the middle of the street under a hanging lamp . . . Simpson was making no effort to control his men but waiting rather for that moment when their minds, subdued but never actually helpless, would again take possession of their bodies.

It's this image that has permeated America's understanding of outlaw motorcycle clubs: the fear of vigilantism, that a well-organised paramilitary force could overwhelm civil society. By force of its numbers and wealth, this gang would be almost impossible to stop, even by its leaders. From the 1950s, America began to perceive a threat to its way of life from organised groups, both social and political. The Communist Party of America had stolen the blueprints for the atomic bomb and sold them to the Soviet Union. A network of communist agents was involved in crime to gather resources for the overthrow of democracy, which led US President Lyndon Baines Johnson in the mid-1960s to suggest that 'organised crime constitutes nothing less than a guerrilla attack on society'.

In 1979, US law enforcement unleashed a new gang-busting magic bullet on the Angels. The Racketeer Influenced and Corrupt Organizations Act (RICO) of 1970 had been originally written to target the organised crime families of the Mafia. It allowed the courts to attack 'enterprises' that engaged in a 'pattern of racketeering'. Prosecutors could demonstrate a criminal 'enterprise' existed by linking 'predicate acts': old convictions for drugs, violence and extortion, virtually anything at all could be in effect re-tried in a federal court. If membership of the enterprise could be proven (and that was the easy part), even the most tenuous links to crime would result in prison sentences of twenty years per count.

The move to charge eighteen Hells Angels and their associates under RICO in 1979 followed the attempted murder of two California police officers in separate bombings. The officers had been involved in prosecuting James 'Jim Jim' Brandes, a member of Sonny Barger's Oakland chapter, though he was never charged over the bombings. It seemed the perfect device to dismantle the Hells Angels, many of whom had a long history of convictions for drugs and violence. Now even members without convictions could be roped into the conspiracy, simply by association.

Barger himself believed it was an attack on the club's First Amendment rights under the US Constitution, which guaranteed freedom of religious expression, speech and the right to peaceful assembly. The prosecutors needed to prove to the jury that, when the Angels got together to ride motorcycles, get high, fight and fuck, this was just an elaborate cover for a criminal conspiracy.

Ironically, the RICO charges would be a test of whether the Hells Angels actually believed in their own credo of brotherhood. A not guilty plea would lead to a minute examination of the structure and rituals of the club. 'Now was when we were going to really act like a club and stick together,' Barger later wrote in his autobiography *Hell's Angel*.

Nobody had ever taken a RICO charge to trial before. The law was so well crafted that most attorneys advised their clients to cut deals with prosecutors. When the Hells Angels and their associates rejected a deal to accept five-year jail terms, it was a massive gamble. If they lost, each would face up to 100 years' jail, because sentences on RICO convictions were served consecutively, not concurrently.

In July 1980, after a nine-month trial, the Hells Angels were found not guilty under the RICO Act. As the state tried to find ways to keep Barger in custody on the predicate acts, his lawyer Kent Russell addressed the press. 'No Angels have been found guilty of being racketeers. The Hells Angels Motorcycle Club has been vindicated. The government failed to prove the club itself is an illegal enterprise,' said Russell. 'Conspiracy is easy to prove and the government failed to do it after two years of investigation, millions of dollars, and buying witnesses that we proved lied on the stand.'

In a quote regularly attributed to Barger, he once boasted that US law enforcement had no chance of bringing down the Angels. Police and politicians must have seen this as an outright challenge: 'We can't be infiltrated, no cops can get inside on us, they don't have the resources, the manpower, or the time to wait. We're unbeatable and untouchable,' he reportedly said.

Over the years getting behind that wall of silence and inside an outlaw club has become as much a goal of law enforcement as convicting the members of crimes. The existence of these clubs was a slap in the face to any police commissioner arguing he could control organised crime. But at the turn of the century as Barger and other California Hells Angels followed the tide of new arrivals into Arizona, law enforcement saw an opportunity to infiltrate the new chapters being set up there. 'Operation Black Biscuit' has been touted in numerous books and television programs as 'the most successful undercover operation ever pulled on an outlaw motorcycle club'.

This joint operation in 2003, between the US Bureau of

Alcohol, Tobacco and Firearms (ATF) and Arizona state police, was the first time that law enforcement had ever successfully infiltrated the Hells Angels. Subsequently, veterans of the operation have become minor celebrities, yet the operation itself is today only a footnote in law enforcement history.

The team, led by ATF agent Jay Dobyns, posed as members of the Solo Angeles, an outlaw club based in Tijuana, Mexico. The team got so tight with the Mesa chapter in Arizona that two ATF agents and another associate were patched into the club. Dobyns even pulled bodyguard duty for Barger.

Their success made Barger's earlier boasts seem foolish. They had beaten the Angels' sophisticated security systems and information network to get right inside the organisation. Dobyns' crew spent a year undercover inside the club, enough time to gather evidence to deal the Angels a crushing blow.

It came early on the morning of 8 July 2003. Across Arizona, more than five hundred federal agents and local police launched simultaneous raids on Angels' charters and homes. A total of fifty-five bikers were arrested, and 650 guns, 30,000 rounds of ammunition and one hundred explosive devices, including hand grenades and napalm, were seized.

One of the most dramatic raids took place at Barger's Cave Creek charter at 4.42 a.m. According to reports in the *Arizona Republic* newspaper, the assault team, which included a Glendale Police SWAT unit with an armoured vehicle, struck like an invading army. Club prospect Michael Coffelt was alone inside on guard duty.

'A voice yelled, "Police! Police!" The armoured vehicle rammed through a wall. Officers shot a dog in the backyard. Every window in the place was broken as flash-bang grenades sailed into the clubhouse.'

Coffelt opened the front door. Amid the confusion, Glendale police officer Laura Beeler, stationed just outside with a rifle, 'pulled the trigger repeatedly, hitting Coffelt with bullets and shrapnel,' the *Republic* reported.

The raid had lasted just fourteen seconds and nearly claimed the life of the prospect. When Coffelt recovered, he was charged with aggravated assault. Beeler claimed Coffelt had fired first, but a judge later dismissed the charge after it was established that the biker's gun had not been fired.

In dismissing the charges against Coffelt, the judge ruled that the police raid was really an unlawful 'attack'. However, the judge found that Beeler's actions were understandable under the 'chaotic circumstances', which of course the raiding party had created. It was a massive show of force for a measly prize. The warrant specified that the cops could only take away the chapter's computer and filing systems. No doubt they expected to find the books for the Angels' criminal empire.

This rap on the knuckles did little to dampen the triumphalism of the stakeholders in Black Biscuit. 'Today, the Hells Angels Motorcycle Club appears to be a shambles: leadership behind bars, mystique broken, organizational records in government hands. Prosecutors are trying to gain ownership of chapter houses by having the entire Arizona club labelled a criminal enterprise,' wrote Dennis Wagner in the *Arizona Republic*.

Black Biscuit had amassed what appeared to be a treasure trove of evidence to prove the Angels were a highly sophisticated, centrally organised crime gang. The media was told that, in Arizona alone, the government 'assembled 800 hours of bugged conversations, 92,000 phone calls and 8500 seized documents to prove that Hells Angels is a criminal enterprise'.

Wagner wrote, 'Confiscated computers and files contained drug ledgers, membership lists, meeting minutes and bylaws . . . The combined evidence paints many Hells Angels as violent, cop-hating, drug-dealing, gunrunning criminals.'

But then things began to fall apart.

ADAM SHAND

Of the original fifty-five Angels arrested, only sixteen were finally indicted on racketeering, conspiracy, murder and drug dealing. It was still an impressive haul—it included several chapter presidents and some leading members. But by the time the indictments got to court, most of the cases were thrown out amid accusations by the Angels' lawyers that the investigators, snitches and informants had themselves broken the law. Two Angels eventually stood trial for the murder of a woman who had allegedly disrespected the club colours inside the Mesa chapter.

And that was the sum effect of Black Biscuit. Most critically, the authorities had once again failed to prove the club was a criminal enterprise, despite a year inside with access all areas.

Jay Dobyns, despite his willingness to preen for the cameras, was a tough, experienced undercover operative. An 18-year ATF veteran, he had served with distinction on the investigations of the Oklahoma Bombing and the September 11 terrorist attacks. He had apparently also nabbed a leading Mexican drug cartel boss and bought firearms from right-wing gangsters. If anyone could have proved racketeering against the Angels, it should have been Dobyns. He blamed the ATF for failing to support him during and after Black Biscuit.

There has never been a motorcycle club that has ever reached the pure structure or uniformity of Johnny's Black Rebels or Simpson's Angelenos. Equally few clubs like Chino's wandering and lawless Beetles have survived for long either. The reality is the most enduring clubs have successfully integrated both ideas into their ranks. The Hells Angels are the most evolved example of that, creating an entity that is neither criminal gang nor pure social club. And Sonny Barger was still the standard bearer of this quite unique group. While the beatniks and the hippies had disappeared, the Hells Angels were (with the help of lawyers, lobbyists and bail bondsmen) still riding the range like latter-day bad guys.

In the age of terrorism after the September 11 attacks on New

York and the Pentagon, many Americans had willingly sacrificed freedom for security. However, just as many pined for the values that Barger represented. The Angels' philosophy had come back into fashion.

While some authors described the Hells Angels MC as the leading player in the world's biggest criminal empire, Barger had just released a self-help book, *Freedom: Credos from the Road*, which elevated his chopped Harley-Davidson to a symbol of what America had lost. It was full of practical advice for living a fiercely independent life, with chapters such as 'Customize Yourself; Originals Don't Come Off an Assembly Line' and 'Treat Me Good, I'll Treat You Better; Treat Me Bad, I'll Treat You Worse'.

9

CAREFREE HIGHWAY

The saguaro grows only in the Sonoran Desert of south-west Arizona. Yet the directors of cowboy movies have placed the towering green cactus with its trademark side arms in locations all over the American west. In hundreds of films, the saguaro is always a sign the outlaw is near. It's cover for the black hats waiting to ambush the brave sheriff riding by.

'Where else would I expect to find you?' I thought, looking at the Hells Angels patch on Sonny Barger's back in front of me. Riding down Carefree Highway into Cave Creek, Arizona, on the back of a Harley, I thought this was a scene to fit the outlaw's romantic vision of himself. Like the saguaro, he was an American icon making his stand before these painted buttes and mesas. Under a vast blue sky, the supreme leader of the Hells Angels could cherish and defend an idea, half-true, half-imagined, that had travelled all over the world.

For the reporter riding pillion on a cold, crisp sunny morning,

OUTLAWS

this was just a taste of Barger's freedom at a safe and respectable 35 miles per hour. We had met an hour earlier at his home, where 'the Chief' had made us coffee in his scrupulously neat and tidy kitchen. It hadn't been an exactly rapturous welcome. He was a serious, intense man, not given to spontaneous levity. It was clear that representatives of the non–Hells Angels world, like us, would take years to get to know him, if they ever could. But he would give us qualified access to his life so as to demonstrate that bikers were not the demons that his legend suggested they were—at least not always. The problem was that, in this orderly domestic setting, he didn't look the part at all, in fact nothing like the image that reading Hunter S Thompson's work had prepared me for.

He had been out feeding his horses that morning and was wearing a lumber-jacket, a sweatshirt, jeans and an old pair of Cuban heel boots. He looked more like an old cowpoke than an outlaw biker. That is, until he suggested we take a spin around the district on his bike. He swapped the jacket for the Hells Angels colours that had been hanging on a coat rack. In the past decade, he had done hundreds of interviews promoting his books, so he knew what reporters expected.

A biker sipping coffee in his lounge room wasn't quite real until he slipped on his colours and sparked the engine of his Harley. Within a few minutes, we were puttering down Carefree Highway doing drive-bys for the cameraman on the side of the road. It seemed a well-practised routine, which he had been performing for film and TV producers since Hunter S Thompson had made him famous forty years earlier.

We turned in to the Buffalo Chip Saloon and Steakhouse, his favourite local watering hole in Cave Creek. It looked like the scene from a spaghetti western and Barger, in his colours, seemed to have stumbled in from another sound stage. I started to feel I had let this interview become a carnival ride, a photo-op with an American Legend. A spin on the back of Barger's Hog, a visit to

106

the saloon, a few innocuous questions would make a neat package, but it would never get near the truth. I'd get some books signed and a picture with the man, and I'd be on my way.

Then he just offered it up unprompted—a Hells Angel's credo of life, justice and perpetual conflict: 'There are a lot of people in this life who need to be murdered and if you don't believe it, ask the cops; they are murdering people every day,' he told me, casually.

In every Angels chapter, the Barger whom Hunter S Thompson had described in his 1966 book was still their role model: 'The coolest head in the lot . . . a tough quick-thinking dealer when any action starts . . . a fanatic, a philosopher, a brawler, a shrewd compromiser and a final arbitrator'. Though he held no official title now, Barger would always be the Chief and the Hells Angels would always be cast in his image.

Forty years later, Barger was still at the helm, and his legion of outcasts had become a global phenomenon, but Thompson was no longer around to share his thoughts. In fact, earlier that year, the ashes of the late Doctor of Gonzo were shot from a cannon over Woody Creek, Colorado.

Barger seemed pleased to have outlived Thompson, though he took credit for the author's fame: 'We made him the greatest writer in the world, but I didn't care for him as a person,' he said. Thompson had been a punk and his book a manual for law enforcement for decades to come. Back in 1966, when the Angels got into strife with the cops on a run, Thompson had locked himself in the trunk of his car. He had turned out to be 'a real weenie and a stone fucking coward', so it hadn't surprised Barger that he had taken the soft option of killing himself.

And 'the cheap asshole' had welched on a promise to buy the Angels a keg of beer when *Hell's Angels* was published. Thompson had tried to deliver the keg in 1992, but Barger declined. 'It was too late, 'cos that was supposed to happen way back in 1966,' he said.

Unrepentant, Barger had stood the test of time, a testament to his own saying 'Freedom ain't free'. Nearing seventy, he was still fit and sinewy; his leathery, weather-beaten skin had a patina of scars and tattoos. On his right shoulder, there was a tattoo '4/1/57': the date he joined the Angels' third chapter in Oakland, northern California. A faded green tattoo on his left forearm, a snake coiled around a dagger, told of his stint in the US infantry as an under-age enlistee. On his right forearm there was a cross in memory of his first wife Elsie, who died in 1967 after trying to self-abort Sonny's baby.

He regretted nothing in life, except smoking three packs of Camel non-filters a day for decades. Surgeons had taken out his vocal chords and larynx after throat cancer. He now spoke by placing a thumb over a one-way valve in his neck and vibrating the remaining muscles. In a concession to this infirmity, his bike now had a windshield and he wore a full-face helmet.

In June 1996, the Organizational Intelligence Unit of the FBI had compiled a dossier on the Hells Angels. It was part of a wad of documents that seemed to have passed through some important hands before an ABC reporter slipped them into my mine as a useful backgrounder. This dossier contained a 1995 New Zealand police report called 'The Fat Mexicans Are Coming'; it detailed mergers between the New Zealand Bandidos and some smaller clubs, and it bore a compliments stamp from former Kiwi Prime Minister Mike Moore. Before leaving New Zealand in 1977, the future South Australian Premier Mike Rann had worked on some of Moore's campaigns, which led me to suspect that I was reading selections from Media Mike's personal biker archive.

The Hells Angels dossier, which formed the bulk of the material I received, appeared to have been a souvenir Rann brought home from his visit to the FBI's Washington, DC headquarters in November 1996. It was a remarkable grab bag of non-forensic information drawn from official and unofficial sources: local police reports, newspaper articles, Hells Angels internal documents, gossip, rumour and even fictional movies. But through its dubious and recycled conclusions one point was hammered home: Sonny Barger, a one-time warehouseman from Oakland, California, had created the template not just for the Hells Angels MC but for all the outlaw clubs that followed.

Yet, despite all the power of the Hells Angels brand, its supreme leader seemed to be a man of modest means. The sun-bleached Stars and Stripes high on the flagpole outside his house lent an impression of benign conformity. If he was the head of 'the world's greatest criminal empire', the spoils had been spent or well hidden.

We had come back from the saloon and, after more coffee, Barger seemed content to let us hang around for as long as we wished. As long as I could keep coming up with ways to film him, he was happy to comply. What followed was a rather mundane tableau of a biker's domestic life. It wasn't a lavish existence but he could say that the day was his own.

It was clear he had taken a lot of physical punishment and done a lot of jail to enjoy this rather low-key freedom. Just watching him go through his daily routines, the apprehension I had felt before meeting him seemed to melt away. This was the common reaction when 'citizens' spent any time inside the Big Red Machine, he said. 'People don't know us, they fear us. Everybody who knows us don't fear us. That is the big problem. Our fear of the unknown,' he observed as he inspected an oil spot on the garage floor where he parked his bike.

The Barger residence was a modest ranch-style home with attached garage on an acre and a half of desert wasteland at Cave Creek, thirty miles north of Phoenix. The FBI intelligence document had prepared me for something else. 'Many HAMC members are millionaires from their drug dealings. Some own lavish ranches complete with thoroughbred horses.' The three mares in the dusty back paddock were hardly Kentucky Derby material, just honest examples of the quarterhorse breed you see right across the country.

I couldn't resist asking the obvious question. So, if the club was the richest motorcycle gang in the world, how had he missed out?

'I wish they would give me my share of the money,' he said, unsmiling. I immediately knew he was serious. If there was loot to be divided, you wouldn't get away with lashing 'the Chief'.

Without further prodding, he launched into a full inventory of the Barger empire. 'Here is where we are at,' he said. He had paid US$150,000 for the house, but still owed $120,000; he would be making monthly payments for thirty years. He pointed to a pick-up truck in the driveway—it was a couple of years old and he was making payments, he said. The only thing he owned outright was the Harley in the garage. He estimated that in the past three years he had paid $250,000 in income tax from the proceeds of his bestselling autobiography, *Hell's Angel*, speaking tours and a range of four hot sauces that marketing promised were 'Hotter than a Harley Davidson's manifold'. Even with all that tax, he still wasn't allowed to vote, because of his criminal record. 'Isn't that what we revolted against England for—taxation without representation?' he asked.

Even the horses weren't his. They were the property of his third wife, Noel, but she had apparently taken off not long before with his stepdaughter. Soon the horses would be gone and he would be alone again with a couple of old hound dogs, he said.

He didn't seem too cut up about the loss of a third wife. Women could come and go, but the club was a constant in his life. Arizona had been a new page in the story of his life as a Hells Angel. He moved out here in 1998 after spending fifty-nine months in the

Federal Correction Institution in Phoenix on a charge of conspiring to blow up a chapter of rival club the Outlaws. He insisted the charge was bogus; he had been entrapped by a federal informer, Anthony Tait (one of very few to have ever infiltrated the club). He fell in love with the hot dry climate of the south-west, and joined the small Cave Creek chapter, not as boss, but as a rank and file member. It was a small tight-knit chapter of only half a dozen members.

Barger's move from the Oakland chapter was one of several factors that had excited federal and state law enforcement interest in the south-west. The Angels had patched over a local club, the Dirty Dozen MC, in a friendly merger in the mid-1990s that consolidated Arizona as Angels territory. Soon they were opening new chapters across the state. At the same time, the south-west corridor was becoming one of the great narcotics routes of the world, linking Mexican drug cartels with voracious customers in the US.

Mexico had long supplied America with heroin and cannabis, but in the 1980s a former Federal police agent, Miguel Ángel Félix Gallardo, known as The Godfather, established a connection with the Colombian cartels to transport cocaine into the US. Eventually, he divided his business into several subsidiaries, each working a specific corridor into the US. The Sonora route through Arizona became one of the busiest and most lucrative.

To organised crime analysts, the Angels' south-west push was much more than a lifestyle decision. It was a business decision aimed at getting a slice of the narcotics action coming in from Mexico. They weren't fooled by Barger's cover story outlined in his 2000 biography: 'I dig the desert; it's the new California. It's wide open and free . . . The Southwest is a growing area for the Hells Angels, as we look toward moving into New Mexico and Colorado. We're shaking it up good,' he wrote.

It wasn't long before Barger got the feeling he was being

watched, he said as we walked over to his hay shed to prepare feed for the horses. As he weighed the bales of hay on a scale, he spoke of how law enforcement had made an industry of the Hells Angels: 'The police make a living off of us. They have squads of agents, DEA [US Drug Enforcement Agency], FBI, the ATF, whose sole job is following us. What a sweet job.'

Through a long-range lens, a Hells Angel weighing bales of anything must have been a tantalising sight, I said.

So curious had the DEA become about the daily activities in the shed that they bought the house next door, to set up surveillance. Barger had quickly twigged to their presence. If there's one thing you learn as a Hells Angel, it's counter-surveillance. 'They had a man and a woman living in there, so I showed them around the shed. Two weeks later they moved and sold the house,' said Barger.

Much of the attention the club received came from a lack of understanding, perhaps deliberate, on the part of law enforcement. 'If people really stopped and looked at what the government and the police are trying to say about us—that people join the Hell's Angels to be involved in organised crime—they will realise that anybody who really wants to be a criminal, the last thing they should join is a club that is under the scrutiny of law enforcement,' he observed. 'My personal opinion is that, if you really want to be a criminal, you have to be a cop or a politician.'

Of course, there were criminals in the club, plenty of them, I countered. Unprompted, my discussion with Barger was taking the same direction as with the bikers in South Australia.

'I have a criminal record, but I'm not a professional criminal. If I was a professional criminal, I would not have a criminal record,' he said, with all the glibness of a well-worn script.

Barger's rap sheet went for pages, covering violence, drug peddling, kidnapping and firearms charges. He also beat a triple murder and racketeering beefs in the 1970s, a time when, in his words, the criminal shit had stacked so high he needed wings to stay above it. He sheeted home the cause of his actions to cocaine abuse.

He had loved the 'blow' so much he had called his Harley 'Sweet Cocaine'. While all Hells Angels were banned from using needle drugs, Barger had established himself as a mid-level heroin dealer to pay for his coke habit. As the Chief, in a haze of cocaine, descended into the drug trade, the club became isolated.

I asked him whether that was the moment the Angels lost their way.

'Well I'm not sure that club did, but I certainly did. I have always admitted that. I am positive the reason I went to prison in 1972 was because I was using too much cocaine. From 1972 until this day I have never used cocaine. I learn fast.'

In the mid-1970s crime had become a game, a battle of wits, with the authorities determined to deprive Barger of his freedom. There was no doubt that Barger was an accomplished crook by then but, despite thousands of hours of covert surveillance and the testimony of infiltrators and club snitches, authorities had never gathered enough evidence to prove the club was a criminal organisation. This was hard to dispute on the evidence, but the 1996 FBI briefing document had an explanation for this.

'Their crude criminal behaviour has given way to the more sophisticated methods used by traditional organized crime,' the FBI analyst suggested. '[Some] gang leaders give the appearance of living very straight lives, living in suburban houses and raising families, while at the same time controlling multi-million dollar narcotics distribution networks and legitimate businesses used for the diversion of illicit profits.' The FBI suggested that the Angels kept their drug business secret by never discussing business in club meetings, but only between individual members.

Yet, while the US had never been able to make the criminal gang tag stick to the Angels, Barger has since conceded that the

1970s were 'a gangster era' for the club. In our interview, I suggested to Barger that the Angels had 'beaten' RICO—another way of saying they had been lucky.

He levelled me with a stare that could have blistered paint. 'We didn't actually beat RICO—we were found innocent on RICO because we were innocent,' he said. The prosecutors had never expected the Angels to fight the case in court and they had called their bluff. They had been tried on the hearsay of informers, mostly myths and legends, and been acquitted on the facts. 'An informant will say whatever the government wants them to say. To get out of the charges he has or the problems that he has. Or the money he's going to get it for doing it,' said Barger with disgust.

Barger is not given to extravagant displays of pride and ego, but the RICO victory seemed to have been his finest hour. A biker—a hoodlum who had only received his high school diploma in jail—had stood up to the best legal minds in America and come out victorious. But he didn't do it on his own: the solidarity of the club had been crucial to the success, he said. If one of the eighteen charged had cut a deal, the rest might have been found guilty. As it was, more than fifty California Angels alone had dropped out of the club as a result of the RICO pressure. But the rest had been prepared to defend the principle of fraternity the club had been founded upon.

'We were the first group to stand up as a group and say "Bring it on!" And when they did, they lost. They couldn't believe it. Other groups began to fight and soon people were beating RICO left right and centre,' he said quietly.

How ironic that an outlaw had made legal history, I suggested.

Again he bristled. He didn't consider himself an outlaw. In fact, the concept did not even exist in modern society. It was a relic of a bygone era 'maybe in England during King Arthur's time': 'In the United States an outlaw is a person who lives outside of the law and has been declared by a federal judge to have no recourse through law,' he said. Anybody could kill an outlaw, said Barger.

The biker was not an outlaw but he was certainly in a different legal category to the citizens, as Barger called the rest of the population. When police arrested citizens whom they believed were innocent, they treated them well; if they believed the citizens were guilty, they treated them badly. It was a form of vigilantism that the bikers always experienced when dealing with police: 'When they start doing that, they are no longer officers of the law. They are vigilantes. And people like myself will not put up with vigilantes.'

Despite the RICO win, people still found it hard to accept that a Hells Angel could act as an individual, Barger said. An Angel could be bad without being a gangster. A biker prided himself on being his brother's keeper, but that didn't automatically mean he was also their partner in crime.

This notion is not exclusive to bikers. Barger cited the case of a Louisiana police officer who had recently been charged with raping a woman in the stationhouse. This had apparently taken place while two of his buddies had kept watch for him. 'How come the rest of the police department didn't know about it? Anybody can do anything. We do have criminals in our club. I was a criminal in our club. Whether anyone wants to believe it or not, if you want to be a criminal you do not want to be a Hells Angel. You know how we are watched—if you are watched like that, do you think you get away with anything illegal for very long?'

But then again, I countered, members had used the cover of the club and its code of silence for their own purposes as well.

'It can be done but only for a short time and then you are caught and in jail,' he replied, before reminding me that there had been hundreds of allegations of child molestation levelled at priests all over the world in recent years, and yet people did not assume that the Catholic Church was a criminal organisation.

Despite the failure of the successive legal actions against the Angels, law enforcement continued to promote the idea that the Hells Angels MC was one massive international gang. If only they could get inside the club, the argument ran, the evidence would surely be found. By the turn of the century, omerta, the Mafia's code of silence, had been smashed. Mob wise guys were queuing up to snitch on each other, leading to the demise of all the New York crime families. Only the bikers had held firm. Discipline and a rigorous selection process had kept the informers and undercover cops out.

Hunter S Thompson wrote in *Hell's Angels*: 'Chapter presidents have no set term in office, and a strong one, like Barger, will remain unchallenged until he goes to jail, gets killed or finds his own reasons for hanging up the colours.' Thompson had got that part right, said Barger. He would never hang up his colours until death, but he conceded the Hells Angels had become too far big for one man to control. Even though authority had now been decentralised, the Angels were still a much more rigid and defensive organisation than the one he had joined in 1957. But freedom ain't free, he shrugged. A member had to submit to the rules that came with it, even the Maximum Leader.

As he bade us farewell, Barger said he would actually probably prefer to ride a Suzuki or Kawasaki, but club policy was that everyone ride a Harley, the machine that Barger had turned into an international icon. He wished he had the guts to ride something else, but he was kind of trapped in his own legend, he said. I sensed that this weighed upon him, causing a restlessness. He never saw himself as the head of a social movement, much less running the corporation the club had become. It was still all about riding high and living free for him.

As he stood under the Stars and Stripes, I asked Barger whether this place would always be home. He shook his head: 'I gotta move a little further north.' He looked out to the desert: 'This is not going to be horse property very much longer. Civilisation is moving in on us.'

But wherever he went, the death's head logo of the club would follow, he said. The sun never set on a Hells Angel's patch.

In 2010, a Melbourne-based consultancy, Bastion, ranked the Hells Angels as Australia's number-two brand, behind only the Salvation Army, for the second year running. The Angels beat brand icons like Coca-Cola, McDonald's, Google and the Catholic Church.

The Angels had 'a clearly understood belief', according to Bastion.

> We know what they stand for, brotherhood, freedom, life beyond the law; we know they're a tribe and take their belonging very seriously. Indeed we can see who belongs by their colours. And we have a damn good idea of what their behaviour is going to be if prompted. Say no more.

In the years after I talked to Barger at Cave Creek, while controversy raged in the south-west over the Hells Angels' involvement in drugs and murder, another less visible threat (at least to Americans) was looming just over the border in Mexico. The Mexican drug cartels were taking over the operations of the Colombians after the death of Medellin cartel boss Pablo Escobar. In the years 2005 to 2010, the Mexican cartels would expand their US operations into the Florida/Caribbean, the Mid-Atlantic, New York/New Jersey and New England regions, where the Colombians had once been the leading suppliers of cocaine and heroin.

By February 2010, the US Department of Justice's National Drug Threat Assessment released data showing that the Mexicans controlled 'most of the wholesale cocaine, heroin, and methamphetamine distribution in the United States as well as much of the marijuana distribution'. Below them Asian gangs dominated trafficking of MDMA, or ecstasy, and high-potency marijuana, commodities that kept them out of the way of the murderous Mexicans. Cuban crime groups were slowly expanding their operations beyond the Caribbean/Florida area with the cooperation of the Mexican cartels.

For all the hype and fear that had fuelled the Black Biscuit operation, the bikers were not even a ripple compared with the king tide of drugs and murder lapping at the US–Mexico border. When a program called the Alliance to Combat Transnational Threats was launched quietly in September 2009 by US and Mexican authorities, North American TV producers showed very little interest—compared with Black Biscuit's sexy images of motorcycles and tattooed Visigoths, the Alliance was hopelessly unphotogenic.

But in the fourteen months to February 2011, the coordinated training, intelligence-sharing and patrols had resulted in the arrest of 270,000 illegal border crossers, the seizure of 1.6 million pounds of marijuana and the recovery of $13 million in cash in the border's Tucson Sector alone. This was serious organised crime. Meanwhile, the ATF was playing dress-ups with the bikers.

Most telling of all was the mounting human toll from the drug war in Mexico. This had already been happening when I sat with Barger in Cave Creek, just three hours from the border. At the same time as the media was focusing heavily on the prosecution of two Hells Angels for the murder of a woman in Arizona, 35,000 Mexicans were being slaughtered with barely a mention in the press. The disproportionate coverage spoke to the primal fear people had of bikers.

'I am still here and the Hells Angels are still here,' Barger told me. 'Like I said all my life, if they got rid of me and the Hells Angels, if we were wiped off the face of the earth, crime would not reduce in the world by one-tenth of 1 per cent. And whatever club it was that took our place, no matter who they think they are or what they are, whatever their name is, they would still be referred to as those guys who are acting like Hells Angels.'

In 2008, the house in Tucson, Arizona belonging to Jay Dobyns, the agent who had successfully infiltrated the Hells Angels more than half a decade earlier, was destroyed in an apparent arson attack. He also filed a US$3.3 million lawsuit against the ATF, alleging over fifty acts of 'mismanagement, retaliation, harassment and defamation'. Meanwhile, the Hells Angels had allegedly sworn to kill him.

'I am now a man without a country,' Dobyns told a newspaper. 'I am up against the crime syndicate that I infiltrated and the agency that abandoned me . . . My family lives in fear.' Despite its status as the most successful sting against outlaw bikers ever, Operation Black Biscuit is hardly a model other self-respecting undercover agents would want to follow. Despite all the expense and risk, prosecutors were not even able to make charges of trafficking methamphetamine possession stick to the Angels.

As Sonny Barger told me in 2005: 'They have never produced evidence of one meth lab. Of everyone who was arrested for methamphetamine, I believe no-one had more than one gram and that is personal use. Of all these thousands and thousands of laboratories that are being busted every year in the United States there are no Hells Angels being arrested.'

World domination is a complex and difficult thing that few organisations, legal or illegal, have ever pulled off for long. From the Roman Empire and Adolf Hitler's Third Reich to the Mafia and Pablo Escobar's Medellin cocaine cartel, the reasons for decline and demise always relate to the failure to manage scale. The bigger they get, the more unwieldy they become. The provinces of the empire inevitably gain self-confidence and eventually see no further benefit in paying tribute to the capitol. The empire only endures as long as the ruthless mastermind who conceived it remains in charge. To the US Federal Bureau of Investigation, Ralph Hubert (Sonny) Barger was the reason that the Hells Angels Motorcycle Club had become 'the largest, richest, most sophisticated, and best organized outlaw motorcycle gang in the world'.

'Barger's foresight, drive and cunning shapes the Hells Angels into the fearsome gang it is today,' the analyst in the 1996 FBI report I had been handed by an Adelaide ABC reporter noted, not without a hint of admiration.

> Sonny Barger does for the Hells Angels what Lee Iaccoca did for Chrysler Corp—he converts a sloppy, rudderless organization into a lean, mean no crap-taking company. He trims idiot cavemen from chapter rosters and embarks on an expansionist course that swells the club from six chapters in 1965 to 67 in 1987.

Of course, 'the intense sinewy' Barger in time came to far outperform Iaccoca. By June 2010, Chrysler was only able to emerge from a second near-death experience, Chapter 11 bankruptcy, by ceding control to Italian automaker Fiat. Meanwhile, the Hells Angels had expanded to 230 chapters in twenty-seven countries on six continents, devouring inferior biker brands along the way and making the Harley-Davidson the world's leading cruiser motorcycle. 'The assimilation of other motorcycle gangs by the Hells Angels in the 1970s and 1980s differs only in bloodshed from the corporate takeovers that shake Wall St,' the analyst concluded in 1996.

10

WALK ON BY, BROTHER

'When you bring someone in from one of the big rival clubs, something always fucks up,' Sonny Barger wrote in 2000 in his autobiography. Yet the club did not heed the teachings of their Maximum Leader when the Big Red Machine invited Christopher Hudson to join in 2004.

Defection is a serious matter: the traitor takes secrets with him; he knows the inner workings of the club, its strengths and weaknesses. His mere presence in the camp of the enemy is a threat to his former brothers. Hudson had been associated with the Finks since 1998. Once a plasterer, Hudson now made his living on the fringes of crime. He was staunch and had an appetite for violence, often against women. In 2003, he beat his then girlfriend and attacked a security guard who came to her aid.

He had no special affinity with motorcycles, but that was not uncommon at that time. Clubs across the country were expanding. They opened chapters in new territories that brought them into conflict with established powers in those areas. Most of the tension stayed below the civilian radar, but ironically it followed the principle of mutually assured destruction that governed the nuclear politics of the era. Clubs beefed up with soldiers to ensure that any conflict would be long and bloody, which worked as a deterrent to some extent. However, as some clubs discovered to their cost, it was the soldiers who actually caused most of the drama.

Hudson was one of the new breed of soldiers finding their way into clubs, but some suspected his loyalty was only skin-deep, a fashion accessory for a life of crime. Bikers like Hudson had little in common with the old-timers who had formed the clubs. The new bikers spent little time on motorcycles, preferring to move around in sleek custom sedans. People in the scene were calling them 'Nike bikers' because of their expensive trainers, not particularly suited to motorcycle wear. According to Arthur Veno, you could tell a Nike biker just by looking at their Harley: it bore the scratches and dents from being regularly dropped.

Gone were the old grimy jeans, black T-shirts and steel-capped engineer boots, replaced by designer T-shirts, baseball caps and pristine white athletic footwear—fashions inspired by US West Coast gangstas. A generation gap had formed. The new members reflected contemporary values, while the old school clung grimly to their traditions. The old way had been Anglo-Saxon, but now multiculturalism, which had transformed Australia, was working on the outlaw nation.

Kids of diverse backgrounds, who had proved themselves worthy on the streets, demanded entry to the clubs. Their parents had often come from war-torn nations and were well-versed in the notion of fighting to the death, doing what had to be done. Disaffected Middle Eastern youth found solidarity in chapters of some clubs, which became known derisively as the 'Ali-Davidson MCs'. The new brigade also provided entrees to criminal contacts and opportunities outside the bikies' traditional stomping grounds.

There was a blurring of the boundaries between the bikies and other dedicated crime gangs.

The old school viewed much of this with alarm. They could not dictate how members earned a living, nor judge them for their associations, unless they brought conflict into the ranks. Needle drugs had long been banned in all clubs, in the belief that a junky was loyal only to heroin. Leave him long enough in a police cell and he would give everyone up to avoid the screaming meanies of withdrawal. Any member of a club caught injecting heroin or speed faced instant expulsion, the loss of his motorcycle and an old-fashioned flogging.

But a new, more potent drug was sweeping the nation. Seizures of amphetamines—including crystalline methamphetamine, known on the street as 'ice'—had increased ten-fold between 1998 and 2004. A survey of schools found that 10 per cent of kids had tried ice by the age of sixteen. In a few years it had jumped to number two behind cannabis as the nation's illegal drug of choice. Ice posed a huge challenge to outlaw clubs, just as it did to society in general.

In the 1960s, Sonny Barger's Hells Angels turned their bodies into laboratories for testing drugs, from LSD to speed, but in the 1990s they recognised ice as a malevolent new threat and banned it in the US chapters. However, this was a matter of discretion for the Australian Angels, who generally put the issue to a vote chapter by chapter. But almost all Angels worldwide understood the threat ice posed, according to Barger. 'Whatever drugs we were using were drugs that everyone in the world was using. It's the same thing with methamphetamine. I don't like it and I don't like to see people using it,' he told me in our 2005 interview. 'We have probably lost more people from using meth than everything else that people have been kicked out of the club for in [our] history,' he told me.

Most of the other big Australian clubs also recognised the

destructive capacity of methamphetamine, but their moves to restrict it were rather equivocal. In many chapters, rules were adopted banning members from smoking ice through glass pipes, but snorting was exempted. To ban the snorting would be a double-standard, given the predilection of older wealthier members for cocaine. The clubs that banned ice outright also risked creating factions in the ranks. Members 'on the pipe' could do almost anything once a stimulant-induced psychosis set in, and they concealed their meth use by getting friends outside the club to buy it on their behalf. It became a pernicious divisive influence in the clubs.

Christopher Hudson was unemployed, living with his father, who was a Gold Coast tradesman. He had a string of previous convictions, including assaults, occasioning bodily harm, possessing weapons, causing grievous bodily harm, drug possession and driving offences. He now had a sideline in identity theft. Despite later being assessed as being of low intelligence, Hudson was resourceful. In 2004, he stole the details of a man who had left a photocopy of his driver's licence with a Gold Coast dealer in second-hand video games. He created enough points of identification to successfully obtain a driver's licence in the victim's name. This was enough to fool up to ten credit providers: he bought a car, took out personal loans and opened mobile phone accounts in the name of the hapless victim. He served only four months' jail over the issue, which apparently left the victim's life in a shambles.

From 2004 Hudson's love affair with amphetamines took over his life. His relations with members of the club soured as his self-centred drug-induced behaviour intensified. His departure from the Finks in 2005 would have been welcomed by many, had he not then joined the Hells Angels and then reportedly tried to recruit other Finks to join him.

A family club. A prison psychologist once lamented that the Descendants MC was the pivot around which Tom Mackie had arranged his life. By 2011, four of his sons, including Matt, had joined the club. (Photo: © Chris Randells)

If you can't sleep on the ground, you aren't drunk enough. The Descendants MC on an early club run. While revolted by the bikers' wild and unkempt appearance, the South Australian community had never held any burning objection to them until a famous confrontation took place on a lonely beach at Port Gawler in June 1974. (Photo: © Tom Mackie)

Fat Sam. In December 1976, Bass (second from right) and his squad had made a seven-hour round trip to Minlaton on the remote Yorke Peninsula to catch the Descendants hanging out together in contravention of the consorting laws. (Photo © Tom Mackie)

Riding high, living free. The Hells Angels with friends and associates on a run in country South Australia. Critics say the motorcycle is now a prop for organised crime, but nothing comes close to the unity generated by sharing the risks of the road. (Photo: © Chris Randells)

After a titanic battle with Sam Bass's 'Bikie Squad' the Descendants MC moved their focus back to the motorcycle and away from crime. Their club is stronger than ever, but content to remain as a single chapter. (Photo: © Matthew Turner)

Standing staunch. From left, Descendants Perry Mackie, 'TB' and Tom Mackie. Having survived the consorting laws of the 1970s, the Descendants told Premier Mike Rann to bring it on, if he wanted to ban them. They weren't going anywhere. (Photo: © Chris Randells)

The Maximum Leader. Sonny Barger, legendary standard-bearer for the Hells Angels Motorcycle Club. 'Those who know us don't fear us,' he told the author in 2005. (Photo: © Getty Images/Scott Olson)

Cop cluster. South Australia Police's dismantle and disrupt tactics against motorcycle clubs generated traffic tickets and media headlines but at an estimated cost of $5 million a year did little to address crime. (Photo: © Chris Randells)

Outlaws welcome. As Adelaide's bikers took to the streets in protest at Premier Mike Rann's campaign against them they found an unexpected level of public support. By the end, Rann was gone and they were still riding the highways. (Photo © Matthew Turner)

Pigs on a Poker Run. During Premier Mike Rann's campaign against the bikers they always expected plenty of heat from police if they rode in club colours. Soon bikers from all walks of life joined events like this Poker Run hosted by the Hells Angels MC in 2008. (Photo: © Chris Randells)

A Rebel army. Australia's biggest club the Rebels MC diverted its National Run in May 2009 to Adelaide to ride on the South Australian parliament with other clubs. (Photo: © Chris Randells)

Terror in the CBD. When Hells Angel Christopher Hudson opened fire on a Melbourne street murdering solicitor Brendan Keilar and wounding Dutch backpacker Paul de Waard and his own girlfriend Kara Douglas, every biker was cast in his barbarous image. (Photo: © Newspix/Craig Borrow)

A united front. In November 2008, the Descendants hosted a media call for the clubs that would soon found the United Motorcycle Council of South Australia and the FREE AUSTRALIA Party. The unity process had begun months earlier away from the public eye at the Tattoo Club of South Australia. (Photo © Matthew Turner)

The pushback. The United Motorcycle Council hosted highly successful protest runs across Australia which drew contingents from most of the outlaw community. By trying to break them up, authorities had brought them together.
(Photo: © Matthew Turner)

A real outlaw? In 2011 the Assistant Commissioner of the NSW Crime Commission Mark Standen was convicted of conspiring to import 300 kilograms of precursor chemicals for the manufacture of methamphetamine. While the bikers aren't saints, nothing they have been caught doing comes close. (Photo: © Newspix/Ross Schultz)

Numerous journalists and writers have wrongly relied upon a legendary conflict between the two clubs dating back to 1971 to explain the repercussions that arose from Hudson's decision to join the Angels. The image projected in the media was one of almost ceaseless conflict between the Finks and Hells Angels when in fact the reality was almost nothing of the sort.

The 1971 blue had apparently escalated from a simple fist fight between senior members of the Sydney chapters of the Angels and the Rebels at a New South Wales camping ground during an outlaw run that had brought a number of clubs together.

The Angels had taken exception to the Rebels' use of their club's death's head logo, which was reversed on their colours. The Rebels' senior member had suggested sorting the issue out with a one-on-one fight. However, according to legend, the Rebel was set upon by some other Angels during the fight, offending some observers' sense of fair play. In the aftermath, members of the Finks and Mob Shitters joined forces with some Rebels to pay a visit to an Angels president at home. The resulting fracas left the man shot dead in his front yard.

Thirty-five years later, some writers were still talking up this so-called feud even though many of the original players were dead or long-retired. While there was still no love lost between the clubs, there was certainly no state of war between them either, I was told in 2011. The members largely kept out of each others' way, but for the occasional skirmish in a bar. The spark that set a blaze on 18 March 2006 had little to do with the events of 1971 and a lot to do with the personal conduct of Christopher Hudson.

The Hells Angels might have suspected something was up when forty-three Finks began filing into the ballroom of the Royal Pines Resort at Carrara on the Gold Coast. The room was packed with 1800 guests enjoying a mixed martial arts tournament, but the real show began when a member confronted Hudson, sitting ringside with fellow Angels.

Police alleged in court later that this had the hallmarks of a pre-planned showdown between the clubs but media reports later indicated there were more personal issues at stake. Hudson had been reportedly accused of attempting to steal a valuable sapphire from an elderly couple associated with the Finks.

Cameras from cable network Fox Sports captured the action of what became known as 'The Ballroom Blitz'. A Fink approached Hudson sitting ringside with a table of Hells Angels and invited him to open proceedings. 'C'mon, cunt! Let's fucking go,' he shouted, before throwing the straight right that set off the melee. Within seconds, the room had descended into chaos as chairs, crockery, glassware and cutlery flew like missiles. The Fink and Hudson were wrestling as other rivals came in to rain blows down on the traitor. Terrified spectators scrambled for the exits as bikers sprawled across tables, grappling and pounding each other. Then, as shots rang out, there was uproar.

Hudson was shot in the back and also the jaw, the bullet exiting out of his chin. The bleeding Hudson was then held against the apron of the ring while others came in and dealt him further punishment. At one point, Hudson tried to crawl away on all fours, but he was dragged back and attacked with an unbroken beer glass.

Meanwhile, smaller brawls were breaking out all over the room. An Adelaide Hells Angel, fired three shots 'indiscriminately into the crowd'. It was never proven that the shots he fired had hit anyone, though a bystander who was hiding under a table was shot in the foot.

Hudson later showed up at hospital with cuts and gunshot wounds, including a hole in his chin where the bullet had entered and exited through his jaw. He was taken into custody on an outstanding warrant, but he remained staunch to the code of silence. He refused to make a statement to police on what had occurred at the Royal Pines.

The media speculated feverishly that the Ballroom Blitz would spark a new bikie war, but the heat from the incident subsided quickly. The leadership of both clubs appeared to believe that honour had been served.

One senior Queensland Hells Angel told a court in 2009 that, despite being bashed over the head with a chair and choked during the Ballroom Blitz, he held no grudge against them: 'The Finks and the Hells Angels are not enemies,' he testified. This Hells Angel was a key member of the United Motorcycle Council of Queensland, which became instrumental in helping resolve long-standing enmities between clubs.

Believing his enemies were still after him, Hudson began carrying a handgun at all times. He had already moved down to Sydney where he was a prospect in the Angels' City Crew chapter. He was spending less and less time on his Harley, preferring to move about in a black CLK 320 Mercedes sedan.

In June 2007, during a three-week binge, he ended up in Melbourne and linked up with the club's East County chapter.

It was 18 June 2007. In the chill of early morning in Melbourne's CBD, the barrel of the gun was hot under the biker's chin. He could not be sure how many rounds he had fired in that deadly fusillade. Christopher Hudson had been shot in the face by someone else before and survived, but this time the .40 calibre bullet would rip through his brain and explode out the top of his head in a geyser of blood and gore on the shop window behind him. It would all be over then, all this drama and bullshit that had consumed his life.

With four spurts of orange flame from his gun, solicitor Brendan Keilar, Dutch backpacker Paul de Waard and Hudson's sometime girlfriend Kara Douglas had fallen at his feet.

He turned his back on the carnage and began walking

along Flinders Lane towards Queen Street. The No. 55 tram to Coburg rattled up alongside him. The passengers had heard the shots and were now confronted by the killer. Hudson pointed his firearm at the tram, sending people diving to the floor in wild panic.

Shooting three people had been a jagged impulse, but Hudson apparently knew what he had to do now. This Hells Angel's last act would be pure free will. And Hell would be well populated with brothers.

But when he pulled the trigger, nothing happened. He was out of bullets—in his psychotic rage he had emptied the six-shot magazine, police said later.

He ran down the street, waving his gun at people in the way, but it was an impotent gesture. Despite his fearsome tattoos, his bulging physique and his firearm, the power and rage were draining out of him. He was a true outlaw now—a lone fugitive from justice. He was a solitary figure in an alien landscape. He took off his jacket and carefully wrapped the gun in it, then he left this small bundle on a building site on Flinders Street.

It had been the most horrific collision between two worlds. At 8.20 a.m. Brendan Keilar, a 43-year-old property lawyer, reached William Street after parking his car on Alexandra Parade to walk to his office in Collins Street. He had a neatly pressed business shirt in his bag for the day ahead. Backpacker Paul De Waard had slept the night in Southern Cross Station to save money. He was headed to McDonald's for breakfast, a newspaper and free coffee refills.

Meanwhile, Hudson had been drinking and doing speed all night in the fleshpots of King Street. First he was at the Spearmint Rhino. Then, after 5 a.m., he and others had moved to Bar Code next door, where the management regarded him as a VIP, so long as he bought their overpriced spirits by the bottle. 'Huddo' was a cool dude compared with the rest of the dregs and losers that habituate strip clubs at eight o'clock in the morning. He was a sharp dresser and had a good line in banter with the ladies. He had only been in town a short time, but he fitted comfortably in to the place. He settled into another drinking session with Spearmint Rhino manager Stephen Kyriacou and one of his employees, stripper Autumn Daly-Holt.

Daly-Holt was a gifted artist. In 2001, she'd been good enough to be included in an exhibition of the best Year 12 work at the National Gallery of Victoria. Now she was 'Savannah', a stripper and pole dancer whom Christopher Hudson regarded on this particular morning as his personal property. When she performed an informal routine in the lap of her boss, Kyriacou, stripping down to her G-string, the bile rose in Hudson and he dragged her away by the hair. When another patron tried to intervene, Hudson lifted his shirt to reveal a Hells Angels tattoo on his abdomen and the gun tucked into his pants.

When Daly-Holt tried to flee, Hudson kicked her in the head and then, grabbing her by the hair, smashed his fist into her face. He threw the topless, sobbing woman into the street, and hurled her handbag and tote bag after her. As she struggled to her knees, Hudson took a three-step run-up and with all his might kicked her straight in the face again, this time shattering her eye socket and nasal bones. Nobody stepped in to help.

It was her friend and fellow exotic dancer, Kara Douglas, who some minutes later found Autumn broken, bleeding and unconscious on the steps of the strip club. She called an ambulance for Autumn but didn't stay with her. Hudson had summoned her and she dutifully met him on the corner of King Street and Flinders Lane. They were having an on-and-off sexual relationship despite the fact that, during their two-month relationship, Hudson had twice broken Kara's nose and given her black eyes. Kara had gone back to him but she had never seen him like this. 'He was just completely out of his mind insane, just completely gone,' she later told police.

He frog-marched Kara up King Street to William Street, jabbering incoherently at her all the way. He dragged her down into an underground car park, pinned her against a wall and threatened her with his gun. When a building manager appeared, Hudson pointed the gun at him, allowing Douglas a moment to flee up onto the street. She saw a waiting taxi and desperately tried to get in, but the driver had locked the doors. Hudson caught up and resumed his assault on the street now filling with people on their way to work.

That's when Brendan Keilar and Paul de Waard stepped in. All it took for Keilar to die was to ask the simple question: 'What's going on here?'

Hudson let his pistol do the talking. Keilar, a father of three, died there on the road. De Waard and Kara were lucky to survive.

Christopher Wayne Hudson was a new face for an old bogeyman. The public was well accustomed to bikie violence but, until this Melbourne CBD outrage, it had usually been kept in-house. In the 1970s, Australian clubbies had squared off on pre-arranged battlegrounds to settle scores with fists and motorcycle boots. There were strict rules governing combat: no attacks on members' homes or workplaces; no ambushes in places where citizens could be pulled into the play. If some foolhardy 'squarehead' chose to provoke a bikie, well, that was a different matter.

But this was a brutal, callous attack on bystanders who had simply tried to protect a woman from assault. It broke so many rules, the leadership of the Hells Angels had no option except to take action. But it was an extremely delicate situation. Hudson had become a New South Wales member, a prospect in the Sydney

City chapter. He had committed this heinous act in Victoria, so the Victorian Angels would be copping the heat from this. Up until now, as the moral panic swept the nation, Victoria had been an island of calm.

Some bikers called Victoria 'Switzerland'. The Melbourne chapters of national clubs at war had remained aloof from these conflicts. Victoria had more bikies than any other state, barring New South Wales, but they had mostly stayed out of the headlines. Now, after what Hudson had done, the media, police and politicians would be crawling all over the club.

It would have been better for all if Hudson had counted his ammunition more carefully, saving one round for himself, one policeman told me. Alive, one way or the other, the club would have to take responsibility. The choice was stark. The Angels could give him up to the police, a move unthinkable to most. Or they could deal with him: they could resolve this drama by killing him. According to police sources, there was deep division on the issue within the Angels.

It's probable that Christopher Hudson's appalling conduct in June 2007 had been a product of ice use. Certainly, his voracious appetite for go-fast drugs was a key factor in his journey to infamy. The week before the shootings had been a blur of alcohol and drugs, all-night sessions in sleazy strip clubs and downtown bars. On 12 June he had met Collingwood footballer Alan Didak at the Spearmint Rhino strip club. After drinking at the club for a while, Hudson offered the inebriated footballer a lift home, but he wanted to show him something first.

As the black coupe sped across the Bolte Bridge, Huddo told Didak he was taking him to the Hells Angels' Campbellfield clubhouse in Melbourne's north. He pumped the music on the car stereo and lifted his trouser leg to reveal he had the .40 calibre strapped to his leg. Didak was terrified. 'I remember the bridge in the background when Huddo . . . put his right arm out the [driver's side] window, still holding the handgun. Even though the music was blaring I could hear Huddo firing shots. I don't remember how many shots Huddo fired, but by this stage I was shitting myself,' Didak later told police.

After a few drinks in the clubhouse, Didak asked to be taken home, but his ordeal was not over. As he drove back to the city, Huddo fired upon a factory near the Angels clubhouse, attracting the attention of the police. When officers gave chase, he fired several shots, causing them to cease the pursuit. For days after his wild ride, Didak pondered whether he should report the scary gun-toting bikie. It was only after seeing Huddo's picture in the paper, the day after the CBD shootings, that he came forward.

'I had considered going to the club and telling them about the incident, but I was scared and just didn't have the guts to go through [with] it,' he told police ten days after Hudson's deadly rampage. To tell on Hudson would have certainly put him in peril from the Hells Angels, but it might have saved at least one life, not to mention a lot of drama for the Angels.

Two days after the shootings, Hudson surrendered to police at Wallan, an hour north of Melbourne. It was an intriguing choice of station. Wallan is 30 kilometres south of Broadford, where the Hells Angels previously owned a property, the venue of club-sponsored rock concerts for many years.

When he gave himself up, Hudson was sporting a heavy bandage on his left arm from the wrist to the elbow. Sydney's *Daily Telegraph* ran a story quoting 'bikie insiders' as saying senior Hells Angels had removed Hudson's club tattoo with a blow torch 'as part of a ritual of punishment for bringing police attention to the club'. The *Telegraph*'s Paul Kent wrote of Hudson's punishment in lurid detail: 'They chained Hudson up and, wielding the hot blue flame of an oxyacetylene torch, seared the tattoo from his arm.'

To the media, this seemed to confirm the Angels' reckless indifference. A father of three was dead, two other people were fighting for their lives and the Angels were only concerned for their image with police. It wasn't until May 2009, when Hudson's mother released a picture of her son in jail sporting his Angels tattoo just below his left elbow, that the blow torch story was put to rest. By then it had already passed into common knowledge. It's understood that the injury was self-inflicted. Hudson had twice tried to kill himself since the CBD shootings—first with the empty handgun and then by slashing his left wrist.

But others believed that the club owed it to him to take responsibility. He had been a righteous Angel, a warrior for the club, allegedly shooting a rival in a club feud in Kings Cross the previous year. If they abandoned him, perhaps he might turn informer against other members. Moreover, if the Angels started kicking out members for being involved in crime, where would it end?

There is an old Hells Angel maxim: 'Your brother might be wrong, but he is always your brother.' In the end, after two tense days, it was decided that the club would stand by Hudson, right or wrong. They had made the decision to recruit him into the club and therefore they shared some responsibility for his actions.

Hudson would now become a member of the Angels' 'Big House Crew', receiving regular jail visits from visiting members. What he had done was wrong, and jail was the right place for him, but they would not condemn him for it. Some even suggested the good Samaritans should have stayed out of the matter—they had brought their fate upon themselves. According to this tortuous argument, Kara Douglas knew the rules of the game. Hudson had bashed her and she had come back to him. He hadn't forced her to meet him on that corner. Like so many girls, she had wanted to walk on the wild side with a biker and discovered it could be rough. But nobody could have expected Hudson to explode in the way he did. No-one deserved to be treated like his victims.

When Hudson appeared in court, charged with the murder of Brendan Keilar and the attempted murders of Paul de Waard and Kara Douglas, there was always a contingent of Hells Angels there to support him. Six were on hand in September 2008 when Hudson was sentenced to life imprisonment with a 35-year minimum.

Reporters in court described an unrepentant bully who did not flinch when told he would spend the best part of the rest of his life behind bars. 'He puffed out his chest and held his handsome head high as Justice Paul Coghlan ordered him to stand to hear his fate,' the *Age* reporter wrote. He seemed indifferent to what he had done.

A consultant psychiatrist, Danny Sullivan, had found Hudson had no psychiatric disorder. His anabolic steroid abuse and lifestyle suggested narcissism and antisocial attitudes, but these factors could not alone explain his actions. Dr Sullivan suggested that there might be something selfish and cruel in the psyche of the outlaw that made such explosions of insane violence possible; that his 'peer group and lifestyle encouraged self-centred and aggressive attitudes'.

This seemed to be an assessment based on popular perceptions of bikers, rather than any clinical observations of the defendant as an individual. However, Justice Coghlan declared that Hudson had shown no remorse for his crimes and this was a factor he had taken into account when handing down the maximum sentence available. Certainly, in the dock Hudson had appeared to be inured to the pain and suffering he had caused. But club sources say he was deeply remorseful at what he had done.

It was widely reported that Hudson had showed no emotion during his initial police questioning, giving what cops call 'a no comment interview'. However, this was not entirely true. At the end of the interview, police told him that a doctor was on the way to attend to his wrist injury. Unprompted, Hudson had said: 'I just wanted to say . . . to say sorr . . . just say sorry for anything that has happened.'

Asked to whom he wanted to apologise, Hudson replied: 'Just the . . . No comment.' The macho mask, having slipped for just a moment, was firmly back in place. He had got the same sentence, 35 years, as gangland serial killer Carl Williams who was convicted of ordering the murders of four people and various drug offences.

11

A POLITICAL OPPORTUNITY

It was hard to see how the public relations crisis facing Australia's outlaw bikers could have become any worse after Hudson's rampage in Melbourne. The killing had nothing to do with a motorcycle club per se. It had been a brain snap by an individual in the grip of a drug-induced psychosis. Yet now in the popular imagination all bikies were cast in Hudson's horrifying, brutish media image. They were callous, muscle-bound, gun-toting goons; degenerate drug fiends and a dire threat to civil society. And there were thousands of them, waiting like a full-scale satanic cavalry for the command to sweep into our quiet streets. This had become a national emergency.

Even before Hudson surrendered to police, South Australian Premier Mike Rann had capitalised on the political opportunity the CBD shootings presented. He wrote to Prime Minister John Howard suggesting that 'a national comprehensive strategy' was required to combat bikie 'terrorism'. He urged Howard to consider using the recently enacted National Counter-Terrorism laws as a basis to ban and control outlaw bikie gangs.

Under Howard's terrorism laws, membership of outlawed groups, or even an association with them, became a criminal offence. New powers gave police the right to hold suspects without charge for two weeks at a time. They could be tracked electronically for twelve months, also without any charge being laid.

Australian civil rights lawyers (who had never experienced the horror of seeing loved ones blown to bits) squealed and whined at the death of liberty and free speech. However, there were already grave doubts that the courts could enforce such a law, which effectively gave government a role in how individuals chose their friends. The Australian Law Reform Commission recommended the association clauses be repealed because 'the interference with human rights [created by the offence] is disproportionate to anything that could be achieved by way of protection of the community if the section were enforced'. In other words, the risk of the power being abused was high and the potential reward negligible.

Nonetheless, Rann said he would follow Howard's national terrorism package when he wrote new organised crime laws for South Australia and he hoped other states would follow suit, preventing bikies from simply moving interstate to avoid justice. The harmonisation of gang laws across Australia had long been a cherished goal among police chiefs. The national anti-terrorism laws had shown what was possible under the constitution, even if the federal government had rammed them through parliament with indecent haste after a one-day Senate inquiry. Police now had the power to lock people up during times of fear or when it was convenient to have certain groups off the street. These moments could include anything from major sporting events to visits by foreign heads of state. The opportunity to apply this approach to Australia's $10 billion-a-year organised crime problem would create a new jurisdiction out of thin air.

Not surprisingly, the Australian Crime Commission was an enthusiastic supporter of harmonisation. And the rapid growth of the 1 per cent nation provided an ideal premise on which to pitch a case for it.

The ACC established a national taskforce in 2007 after an intelligence report had indicated an explosion of new bikies on the scene in 2005–06. The ACC reported that ten clubs had established twenty-six new chapters across Australia, taking the total population of bikies to more than 3500. A United Nations Office on Drugs and Crime report (released in 2002) had indicated there were about 7000 'associate members' of outlaw motorcycle gangs in Australia. This was a sharp drop on South Australian police estimates that up to 200,000 were aiding and abetting the outlaws, but it was nonetheless alarming.

Of more concern, however, was the notion that bikies were becoming 'more dynamic and sophisticated', able to operate across state and international boundaries. Another ACC report in late 2006 had revealed bikie involvement in legitimate industries, including Australian mining and Indonesian oil rigs: '[Bikie] involvement in outwardly legitimate business enterprises is potentially impacting adversely on a number of key market sectors in Australia, including finance, transport, private security, entertainment, natural resources and construction.'

To the average citizen, it must have appeared that bikies were on the verge of taking over the world. After reading press articles about the report, I phoned the ACC to get the source material for these conclusions.

Expecting a big fat brief in response to my query, with lots of heavy type and appendices, I was to be disappointed. The ACC dossier was just a page and a half long. I called the ACC back and asked for clarification—for some examples of Bikie Inc.'s evil conglomerate. I emailed questions and they promised to respond— but they didn't. Finally I spoke to an official ACC spokesman;

strangely, he was not allowed to speak, but he broke ranks long enough to say they were all too busy to discuss the matter.

By now I was familiar with the PR staff of state governments and police forces treating me in this manner. The media was being asked to take on faith that the clubs were an elaborate front for organised crime. 'There appears to be a new generation of OMCG [outlaw motorcycle gang] members emerging who appear less interested in the historical "ideals" of OMCG membership and more interested in using the OMCG club to facilitate criminal enterprise,' the ACC warned. But evidence that the ideals of the clubs had been consigned to history was hard to find.

'If you knew what we knew, then you wouldn't be arguing the toss,' one South Australian policeman admonished me. It seemed a fair proposition. I resolved that I would wait until that evidence was provided before reaching a final judgement.

From its roots in the late 1940s, an Anglo-Saxon elite had dominated outlaw biker culture. The ex-servicemen who had fought the Axis powers in World War II enforced a cultural chauvinism on their members. They were allowed to ride only motorcycles manufactured in countries that had fought on the Allied side, leading to an early dominance of Harley-Davidsons and Indians from the USA and Nortons, Triumphs and BSAs from England.

Despite the swastikas, iron crosses and other Third Reich paraphernalia they wore, the early bikers weren't Nazis—they just liked to shock the citizenry. But, as mass migration changed the world in the decades after World War II, the old guard had clung tenaciously to its origins.

Australian motorcycle clubs, even those that had become the local chapters of US outfits, retained the indigenous working class values that spawned them.

If you proved yourself dependable over a long period of time and were willing to uphold the values, the club would eventually give you a go. Even better, if polite society had deemed you an outcast, you would fit right in. Some founding members in the 1960s had joined clubs as a protest after being denied the chance to enlist to fight in Vietnam, but the overwhelming motivation was a search for personal freedom and a peer group where a member could fit in.

The conventional wisdom in the media was that the local chapters of international clubs had all the independence of fast food franchises like McDonalds. It was regularly suggested that the local members would snap to attention if overseas powerbrokers delivered an edict on anything from crime to the design of emblems in the club colours. It's often stated as fact that if clubs are warring in one particular country, there must be conflict between them everywhere. There was no evidence to support this. For example the Hells Angels have been at odds with the Outlaws MC in the US for a long period but there have never been local outbreaks of the conflict.

In reality, there was very little direct control from the US parent chapters of these Australian chapters. There was complete deference to the traditions and the symbols of the club but in most cases decision-making on everything else was stubbornly localised.

The idea that these outlaw clubs were in fact international conspiracies was seductive to headline writers, but unsustainable in practice. Apart from a few documented examples where criminal opportunities had been shared, it was hard to mount a convincing case that the international outlaw movement was in fact the world's largest criminal conspiracy, as other writers had suggested. Certainly there had never been examples proven of overseas chapters sending money, guns and troops to help their Australian colleagues. That wasn't to say the local clubs were crime-free, just that bikers here didn't need the help of foreigners to get into trouble. The esprit de corps of the local chapters had its roots in shared experience and friendship, not allegiance to some overseas cult. This sense of oneness had often been expressed in violence with other clubs and these incidents helped create the mythology of the local outfits. What happened in America or Europe would have little significance here, they had their own war stories to share around the bar.

For the members of outlaw clubs, a good punch-on is the only activity that comes close to the feeling of unity generated by the club run. It is this shared risk and danger that bonds them so tightly. A club that did not spend a good portion of its time either riding motorcycles or defending its colours would not remain a vibrant brotherhood for very long. The camaraderie generated by getting drunk or high together each week would soon wear thin without the X-factor of shared danger. No amount of sex, booze or drugs could match the high of combat.

Most blues happened spontaneously late at night in bars. Blokes mouthing off, putting shit on the patch, were guaranteed a slap or two. If they backed up with reinforcements, there would be a ring-around and members would turn up to support their brother, but it rarely got to that these days. Most club leaders were advising members to stay out of bars where other clubs drank. With the police watching night and day, they couldn't afford the dramas. Still, active members were required to front up if it came down to a stink, even if it was one of their members in the wrong. Like the club run, the only excuse accepted for missing a call-out was being in hospital or jail.

It was the same for all clubs, all over the world. The brother might be wrong but he was always a brother. A club that did not back its members in battle was weak and vulnerable. In the 1980s, dozens of clubs had disappeared in a Darwinian survival of the fittest. If a dominant club sensed weakness, they would march into the rival clubhouse and demand the members hand over their patches. To have your colours lowered was a humiliation that no club could ever recover from.

One club member told me: 'This club is not set up for the

purposes of organised crime. Among the members there are businessmen, tradesmen, guys who drive heavy machinery. There are
students and apprentices. We are not a street gang.' This man had
done jail time, but now he had a wife and young family and was
working a solid week; that was the case with many of the members, he reckoned.

But there were also active criminals too, I had said.

'Well, we aren't a bowling club either,' another biker had
retorted. 'We're a bike club—a brotherhood.'

So what is that, I'd asked.

'See for yourself,' he'd said, implying that, if I could get beyond
the stereotypes, there would be some surprises. 'Have you ever
been arrested?' he asked me.

Why yes, I was forced to admit, remembering that drunk and
disorderly night in Gove, Northern Territory, back in 1981, weav-
ing home on a suspected stolen bicycle.

'Well imagine that!' said the biker, laughing and clapping a
meaty hand on my shoulder. 'I've never been nicked in my life.
Been raided plenty of times, but never arrested. So who's the outlaw now?' he had asked.

In the wake of the Hudson mayhem, it would have been sensible
for outlaw bikies to keep a low profile, in order to preserve their
alleged criminal enterprises. But Tom Mackie of the Descendants
saw more and more were ready to tell their stories and to explain
what their membership meant to them. Just as many were going
under the needle to get new club tattoos to highlight their membership. Going underground was just not their style. They were
not going to hide away, nor submit to the labels society and the
politicians might place upon them. They might have had criminal
records and had done time, but they refused to be typecast.

To the founders of clubs like the Descendants, the club patch was not a fashion item, like a suit or a piece of jewellery worn for show or profit, and then put away in the cupboard. It was a commitment for which a member had to be prepared to sacrifice his liberty, and possibly even his life. There was no life membership in the Descendants where someone could step back from weekly duties after 15-20 years but still participate in club activities. Once you were in, it was for life.

'When we wrote our constitution all those years ago, we never thought we would make it past 30 years of age, so it wasn't really an issue,' said one of the earliest members.

There was no element of disrespect intended to other clubs who did offer it. In fact there was no knowledge of other clubs' guidelines in those formative years. Each club had its own situation but this rule had worked for them as a single chapter club.

'It takes a lot of effort to get in this club and it takes a lot of effort from the right bloke to stay in this club,' he said.

Staunch bikers operated on a different plane. They were willing to do jail terms to maintain this life of knight errantry on a motorbike. Sending them to prison for associating with their brothers was no punishment at all. They would come out of jail straight back into the arms of their club. It was the only life they knew. In fact, the more fellow members the state locked up, the better it would be inside. It would strengthen the bonds between members. Once jail no longer holds any terrors for someone, it's difficult to punish them.

If their lifestyle was going to endure, it would require members to show discipline and loyalty. The task of gaining consensus among the members was often difficult. The internal politics inside clubs could be ferocious. Some of the best fights members had ever seen had been among club brothers. Somehow, out of the anarchy and emotion, the clubs moved forward.

In the climate of fear that followed the Melbourne CBD shootings there was public assent for a push to break the bikies, to send what Mike Rann had called the 'pond scum' back to the swamp once and for all. When faced with this pressure, it was assumed the clubs would fold and its members would retreat to their underground criminal pursuits.

'A lot of people who just go to work and then go home, maybe go out on the weekends, they fold to pressure. Whereas we won't fold to pressure,' one biker told me. 'We will fight. Our heart and soul is in this. It's just like your family: you put your heart and soul into it. If they are going to try and take your family away, you are not going to watch your kids get taken away. We will stand up for ourselves and I think they fear that.'

Club philosophers believed this assault on the bikers could prove the club's finest hour: 'I swore as a child I was in search of brotherhood and unity, because all I could see in the world was actual terrorism and public uncertainty and problems with governments and I felt like this was the last stance of a true democracy. Here I found strength, unity and a brotherhood, and I could help other people,' said one member.

Rann's anti-biker rants gave Adelaide's bikers a focus for their anger, said Tom Mackie of the Descendants. Here was the reason that clubs existed in the first place. They already believed that, if you were poor and uneducated, from a dysfunctional family, you didn't have a chance in Rann's world. Your vote, your voice— even your existence—had no value at all. There was no justice for you. So the motorcycle club offered a true alternative, a form of participatory democracy.

Society had short-changed the bikie, but, if he complied with all the rules and regulations of the club, he would be rewarded with a kind of enduring freedom. And if he went to jail, which was a stone-cold certainty for many the club would be waiting for him when he returned. The club was worth fighting for, because it would fight for him.

12

LAST STAND AT STORMY'S

In October 2007, it felt like things were falling apart. South Australia was facing another summer of crippling drought and economic stagnation. Yet the Rann Government was enjoying record popularity. The law and order campaign had been either a miraculous diversion, or yet more evidence that people need something to hate. Either way, it was a state at war with itself.

The drive from Melbourne had been a bleak eight hours of parched country and fierce heat. Outside the car, a cloud of bush flies descended on anything with a hint of moisture. The mood in the towns and truck stops was malignant. The big dry had produced in people a kind of spiteful rancour looking to vent. Mike Rann's War on Bikies was guaranteed to provoke an outpouring of spleen.

'Oh, yeah. We've had those bastards here, all right,' the owner of a roadside nut stall said with supreme authority. There had been 'goings-on in the night', he confided. Someone on a motorbike had been going round nicking stuff in the district, but they had caught him recently. 'Some blokes chased him in vehicles till he got hung up on a barbed-wire fence,' the man said with a chuckle.

It actually turned out to be a local kid on a trail bike. But there had been other things: shipping containers that had mysteriously appeared in a nearby paddock and then later vanished; a group of thugs and their girlfriends that had camped under the bridge a few years ago. And what had they had done under the bridge, I asked.

'Well, they were just like animals, they were,' he replied, deferring to his wife. The government could eliminate every last one of them as far as he was concerned. But they're too rich, he said. And way too clever. He pointed out to the busy highway: 'Every day, there's trucks out there haulin' the bikies' dope to Melbourne and Sydney. They got tanks with false bottoms and secret compartments. And they come back loaded with speed and guns. If you don't believe me, you're kidding yourself. Just ask the government,' he said, his face reddening.

In Adelaide, the atmosphere wasn't much better. The fatwa on crime and sin was in full swing. Even bastions of vice regarded as part of the fabric of Adelaide were feeling the heat. Stormy Summers' bordello had been the first to go.

In December 2006 the sheriff, backed by the might of the STAR Group, had descended, blocking off Waymouth Street for a tactical assault on the brothel. They had come to evict Stormy from her den of iniquity. With the title to the building transferred to her manager there was the pressing matter of non-payment of rent. The manager was now kicking her boss out of Stormy's.

SAPOL was only too happy to assist in shifting the former madam and her motley crew out of the CBD. While Steve Williams had been in residence, the place had been a rallying point for those opposed to the moral panic sweeping the state. With him gone, this was a good chance for the state to sweep the rest of the vermin from the street.

At least Stormy's last stand would be a spectacular event, the remnants decided. They wouldn't go quietly. Stormy's son had died in there and she was prepared to follow him defending the place.

The posse tried to storm the complex but Stormy's husband, Marky G, had welded the front doors shut. Hurling abuse, he laid a withering fire on the officers with a slingshot from the top floor, while the working girls bombarded them with their underwear and used condoms. When he was out of ammo, he hurled a fire extinguisher down on them. He was frothing and howling, just totally gone.

If police had not confiscated his firearms in an earlier raid, the siege would have certainly ended in bloodshed. Death by cop was an honourable end, compared with being herded out like cattle to the slaughter. However, the bordello suddenly went quiet as Marky G regrouped.

The STAR Group officers must have thought he had passed out or expired; methodically they cut through the front doors with an angle grinder, showering sparks into the mirrored foyer. Imagine their surprise when Marky reappeared at the top of the stairs with a jerry can full of petrol. He was grinning maniacally, threatening to send everyone in the brothel up in flames. A simple eviction was about to turn into a police killing. His eyes were rolling in his head as he stood bellowing and spitting abuse at them. Pushed into a corner, he was capable of anything. The cops backed off then, but it was only a temporary victory.

A week later, after much negotiation, Stormy and Marky reluctantly quit the premises, leaving most of their possessions behind. She had lost her son and Steve Williams while in that place; she wasn't about to sacrifice her husband. Some of the best prostitutes in town hit the bricks too, in a bonanza for Stormy's competitors.

It was heartbreaking for Stormy herself, whose entire life had been tied up in that place. She ended up in a one-bedroom Housing Commission flat down at Port Adelaide. The loss of status for this grand dame of sin must have been crushing. But somehow Marky G avoided jail.

By 2007 Adelaide's underworld was riven with conflict. New feuds were developing between street gangs popping up in the suburbs. There had been seven shootings in the past seven months, which for a quiet town like Adelaide was a veritable crime wave. Trouble was coming to the boil between the Hells Angels and a crew of ethnic gangsters who called themselves 'The New Boys'.

Rann's security industry laws had taken the bikies out of Hindley Street and the vacuum had been filled by the New Boys, whose charismatic leader, Vincenzo Focarelli, ran operations from a tattoo shop, Ink Central, on Hindley Street. Focarelli had been a nom for the Angels' North Crew, but reportedly hadn't made the cut.

Like Carl Williams in Melbourne's underworld, Focarelli saw his crew as the vanguard of a new generation sweeping away Adelaide's old guard, represented by the bikies. Through social media like Facebook, the New Boys had forged links with other ethnic street gangs around the nation including Sydney's newest bikie club, Notorious MC, and the surf gang, the Bra Boys.

They were quietly establishing a network in other Australian cities too. Unlike the bikies, they did not announce this by building forbidding fortresses or wearing club colours. They were underground, revealing their membership only through cryptic tattoos and the letters 'NB' inserted into Facebook profiles. When they came out of the darkness, it was said, the nation would be amazed at how large and pervasive they had become. While everyone was focused on the bikie menace, the New Boys would lay all before them.

The New Boys had big plans to turn their notoriety into a marketing powerhouse like the Sydney surf gang the Bra Boys had. There would be New Boys–branded clothes, music, documentaries and films. They would establish a conglomerate, providing employment to all the brothers and their families.

Focarelli had another trump card that would further unite his club: Islam. While the godless bikies destroyed their edge with booze and drugs, the New Boys would be disciplined and devout, fearful only of Allah. More of the crew were converting to Islam by the day.

While the bikies still had their differences, the problems posed by the New Boys threatened to unite them. Some bikies wanted to go down to Focarelli's shop and beat the shit out of anybody they found there. A short sharp lesson, it was felt, would restore the fear that maintained the balance of power in the jungle.

The stage had been set for a heavy beat-down of the New Boys, but wiser heads prevailed for now. More bad publicity would only be a bonus for the state government in its campaign against everyone. There was also a sneaking suspicion that Focarelli's ethnic army would be no pushover. It's difficult to defeat an enemy who is prepared to lay down his life for his god.

Meanwhile, SAPOL's bikie squad, Avatar, were taking any opportunity to get in the face of the bikers. The tension was rising every time the two sides met. A ride across town in colours could mean half a dozen stops by officers. There were routine raids on homes and businesses calculated to cause maximum grief and embarrassment. The cops were determined that the entire street would know there was a bikie living next door. They could turn up at a workplace where a bikie was applying for a job to let the boss know they were hiring a villain. Some employers found the heat too great and withdrew offers. Others that stuck by their word risked being classified as associates and opening themselves up to the same treatment.

The Adelaide media began to report bikie involvement in legitimate industries as something sinister. A bikie-aligned business could not be taken at face value. There was always a suspicion that it had to be a front for laundering the proceeds of organised crime. The fact that many of these business owners employed their club brothers seemed to confirm the sham nature of the enterprises. The stories ignored the fact that it was this very pressure that was driving the economic links between club members. The links between employers and employees was enough to base a story upon. As the heat rose, companies with bikie links were quietly told they would not be considered for government business, though they were squeaky clean.

This style of journalism had begun to spread across Australia as the moral panic really set in. In 2008, four men turned up at the Lodge, the Prime Minister's residence in Canberra to carry out maintenance work. They had all the necessary identification papers and documentation from the department of the Prime Minister and Cabinet. The one-hour job went off without incident. That is, until the ABC got hold of the story some time later.

'The police on duty . . . were uneasy, given that the men were tattooed and dressed like bikies but they had what appeared to be legitimate documentation and it all checked out, so the police eventually let them into the grounds and into the care of Lodge staff,' the ABC reported.

This story caused a minor storm. Men coming to work had been transformed into bikies who had 'infiltrated' one of the country's most secure locations. Deputy Opposition Leader Julie Bishop fanned this faux controversy to score a political point or two.

'Not only is The Lodge the home of the prime minister and his family but it also hosts many international leaders and guests at high levels around the world so it does have, potentially, international significance,' she told the ABC.

The fear created by such media beat-ups seemed to justify the police attention. The mere presence of bikies now generated the conclusion they were up to no good.

It was at funerals where the building anger between bikies and the state could be most readily observed. From across the street (as if making sure they were seen), a contingent of police officers would film the members as they arrived. With members often coming in from around the country, it was a valuable opportunity to gather information and fresh images.

The members would scowl at this invasion of privacy. They had been photographed so many times, what was the point, they asked. Perhaps in death the cops could turn their mate into something he wasn't.

To his clubmates, the deceased would be simply a loyal friend, a staunch character. He was someone who wanted to be part of a crew that was all about getting together, whether it was drinking on a Friday night, or riding interstate and seeing buddies, or going riding in the hills on the weekend. If he or any other bikie had a life of crime, that was nobody else's business.

Every member was treated the same in death. The coffin would be taken from the chapel in a hearse flying club flags and escorted by the cortege of motorcycles. Members who had flown in from interstate would ride borrowed bikes organised by the locals. It would not do to arrive in a car on such an occasion. At the cemetery, after the minister had conducted the service, the members would lower coffin into the earth; then each of them would take his turn on a shovel, and soon the grave would be filled in. Burial is the only way for the 1% as he takes his colours into the cold earth. To burn the patch would be sacrilege. And the cops would just take reams of video footage and still photos of these rituals. They must have gathered thousands of pictures of the same heads because the personnel of the clubs wasn't changing and there were too many funerals that year.

By now, I was getting to know who was who in Adelaide's clubland. There were members with serious criminal records. But they were in the minority, as were the handful of members who had a clean sheet. The majority were in the middle—just small-time operators with a few convictions, often from years before. Most members would have been unremarkable in criminal terms had they not donned an outlaw's colours. Many told me that, were it not for the club's calming influence, they would have been full-time villains.

Since 2005, there had been no charges of criminal conspiracy or organised crime levelled against Adelaide bikers. A handful had gone to jail for minor drug offences, and others for violence or weapons charges.

A capacity to do time without whining and complaining is regarded as a virtue among bikies. Police will often dangle the carrot of a lesser sentence for members prepared to tell on their mates; it's worth letting one go free, to get a look inside the club. But to be staunch is the highest praise a bikie can earn.

It was the clubs' paramilitary organisation and discipline that seemed to intimidate civil society so much, just as the spectre of the private army that Frank Rooney had imagined in his seminal *Harper's* story 'Cyclists' Raid' had terrified America in 1951. Today such a group could not exist without being tagged a threat to society, lumped in with terrorists and other treasonous subversives.

Of all the insults and allegations that politicians had thrown at them, it was the description of them as terrorists that had hurt the most. It was a terrible slur on their patriotism, they said. Higher-minded members believed that, on the contrary, they were fighting to uphold founding freedoms the country had been steadily abandoning.

'I don't think I have met a member who hates Australia; if he does he should go somewhere else,' said one biker. 'We'd like to say to the army, give us something to do to help protect our country.'

But while they were outraged to be called terrorists, they conceded that fear had been good for the clubs. Suddenly everyone wanted to join, said a member. On Friday nights the club bars were open to associates and friends, and the attendances were steadily rising. The disaffected, the persecuted, the paranoid and the angry saw common cause with the outlaws. The harder the clubs made it to get in, the more desperate people became to join. In the past when the clubs had expanded, it had been to defend the patch against other clubs, but this was different. This war with the state would be won on discipline and loyalty.

But it was beginning to dawn on many of them that those members who engaged in freelance crime and mayhem were damaging the case the clubs could make for their survival. It was the first clue that the leadership of the clubs recognised there was a need for change. People in the movement began asking whether a bikie could be a righteous brother when his criminal activities rebounded on the rest of the club.

In the US, the RICO anti-racketeering laws had changed the attitude inside clubs to crime. Pre-RICO, Sonny Barger had set a clear doctrine inside the Hells Angels: 'If you are in the club, I don't care what you do, as long as you don't put it on me,' he had decreed. But now, simply sharing membership with a crook was enough for him to lay his shit on the rest. After flirting dangerously with becoming a dedicated criminal gang in the 1970s, RICO had forced a subtle change in the Hells Angels' recruitment policy.

'Well some of us in the club have seen the whole cycle, but

there is nobody that joins the club in America because they want to be a criminal,' Barger told me. 'That's the most stupidest thing you could do. If you want to be a criminal you wanna be as far away as you can be. I'm not denying that you might sometimes need some money quick, so you go and do something stupid. But you aren't going to do it for a living,' he said.

In the 1970s Barger had run heroin and cocaine into the US from Mexico, becoming one of the bigger dealers in northern California. Such a business would not be tolerated today. 'Nobody is going to believe this, but the charter I am under in Cave Creek says that if you are caught selling drugs you are automatically kicked out of the club,' he said. He predicted that any move towards RICO would have similar effects in Australia. The one positive out of RICO—the 'big law with the funny name'—had been that you literally became your brother's keeper. The club had become more manageable as a result, he said.

In Australia, there were already quite enough opportunities to use a club patch that were legal, even if they were perhaps morally questionable. A certain kind of bikie saw a legitimate place for his special skills in the business world.

On the wild frontier of business, debt collecting is a business that relies on some implied level of threat for success. Non-payment of commercial debt is a national sport in Australia. Many foolishly believe the police will recover their money with diligent investigation and stern words; the conmen in business know that police will always direct complainants to the civil courts. The cost of litigation being prohibitive, the villains run up debt with impunity. It's a good life on the lam from the creditors, until that knock on the door.

Bikies are highly effective debt collectors because of the perception that the club stands behind them. Therefore, if a member uses the patch as a tool of trade, most chapters stipulate that they pay a tribute to his brothers, perhaps 10 per cent of the proceeds.

But debt collection is not illegal—some very nice people around town recover money, courtesy of bikies.

The moral panic over bikies coincided with the end of nearly two decades of economic prosperity. During the boom, corporate Australia had extended generous credit but, as sales dried up, even good customers became slow to pay. It was time to chase those bad and doubtful debts as never before. Banks and finance companies, who had built fat margins on lending to small businesses, were now pushing many customers to the wall.

Big clients who owed $10 million or more got the kid-glove treatment. The weight fell on small businesses, which couldn't afford to fight the banks in court. Their debts were often 'factored', sold to third parties at a discount to get them off the books. Then one day a bikie turned up at the debtor's door asking for the money. Collection firms stressed to their agents that they should never threaten the 'clients'. A 2-metre outlaw weighing in at 120 kilos, dressed in full colours, did not need threats to get his message across.

Business had never been so good for the bikie debt collectors. And they had Premier Rann and his fear campaign to thank for it. The 'pond scum' that folks had read about in the newspaper had slithered from the swamp and were now standing stolidly in the doorway. If the South Australian Premier, flanked by his Police Commissioner Mal Hyde, told them that bikers were involved in murder, rape, extortion, drug manufacture and illegal firearms, then it must be so. People had every right to be terrified. These frightening people were the enemy within the authorities said.

The power of the patch was growing. For some bikers, it was only a short walk from debt collection to standover tactics and extortion. The club regalia sent the message that the individual had the backing of the club. Even if he was rebuffed, there would be others following. Any sensible person would just pay up unless he was prepared to wage all-out war.

How much of this was true mattered less than the perception that it was. Even the *spectre* of bikies was enough for some to part with their money, such was the fear. In 2007, a court heard that a Melbourne woman, Debra Lee Bassani, had extorted more than $125,000 from relatives in a scheme involving phantom bikies and an imaginary detective. Three families had lived on the run for nearly a year in cabins and caravans in fear of bikie snipers.

This bizarre scenario began when the grandmother of Bassani's husband died, bequeathing her home to her family. Bassani told relatives that the house's tenants were bikies, who were angry that police warrants were executed at their home. She told them a detective from an 'elite squad' would protect them if they made payments of $5000 a month. Bassani sent text messages, claiming to be the detective and warning them of impending attack by the fictitious bikies. After one such alert, a terrified relative swam across the Barwon River to escape his imaginary pursuers.

Also in 2007, a convicted drug dealer used Steve Williams to explain why he hadn't answered a subpoena to appear at an Australian Crime Commission. He claimed that, on the morning of the top-secret hearing, Williams had bashed him in a service station and warned him the attack would be 'just a start'. Most ominously, Williams had somehow discovered the dates on which the man was to appear at the ACC hearing. Conveniently, the claim was made after Williams's disappearance, so there was no way to verify the alarming security breach.

Some bikies were buying into the myth-making too. It was said that a certain kind of man changed when he was awarded his club patch. He had a new sense of himself. The three-piece patch with the club name, logo and location was like a big gold key to the city. He felt he could walk in anywhere and put his hand out for money. In this climate of fear, even a small man in colours could cast a big shadow.

And Mike Rann, far from quelling the anxiety, was fanning

it. Young men, who were already alienated by a lack of education or by criminal convictions, saw the clubs as a convenient way out, a social achievement. Becoming an outlaw was flipping the bird at a society that offered them no more than a welfare cheque and a jail cell. Once they had been cavemen, fighting for supremacy in a wasteland no-one cared about, but Rann's vitriol had turned them into something real and substantial.

Like terrorists, Rann's bikies were motivated not by crime, but by a deep irrational hatred of law and order. They were part of a highly organised insurgency that aimed to destroy everything. If there was evil in Adelaide, the bikers were at the root of it. If they could be removed, the shootings, bombings and abductions would cease overnight. The City of Churches would return to its innocent past—at least until the next shallow grave was uncovered in the desert.

The supreme irony was that the more Premier Rann high-lighted the lawlessness of the bikies, the less credence the chattering classes gave to his claim that the crime rate was actually falling. The radio shock jocks that Rann had courted were falling out of love with him. 'We are the capital of drugs and cannabis . . . while the politicians lie through their bums,' 5AA's Bob Francis was fond of telling listeners. 'We have a terrible situation with murders. They say crime has gone down; that's crap. They play with stats, they work on the percentages and the numbers, but the government is doing nothing to stop the crime in this state.'

What every analysis failed to take into account was that the percentage of MC members active in crime was relatively small. Over the previous two years, a number of the Adelaide bikers had been charged with various offences, but nothing that seemed to match the soaring rhetoric of the government. Yet every outbreak of crime seemed to purportedly have a bikie link somewhere.

During this visit to Adelaide I had arranged to meet some associates of a particular MC at a bar on Light Square.

One associate spoke of continuing animosity between the supporters of another club and how it would be sorted out in the traditional manner. None of this seemed to have their club's sanction; it was more a side battle, where hang-arounds might prove themselves for later admission.

Two groups of hang-arounds had been hunting one another for some time, but had yet to collide. Then, close to midnight, one of the team I was with received a text message simply saying words to the effect of: 'Don't be outside the club in the next ten minutes.' The meaning was clear: there was going to be a drive-by shooting; we should stay inside for our own safety.

Within half an hour, word circulated that there had been a shooting about 500 metres away, across the Square at a bar called the Gemini Gaming Lounge. At 1.36 a.m., when a man walked out of the club to his car parked out front, a group of four men in a dark-coloured sedan cruised past. One of these men let fly with a volley of six shots.

One round struck the man in the throat, leaving him in a critical condition, paralysed from the neck down. The text had proved eerily prescient. Nobody with me doubted that this was bikie-related and the next day the press agreed.

We spilled out onto the street, looking for the next place where we could quell the adrenalin with a few more rounds. Towards dawn, with all the bars closed, the centre of town was still overrun by surly drunks and speed-addled freaks looking for the meaning of Saturday morning.

As I fled the scene in a cab, I had the slightest pang of sympathy for Mike Rann and his moral crusaders. Adelaide seemed to be an ugly, scary place filled with damaged and angry people. I reflected on my night's headline attractions: after the shooting on Light Square a herd of nasty drunk girls in party frocks had bitch-slapped each other in the street and a pair of steroid-fuelled bullies had picked fights in the taxi queue. And that was just what I was aware of, or had witnessed.

Furthermore, it turned out much later that the Gemini Lounge shooting had been a targeted attack. In the uproar over the bikies in recent times, the cops had missed the fact that tension was rising between two Vietnamese gangs. The victim this night had been no innocent bystander caught up in a bikie war. The ominous text message I had been told about before the attack had been wrong, a practical joke even.

But that would have been little consolation, even had I known it then. Any self-respecting tourist in this town that night would have run screaming into the desert, never to return. It occurred to me that no amount of police and no law, no matter how draconian, could restore civility to this toxic human zoo. Nothing less than an airstrike would do.

13

GOD'S GIFT

In late 2007, as law enforcement agencies feverishly searched for the black box to Bikie's Inc.'s empire of crime, Australian Federal police were closing in on a massive pinch. At 300 kilos, this would be the biggest importation of pseudoephedrine that police had ever intercepted.

Much of the speed produced in Australia was sourced from small to medium backyard operations. By the late 1990s, budding speed cooks could download the recipes from the internet. Typically, they could source pseudoephedrine by buying copious quantities of over-the-counter cold and flu medications and then extracting the 'Susie'. It was a lucrative cottage industry because it did not require any international connections. They could make a quick and dirty fortune from items most people had in the bathroom cupboard or under the kitchen sink.

But the crooks that the AFP agents were chasing were in another league altogether. There was enough Susie headed for

Sydney to supply the national market for six months. The organisers were attempting a dry run. They were to receive a shipping container filled with 17,000 kilos of basmati rice from a company based in Lahore, Pakistan, Elegant Hosiery. The conspirators were not concerned that a hosiery company exporting US$21,275 of rice might set off alarm bells. They knew the system inside and out—customs were flat out checking the contents of just 10 per cent of the containers that came into Australian ports. If the test run went well, three other shipments were planned to follow containing the precursor chemicals.

Such an operation would have been a huge step up in class for most of Australia's alleged bikie villains. This deal would cement the conspirators as the biggest players in the amphetamine industry overnight.

The villains involved in this affair, however, were not bikies. In fact, the mastermind had been instrumental in putting outlaws behind bars.

Mark Standen was an assistant director of the New South Wales Crime Commission, a super-secretive law enforcement body that had enjoyed phenomenal success in attacking organised crime. Standen was one of the commission's best investigators, a friend to some of Australia's most senior police and an ambitious man on the rise. But a tip-off from police in Holland had led AFP agents to place listening devices inside Standen's mobile phone and in the car of a co-conspirator.

A different picture of the assistant director began to emerge from conversations between Standen and his partner, Bakhos 'Bill' Jalalaty, a Sydney businessman. In a Sydney cafe in September 2007, Standen had confided he was under financial strain: his four kids had crooked teeth and needed braces; his wife needed expensive psychiatric treatment; he had a big mortgage; and he also felt pressured to assist family members. He was also lavishing expensive gifts on his mistress, a former Australian Federal Police officer.

'I just want two hundred thousand . . . if I had a hundred in cash I wouldn't have to panic for, say, another year,' Standen told Jalalaty.

Standen had hoped to raise some quick cash with a consultancy on a Hollywood blockbuster in which Russell Crowe was to play a retired FBI director. He had met Crowe in Sydney and they had got on well, but he was disappointed when there was no job offer. 'Maurice', as Standen liked to be called in emails, was looking forward to just getting 'the slate clean'. The legal shipment of rice was the first step, delivering him a profit of $17,000.

Understandably, there was jubilation within outlaw circles when police arrested and charged Standen with conspiracy to import the pseudoephedrine and conspiracy to pervert the course of justice. Standen had been behind the harassment of outlaw clubs in New South Wales and had been instrumental in locking up several members on trumped-up charges. Not only that, but his activities underlined the bikie claim that the justice system was corrupt. While the hue and cry over bikie crime made screaming headlines a member of the New South Wales Crime Commission was doing exactly what they accused the clubs of doing—but on a massive scale. It showed the potential of powerful and unaccountable bodies like the New South Wales Crime Commission. Evidence given in Standen's trial showed how tempting it was for police to dip into the drug trade when official oversight was so inadequate. Standen had shown an insider's mastery of law enforcement techniques in covering his tracks.

In the end, it was not Australian police who had caught up with Standen but Dutch authorities who had alerted the AFP. It seemed reasonable to ask how many other Crime Commission figures were involved in such nefarious activities. Indeed, how many officers had known of the financial pressure that Standen had been under? Bikies were always accused of protecting criminals in their ranks, so it was only fair to ask Standen's superiors the questions: how much did they know of his activities and when did they know it? Standen maintained he had acted alone, but the Commission had stifled further inquiry and criticism. Later, when the *Sydney Morning Herald* delved into a range of questionable practices, the Crime Commission responded by seeking court orders to seize the reporters' telephone records.

To the hardline outlaws, this was a depressing fact of life, reinforcing the dismal truth that law enforcement was a law unto itself. But to the moderates and reformers of the club scene, this was a much-needed morale boost. They began calling Standen 'God's Gift to Bikies'. The Queensland clubs, led by the Hells Angels, had been discussing the creation of a confederation since 2006, when Rann put his anti-association laws on the agenda in South Australia. It was felt that the state Labor governments in Queensland and New South Wales would follow suit. Western Australia was already planning its own legislation.

Standen's fall from grace accelerated the move to unity. He had gifted the bikies a valuable argument in the public debate in which they were engaged. Drugs were a society-wide scourge, not solely the preserve of the criminal class. Standen had put the sins of bikies in perspective. They perhaps naively believed the media would grasp the significance of the bust. People—whether they were cops, bikies or even ordinary citizens—were always divided into the good, the bad and the ugly.

In early 2008, at the first meeting of the United Motorcycle Council (UMC) of Queensland, Mark Standen was a featured topic of conversation. Seventeen outlaw clubs sent delegates to that first meeting, held in a suburban hotel in Brisbane. There were clubs represented that had been fighting for forty years; the original cause of their conflict was long buried in the past, but never forgotten. The old enmities could have flared up again at any moment. But 'Hothead', the national president of the Outcasts—a club with chapters in Queensland, New South Wales and Victoria—set the tone for what was to follow across the nation.

'As of this moment, the Outcasts wipe the slate clean,' Hothead declared. 'Whatever arguments and hostilities exist from the past are forgotten as of now,' he said. There was a shocked silence in the room. It was meant to be simply 'a meet and greet', but Hothead had raised the bar.

'Everyone that night went away considering their own positions. Whether their clubs could forgive and forget the past for the sake of the UMC,' recalls one member. 'Other clubs had not been quite so open about it, but behind the scenes had said: "Yes, it's time to give that [the feuds] up".'

Gradually, over the next few months, a spirit of détente grew within the group. The delegates had come together at first to represent their clubs, but they began to feel a part of something bigger.

The UMC organisers cleverly took something from how each club ran their meetings to make people feel comfortable. The council needed to be a neutral chamber that emphasised the similarities, not the differences between clubs. The meetings were never held in clubhouses and a different club hosted each one, providing the catering. All votes had to be carried with a 60 per cent majority and even clubs who were not UMC members were sent copies of the minutes. It could have been the meeting of any sporting or social association, except for the rough heads and club colours on show. There was a treasurer with a cashbook, a secretary and a meeting chairman. In deference to security and harmony, all mobile phones were handed in at the door, which was always guarded by a nominee or two from the host club.

Although their public image was anarchic, behind the scenes biker clubs had always operated under formal guidelines and disciplines. So the transition to the orderly UMC format was surprisingly easy.

The meetings ran smoothly, working through issues of

fundraising, the planning of lobbying efforts and massed collective rides. There was a printed agenda, reports and audited accounts. Business could be raised without notice, but only after the formal items had been disposed of and always within the meeting protocol. It began to feel more like a single entity than a collection of rivals.

New South Wales was the next cab off the rank, starting a few months after the first Queensland confab. When the manager of the western Sydney hotel they had chosen for their get-together saw members of the state's most notorious outlaw clubs rolling up in colours, he called the police, anxious that his pub was the venue for an organised crime summit. The cops turned up in force and were shocked to see once-mortal enemies sitting together.

For the first time, outlaw clubs were doing something that their critics did not expect. It was easy to dismiss the early UMC meetings as window dressing: another shallow public relations show, much like the Christmas toy runs. 'It's just like putting lipstick on a pig,' one police officer said. 'It might look pretty but we still know what kind of animal it really is.' But the delegates did not feel they were engaged in a sham—quite the opposite.

From the very first meeting in Queensland, an unexpected energy was created, which the delegates took back to their own clubhouses. Their club brothers sensed something new and novel was going on. Some began attending meetings as observers, to see what was happening. The bikies were moving in uncharted waters—there were no international precedents for such a union. A confederation of clubs had been attempted in the US, but had been dominated by a few big clubs. Here was a genuinely representative body, whose decisions were regarded as law by all clubs involved.

As they spent more time with each other, the old enmities began to rapidly break down. There were even instances where the UMC sent a neutral member from its ranks to mediate disputes between clubs from interstate. The beauty of this mechanism was that, if clubs failed to adhere to the decision of the mediator, they risked pissing off the third-party club. They certainly could not continue to be a member of the UMC without respecting its decisions.

Little by little, they were learning to get on with each other again after a long period of isolation and mistrust.

As bikies saw how other clubs did things, the penny dropped for many. Despite all the bloody rivalry and chest-beating about whose club was the best, there was no more than a Coke and Pepsi difference between them all. To stretch the metaphor, there would be no victory in winning the Cola Wars if all soft drink ended up banned.

In September 2008, the South Australian parliament passed the Serious and Organised Crime (Control) Act 2008 (SOCCA), which Premier Mike Rann bragged was 'the world's toughest anti-bikie legislation'.

Under the act, the Attorney-General could outlaw any group or club if he was satisfied the members associated 'for the purpose of organising, planning, facilitating, supporting or engaging in serious criminal activity' and the organisation represented 'a risk to public safety and order'. The Attorney-General was not required to provide any grounds or reasons for the declaration. The 'criminal intelligence' provided by the Commissioner of Police could be kept secret.

Once the declaration was made, the Police Commissioner could apply to the courts for a control order to be made against anyone deemed to be a member of the outlawed organisation. The control order prohibited the subject from associating with other members of the declared organisation by any means including telephone, email, letter, facsimile, or in the flesh. If a person under a control order associated with a member of a declared organisation, or others under control orders, up to six times a year, he faced a maximum of five years in jail. Just being in the same pub was enough to trigger an act of association for the police to add to their running tally on somebody.

The legislation also created new offences of violent disorder (maximum penalty of two years' jail); riot (seven years, ten years where aggravated); affray (three years, five years where aggravated) and stalking of public officials by OMCG members (seven years). Stalking a person with the intention of intimidating a victim, witness, court official, police officer or public servant would now become a serious offence. It would become easier for police to secure orders to dismantle fortifications protecting clubrooms.

An earlier draft of the act had proposed giving the Attorney-General the power to ban insignia and club colours from public display. That didn't make the final bill. Perhaps enforcing the dress code would have been a stretch, given that police were flat out embracing their new arithmetical approach to law enforcement.

Critics warned that the SOCCA would give police and government unprecedented control over the lives of South Australians. Never before had an Australian government sought to regulate social interaction to such an extent. Mike Rann could now determine who you could be friends with. In an interview with this author, Attorney-General Michael Atkinson talked up the novelty of his new law, suggesting the state's bikies would act as lab rats for a range of socially intrusive measures in the future. 'South Australia is a small state. Adelaide is a comparatively small city. I think we can be a laboratory for testing new laws, laws requested by the police commissioner, filtered through lawyers and the department and Cabinet long before they become law,' he said.

There were exemptions that allowed ministers of religion, close family or professional contacts to associate with members of deemed organisations, but Atkinson predicted the law would make South Australia 'a no-go zone for outlaw bikies'.

There was an outcry from civil liberties advocates, defence lawyers and the South Australian Bar Association. Rann dismissed them all with contempt. While he had the media behind him, he could afford to sneer at the fat cats of the legal profession. Lawyers who had grown rich on defending the bikies were part of the problem in the first place, he said.

'The legal community has condemned every action that we have taken to toughen up the law on bikies,' Rann said. 'We've seen legislation being appealed against on constitutional grounds, held up in the courts because somehow we are breaching the civil liberties of bikies. I think that's a good thing, that we do breach the civil liberties of bikies . . . My message today to the lawyers is join us in the fight against people who, in my view, are terrorists within our community, rather than trying to frustrate us.'

Prosecutors, on the other hand, were very pleased with the new powers. Lowering the evidentiary burden would make the task of ridding society of bikies a great deal easier. In fact, South Australia's Director of Public Prosecutions Stephen Pallaras told Adelaide media the new laws didn't go far enough in shutting down the criminal menace the clubs represented. 'Why do we tolerate their existence?' he reportedly asked.

Still riding high in the polls, Rann could afford to play to the cheap seats. He could harness the anger about crime and lawlessness in the streets. It would all go away if everyone backed his campaign against the bogeymen.

The bogeymen themselves mostly didn't feel much different, even if the manner in which the law viewed them had changed overnight. A few members did drop out because they felt they had too much to lose, but they were in a tiny minority.

As Arthur Veno had predicted, it was the moderates, not the

hardcore criminals, who would now be considering their futures. But most wouldn't be quitting, just going underground, as the Hells Angels had in Canada when faced with government attempts to ban them in the 1990s.

Life members of the clubs would not be exempt from Rann's new laws. Many of them had criminal histories with convictions for drugs, violence and theft but a large number of them had actually grown out of their wild ways. It was common to find older members who had not been in trouble with the police for decades.

They now had jobs, businesses and families. As life members they were excused attendance at weekly church meetings; but they still went on runs and were part of the extended club family. They were often influential mentors and sounding boards to the present leadership, explaining the history and values of their clubs. They were proof that members could put aside crime and participate in society while remaining bikers. Now, courtesy of Rann's new laws, they were about to branded as criminals again. All their past sins could be dredged up again if they didn't bend to the new laws and abandon their clubs.

Each man had to make his own decision about the future. They had families to feed and clothe and they couldn't do that from jail. Yet it seemed very few were planning to cut and run. Instead they planned to stop wearing colours in public, perhaps take the stickers off their bike and make themselves scarce for a while. They reasoned that police would eventually weary of trying to catch members under control orders from associating. There would be no surrender. They would just have to get sneaky again, but this would pass.

After decades as bikers, this was a way of life. They wore their patch to show people who they were. They regarded themselves as bikers first and citizens second, but it was a fine line. I reflected on the endless variety of the bikers I had met. They were crooks, drunks, thugs, drug abusers, teetotallers, businessmen, trainee professionals, nightclub bouncers, tradesmen and house husbands. There was no single type that seemed to dominate but their dislike of authority had welded them together. Perhaps someone needed to go the government to explain exactly what this culture was all about.

A few days later, I raised this idea with the SA Attorney-General, Michael Atkinson, There would be no summit between the government and the outlaw nation, he said.

'No, I won't be having a dialogue with the leadership of the OMCGs,' he said, with evident disgust. 'I am not going to consult organised crime regarding laws applying to organised crime.'

Atkinson would bring the authority of the state crashing down on the outlaw nation. On his watch, there would be no room for the clubs to self-regulate their affairs. The government was in charge.

'I just think [self-regulation] is a prescription for defeat. It's a counsel of despair. It is society and government surrendering to the 1 per cent gangs, and we're not going to do that,' he said, resolutely.

14

THE PUSHBACK

The Descendants' Tom Mackie had watched panic and alarm spread through the outlaw nation as the SOCCA legislation passed the South Australian parliament with a minimum of debate.

Members of other clubs regarded Mackie as an éminence grise of the bikie scene. He was only just past fifty, but with his long, flowing grey hair and goatee beard he reminded me of a wizard elder from the Harry Potter books. Certainly, he had a calm, analytical mind and he had seen enough history to know it moved in cycles.

Bikers from other clubs came to Mackie in a state of high anxiety, fearful their membership would place their livelihoods and families in jeopardy. Some declared they were moving interstate, hiding their club gear or even starting a biker church to take advantage of the religious exemptions under the SOCCA. Some railed and thundered with threats of retaliation and violence.

Mackie's advice was simple. 'I told them how we endured the

consorting laws decades before: "Stand your ground. Let the government bring it on,"' he said. If the clubs tried to hide, or engaged in some mad rebellion, they would be doomed. The public would conclude that they were exactly what the government said they were. They should fight for their rights like citizens of any democracy.

The new legislation itself was the greatest threat to law and order, Mackie believed. In the 1970s, he had witnessed his own club become 'criminalised' by an earlier attempt to regulate the association of undesirables. But everyone seemed to have forgotten about that old titanic struggle, when his club and others had found themselves targeted by Sam Bass and his Bikie Squad.

There was an apocryphal story that the Descendants had been formed from members of a travelling tent boxing troupe. The club had never bothered to correct that. Stuff like that had encouraged people to leave them alone. But these days club members were rarely seen downtown, preferring their clubhouse and the company of their circle and select outsiders from other clubs.

One Friday night early in South Australia's latest great panic, a raiding party from Avatar had burst into the clubhouse, armed to the teeth, their red laser gun sights searing into the darkness of the dungeon-like bar. The members sat calmly on their stools as the squad, hyped to the eyeballs on adrenalin, had swarmed through the place looking for guns, drugs and bombs. From bitter experience, Descendants knew not to give an excited cop a reason to shoot them.

Mackie recalls that, having found nothing, one of the officers took the opportunity to lay down a few home truths: 'He said: "Now we're finally going to get rid of you people once and for all. We've got a government that has the balls to take you on and we're going to have laws that will allow us to dismantle your club, member by member!"'

'I looked at him and asked, "How long have you been in the force, buddy?" He replied: "About ten years".

' "Well", I said, "History tells me that five years from now, I'm still going to be sitting in this bar having a beer with my brothers. You, on the other hand, will be writing traffic tickets in a country town," ' said Mackie.

The infuriated cop looked at his mates for support against Mackie's impudence.

'There was silence for a few seconds and then one of the older cops shrugged his shoulders and said: "He's probably right, you know." '

Mackie knew how these circuses ran. He had seen two or three moral panics wax and wane over his time. This would eventually go the same way. But in the meantime, it was going to get very rough.

Three decades on from the climax of the war between the Descendants and the Bikie Squad—the violent showdown at the Arkaba Hotel in July 1979—Mackie could reflect that, while they had got their revenge on Sam Bass and his officers, the Descendants had paid a high price too. Morelli Esposito's accomplices from the ambush at the Arkaba, Mick Carey and David De Angelis, had both succumbed to heroin. Morelli's own raging thirst for smack had led him into the police trap in the first place. Heroin had ravaged them, stripped the dignity of some of the members and at that time diminished the club's reason for being. They had imagined they were invincible—able to 'out-drink, out-drug and out-fight' anyone—but they had learnt there's no winning with heroin; there's only degrees of losing.

The daily business of the club had become an endless schedule of court appearances and the half-madness of addiction and withdrawal. It was sadly ironic. Once free, some Descendants had chosen to become slaves to their addictions. Not all members were on the gear but heroin polarised the club.

It took a long time for the penny to drop. The youthful love of motorcycles had originally brought them to Rundle Street on those Saturday afternoons in the early 1970s. But by the early 1980s, there was a lot of hate and resentment holding them together. The core of original members had realised the only future for the club was astride the motorcycle. They almost subconsciously stopped recruiting members from the drug scene, opting for guys who were into their bikes, first and foremost.

They took their machines to the drag strips, where they mingled with other outlaw clubs and enthusiasts. The same thing was happening in the US, where Harley-Davidson was producing new models that could compete with the Japanese rice rockets for straight-line speed. The Harley 'bungers' could never compete with the nimble Japanese bikes on the circuit, but over the quarter-mile, they were extremely competitive.

For the first ten years of the club, the Descendants had rarely left Adelaide. The crappy old Triumphs and Hondas they rode had made even weekend trips an arduous proposition back then. Now they travelled all over Australia as a club to compete in the drags. Perry Mackie was national champion for three years running. A cabinet filled up with trophies members had won on their Harleys against the once unbeatable Japanese bikes. The racetrack was also a venue for members to mingle with members of other outlaw clubs. Friendships impossible in bars and nightclubs had thrived trackside.

It took several years but gradually the hard drug using element washed out of the club. There were still members being nicked for the odd minor charge, but the hard drugs, and the desperate mentality that went with it, were gone. Members worked straight jobs to pay their dues. For instance, in 2000 'Tony', who had an events management background, was cleared to run a security team at Olympic Games in Sydney, despite his membership of the club.

The members were workers now, or business owners, which

allowed them the freedom to take off when they needed to. The majority had stayed out of jail. Like so many working-class Australians, the Descendants had bought modest homes in the suburbs and watched their paper wealth grow through the eleven prosperous years of John Howard's national government. Some were dabbling in the property and share markets.

The club had recently racked up thirty-five years and had celebrated with a re-design of the club colours. The griffin had acquired a more buff, muscular appearance than the crude rendering of 1974, befitting the struggles the club had overcome. A friend of the club had painted a mural of the club on the wall, depicting the members in heroic pose, hair flowing in the breeze as they stood alongside their motorcycles in a dramatic roadside scene.

Mackie was proud to say that his four sons had become members of the club. Despite the pessimism of the prison psychologist, Mackie had found his niche in life after all. The club was still there as a pivot, the unifying force of his being, but he earned an honest dollar as a rigger in the entertainment industry. The rest of his time was spent ferrying his younger children to and from sporting and cultural activities. Like so many bikies, Mackie had believed in populating the earth with as many progeny as he could manage.

The Descendants had earned much respect for their longevity and stability as a club. So it was to them I came in November 2008 with the mad idea of getting as many bikers as possible from different clubs in one spot for a story. I thought I'd get a few of the old stalwarts, but an amazing cross-section of members answered the club's call. More than thirty guys from half a dozen clubs pitched up at the Descendants' clubhouse as the sun was setting.

There were members present from different clubs who had known each other since those Saturday afternoon sessions in Rundle Street back in the 1970s. They had belted each other a few times since, but a kind of mutual respect had developed between them over the years. While they wore different patches, they had the same heritage and ideals in common. The first half of the 1970s had been one long party for the Adelaide clubs. They had shared the same streets, the same women and the same view of life.

But then hard drugs and the associated crime had poisoned the well for everyone. The clubs had become insular and remote from one another as hardened men from jail began to proliferate in the ranks. Jealousy and hatred bred of ignorance had caused an almost never-ending series of conflicts. Defending the honour of the patch, while denigrating those of other clubs, had been elevated almost to the level of an obsession. So much blood had been spilt in futile attempts to prove that one symbol was superior to another. Even during these crises, though, a select few members could make informal contact with each other, helping to nip some issues in the bud with quiet diplomacy. But this was always done very carefully to avoid charges of fraternising with the enemy.

As one biker said, 'The heritage of the club scene was that we were in a contest to prove who had the biggest dick at the piss trough. A few of us always knew that we were cut from the same stone.'

That night there was also a sprinkling of guys in the room who had been in clubs for ten to fifteen years. These were men who had been attracted by the spirit of the old days and joined up just as the good times were about to end. In the early 1990s, some clubs had still mingled with each other at bike shows and concerts, but soon that had ceased. A deep suspicion of rival clubs had become the norm by the turn of the century. But there were members who had thought it prudent to keep communication lines open. This was not out of love, but necessity. There were times when drama simply had to end, before something much more deadly erupted.

So members of these two generations had maintained a form of contact with each other, but never like this before, openly mingling in a clubhouse. There were still simmering conflicts between clubs, but their attendance sent a clear message. It was time to heal the wounds while the body, ailing as it was, could still be saved.

Mackie had specifically asked that older heads bring younger members along, so they could learn the etiquette of dealing with other patches. Mackie said that the tension between clubs in recent times had meant they had almost forgotten how to mix.

Under the host's direction, nominees from the Descendants had laid out platters of barbecued chicken, meat and salads. The fridges were full of cold beer and a selection of spirits, and fine South Australian wine was on hand. Still Mackie could not predict how proceedings would go.

One ill-chosen word, a misinterpreted gesture or even a spilt drink and the goodwill might evaporate, he warned. There were blood feuds stretching back decades. The setting was suitably dark and foreboding: medieval battleaxes and daggers lined the walls and the griffin overlooked all from high over the bar. As the bikers began rolling through the big black gates of the clubhouse, I was thinking this could have been the most foolish thing I had ever done. Pitching half a dozen assorted clubs into one room might have diabolical results.

But this would turn out to be a meeting of minds that had been looking for its moment. I had provided that impetus, but the men in the room had already decided that unity was the only hope of survival. There would be no winners from the violence and rivalry that had consumed their culture. They craved a return to the easy fellowship and tolerance that had prevailed in the first five years of the Adelaide scene in the early 1970s. And they wanted to take that feeling back to their own clubs. This was the old school reasserting itself right here in the Descendants' clubhouse.

Seven Rebels members, some of them noms and first-year patches, stood proud away from the rest in the bar, staying in their tight circle. Some club members, the memories of recent conflicts still fresh, kept a discreet distance separated by a patchwork of colours around the corner of the bar—Gypsy Jokers, Odins Warriors, Descendants and even some Christian bikers, the Longriders. Early in the evening the men in the bar maintained a studied coolness. Just to be there was remarkable.

'Fuck me,' said Brains, a thirty-year veteran of the club scene. 'We've punched on with some of these clubs and here we are drinking with 'em. Never thought I'd see this,' he said, draining the first of countless beers for the evening.

All the clubs faced extinction under the state government's new SOCCA. It was time to show solidarity. Any club might be the one to face the music. They could gather strength and purpose by sharing their experiences under Rann's unrelenting pressure.

At a personal level, they were all used to being raided, roughed, cuffed and remanded in custody. That came with being a bikie. You needed a good mouthpiece (lawyer) to keep out of jail. You were going to get plenty of experience in the dock if you rode with the outlaws.

But the pressure being exerted on non-bikie friends was harder to take. The Crime Gangs Task Force would sweep through licensed venues where bikies were drinking, and slap them with a barring notice under section 21 of the Liquor Licensing Act. In the past, publicans had occasionally asked police to bar troublemakers from their premises using the section 21 notice, which could keep them out for up to five years. But now police reportedly put pressure on licensees to notify them when known bikies were in the bar so they could swoop in with the notices as part of their 'disrupt and dismantle' campaign. Over a period of weeks, members were finding they were suddenly barred from all their favourite watering holes, one after the other.

Once served with the notice, they were forced to leave. Anyone drinking with them was asked for identification and was then added to the list of the club's associates. Even people a bikie had just met would be monstered by the police. Anyone who refused to give particulars was arrested and then hit with a barring notice as well. The bikies had never realised how much power the cops had over them until now.

The new anti-association laws were not even in operation yet and no club had been declared so far. However, the notice would state that the reason for the banning was the offender's membership of an outlaw club.

'It's not illegal to be a member yet and, if I am sitting there, what laws have I broken?' asked one bewildered outlaw, brandishing a wad of section 21 notices he had been issued with over the past month. 'It's like you are no longer a human no more, being told to leave all the time. And it's embarrassing. I know it's what they are trying to do—they are trying to embarrass, manipulate us. I understand it but I don't see the sense in it.

'If you were in there mucking up, smashing, crashing, making a prick of yourself, fair enough—single that person out. But if you are sitting at a bar, doing nothing, minding your own business, socialising,' he said, the anger rising in him. 'And *that's illegal*! I don't fuckin' *get* that!' he shouted, thumping the bar so hard a row of beers nearly toppled. It would be a brave cop who handed this biker his next section 21 notice.

They had all been through this treatment; sharing their stories of harassment now brought them closer. The room was full of the kind of bikers the government did not want to acknowledge existed. They were workers, business owners, men who sat on industry committees and, yes, there were some people who had no criminal records.

'I have got nothing: a clean sheet,' said one. 'I am forty years old with nothing, and still I'm copping it like a convict . . . but if that's the way it's going to be, then so be it. When my daughter turns eighteen, I can't take her for a drink. If I take the kids for tea at a restaurant that has a bar in the back, I am breaking the law? Are you for real?'

Between them, these blokes knew most of the troublemakers in the clubs, so, if something out of order happened, there was normally a short list of suspects. A quiet word was often enough to pull the miscreants into line. Steve Williams had tapped into the network when he was president of the Jokers and his legacy hovered like a ghost in the room. He had dreamed of hosting nights like this, but had not seen it happen. There was an unspoken vibe that this group was here on unfinished business.

The men shared concerns about the gangster element that had crept into the scene. There was tension between the old schoolers and the Nike Bikers in almost every club, they said. They were scornful of clubs that were recruiting in jail or the gym. You could build a thug with steroids and human growth hormone. You could cover him in tatts and gold chains, fill him with crystal meth, grog and hatred, and he would fight just about anyone.

But in the cold light of morning, the biker was nothing without loyalty and fraternity. And a lot of it was unglamorous. Being a clubbie was also about making sure the families of jailed members were looked after: mowing their overgrown lawns and fixing their leaky plumbing. It was looking after a mate's missus without hitting on her. It was about organising funerals for fallen members. It was about skipping work to travel halfway across the country to show solidarity when a member died. It was getting on the tools when there was manual work to do at the club. It was about being there when you were needed, not just when there was a dollar on offer.

Some younger members were doing business outside the bikie circle these days, mingling with the ethnic street gangs and organised crime syndicates. It wasn't their place to judge, but the old schoolers wondered where the new breed would be found when push came to shove. In the past, the weak links had invariably been the ones who thumped their chest and loudly proclaimed their brotherhood, preaching to lesser entities about respect and courage. But when the shit came down, they chose the money over their brothers.

It wasn't as if the Nike Bikers were sharing the loot either. The clubs usually didn't see a cent of the drug money, nothing in fact except for a member's weekly dues. However, they still copped the heat. They couldn't run these guys out of their own clubs, but in swapping stories they were keeping the old values alive and raising questions the clubs needed to be answered.

That's why they were here this night, and putting up with talking to the damn reporter, they said. They weren't afraid to say that the clubs needed to address their shortcomings. Things had got out of hand in recent years - that was true, but it wasn't all bad.

As the night wore on, I struck up a conversation with 'Mori', one of the Descendants nominees who had been tirelessly serving food and drinks.

This bespectacled clean-cut man seemed an unlikely outlaw: he had no tattoos, or even earrings. He worked a nine to five job in middle management, and had three kids and a wife. He did not join the Descendants to be a crim, but because he loved motorcycles and the camaraderie. He'd hung around the club for fifteen years, before they nommed him up. That Mori could find a place in the Descendants is a measure of where the club was after thirty-five years. It was a natural progression for Mori after making friendships at the drag strips.

He had proved he was staunch; he had gone the distance, said Mackie. After fifteen years of patient waiting, Mori wasn't going to go quietly if the clubs were outlawed. This was the message all of them took back to their clubhouses from that night.

Without realising it, I had been a witness to a key moment in the creation of the United Motorcycle Council of South Australia that night. What I didn't know until much later was that the process had actually begun months earlier. This evening had just been the first public outing.

In 2011, 'Bear', a senior Gypsy Joker, told me he had been fixing the ceiling at the rooms of the Tattoo Club of South Australia, which he had set up. He was there with a group of non-club friends including 'Rambo', Adam Fields and Steve Provis. They were drinking steadily as they worked, talking about how Rann's new association laws would affect them. Soon Rambo, Fields and Provis were doing more talking than working. They had lit on the fact that under the SOCCA laws, there was an exemption for members of churches and political parties. Joining a church seemed a little far-fetched, but why not a political party? Paid-up members of a political party could continue to associate even if their clubs or groups had been banned under the Act. But who would want to be a member of the major parties on offer, they asked.

Bear remembered he was getting exasperated with all this talk. 'Oi, you three! Why don't you stop complaining and go start a political party? Let me get on with fixing this bloody roof!' he roared. They took him at his word, literally.

A few hours later, Bear's friends came back with the papers to register a political party. After paying the fees, the Freedom Rights Environment Educate Australia Party (FREE) was born.

To Bear, FREE had only begun as a way of dodging the anti-association laws, but soon he realised that a political party was the best way for bikers and their friends to make a stand. The first FREE Party meeting had also been held at the Tattoo Club and it was a tense affair. Almost all the clubs in town had sent representatives to hear what this thing was about. They all took a risk being there. The conflicts and mistrust ran very deep in their world. Bear was immediately impressed at the turnout and the desire to work together. This began the second phase of the Gypsy Jokers' involvement in politics. This time there would be no flashy public campaign as Steve Williams' advocacy had been, but a quiet grassroots effort bringing like-minded people together. The club backed him all the way.

However, Bear needed 150 members to start the party and they had to be eligible voters. Very few outlaw club members were registered to vote, not wanting to be part of the mainstream system or to reveal their private details to authorities. So Bear had to ask them to hand over all their details to get them registered.

'That was where the real trust came in. Nobody wanted people from other clubs wanting to know where they lived. There was a big responsibility on my shoulders to do the right thing,' he said.

FREE was going to struggle to get the 150 members it needed in order to be registered. Bear decided to involve Paul Kuhn of the South Australian Motorcycle Riders Association, which represented non–1 per cent motorcyclists. Kuhn was a quirky and determined character who rode a 500cc motor scooter. A justice of the peace, Kuhn had never been in trouble with the law in his life and took up the political cause with amazing gusto. Despite being heavily attacked by some sections of the media, Kuhn was to rise to national prominence, helping other FREE members to organise protest rides through Adelaide that drew hundreds of participants from all walks of life. I could never get used to seeing the outlaws on their Harleys riding alongside Kuhn on his scooter, but it was a measure of the new spirit of openness. Many of the bikers were genuinely shocked at the numbers and profiles of ordinary citizens who came out in support of them.

It was this nucleus of bikers in the FREE Australia Party that would also lay the groundwork for the UMC. Over the weeks and months that followed, the same faces turned up again and again at both FREE Australia and UMC events to discuss the battle with the government. Others joined them until more than a dozen clubs were represented. The pushback had already begun by the time the Descendants hosted this get-together for the media.

As the first meeting broke up, Tom Mackie's sons tried to drag me downtown to a party at a strip bar. I declined, staying at the bar with their father, with Brains from the Jokers and a few other lags from the Rundle Street days.

It was only several hours later that I noticed that Brains' right leg was a stainless-steel prosthesis, the legacy of a horrifying road accident. He had been T-boned by a car and driven into a traffic light. No-one who was fair dinkum came through life without scars, he said. Life in a motorcycle club took its toll one way or another. This latest challenge would test the resolve of the new generation, but he was confident they would come through it. The government could fill the jails to overflowing with bikies, but they wouldn't break them.

Brains, a keen student of history, knew that the State had rarely succeeded in regulating social interaction and cultural tradition through the imposition of draconian laws.

In 1746, King George II of England gave the nod to a law banning the wearing of Highland dress in Scotland. This had followed the leading role of the Highland clans in the Jacobite uprisings against English rule between 1689 and 1746. The so-called Dress Act was one of a series of measures aimed at bringing the warrior clans under government control by crushing Gaelic culture. Overnight, the wearing of clan tartans and the kilt was outlawed. The Dress Act, said Brains, had only served to unite the warring clans and turned Highland clothing and paraphernalia into symbols of resistance. Jailing bikers under the SOCCA would do the same again, he said.

'If the government needs to build a new prison system to house 300 members and another 2000 associates, well go for it,' said Tom Mackie. 'I think most club members will be quite content to do a bit of jail time, if that's what's needed. To say you are going to break us up with a law of association, it's just not going to happen.' He raised a glass to the griffin.

15

A FREE HORIZON

Russell Merrick Oldham was, by all reports, an eloquent, intelligent man and he chose a romantic stage. Under the stars the Bandido loved so much, Balmoral Beach was a tranquil crescent-shaped vista. Walking down to the shore from his hiding place on Rocky Point, he could see the lights on North Head and beyond a glimpse of the open ocean.

It was 11 May 2006 and over the past three weeks he had weighed up his dilemma. He had shot his own club's president in cold blood in an inner-city laneway. He had put two in the head of an unarmed man. It was a heinous act, but he was confident he had done it for the right reasons. The dead president in question was Rodney 'Hook' Monk of the Bandidos' Sydney downtown chapter. Hook was also a key player in the supply of high-quality Colombian cocaine to Sydney. Not to mention the fact that his brother was a high-ranking cop. There were all kinds of people looking for Russell that night.

A former member of the Bandidos told the *Sunday Telegraph* newspaper that 'the best thing Russell can do for himself is top himself. That way he avoids torture and a very slow, painful death'.

So far, he had evaded them all, but he was vulnerable. While he was on the loose, his girlfriend would be a target too. Sooner or later, his club mates would come for her, he believed. He knew how they thought. His girlfriend, Lee Smith, was a parole officer, for Christ's sake—just one rung up from the cops. They would speculate about what he might have told her. Giving up to the cops would only make matters worse. His death might pacify a few of his old mates, at least.

He deemed his life worthless anyway. Lee had aborted his baby just weeks earlier. He couldn't blame her. What sort of life was this? He had squandered everything. He had dropped out of medical school at Sydney University, drifting into the underworld and finally into the Bandidos, all the while looking for some place to belong.

Oldham had been part of the Bandidos' chaotic rise to power in Sydney. The club, with its trademarked pistol-wielding 'Fat Mexican' patch, had been growing in strength around the world and the Sydney chapters had recruited some of the heaviest guys in town to their ranks. However, there was no evidence that the criminal activities linked to Bandidos members were centrally coordinated in the club.

Police believed Rodney Monk had criminal connections with members of the other clubs, and had also forged links with a syndicate that was importing a tonne of cocaine into Australia every eighteen months. In 2005, a former drug dealer had told the New South Wales Crime Commission that he had sold 25 kilos of the drug via the Bandidos president, who was a cocaine 'broker'. However, this allegation was never tested in a court and must therefore be regarded as hearsay from a dubious source, despite the fact it was endlessly quoted in media reporting on Rodney

Monk's death. Considering the criminal activities of the Commission's own assistant commissioner Mark Standen at the time, such information must be taken with a grain of salt.

All was in ruins, Oldham had written to Lee just days earlier in a letter later published in Sydney's *Daily Telegraph*: '*A broken mind and a broken heart. What I have done is horribly wrong and as a result this action shall serve to define my character in the eyes of others.*'

He took his shoes off and waded into the shallows. He was at peace here where he and Lee had come to hide their relationship from the club. '*With every stroke of this pen my heart burns for you and I wish I could hold you once more and let you see the love in my eyes. In the end, my darling, I did protect you with my life.*'

When the water was lapping his knees, he shot himself through the head. He had finally taken control of his life by ending it. It was an achievement, of sorts.

The idea of an egalitarian brotherhood is romantic, but the reality is less clear-cut. Most clubs deal with frequent conflict and political in-fighting as they try to enforce their rules. It's a delicate balance as the leadership risks becoming authoritarian and remote from the members.

Clubs that run into trouble have often become as rigid as the world outside. The Milperra Massacre of 1984, fought out between the Comancheros and Bandidos in the car park of the Viking Tavern, was one such moment. They had all been one club under one roof until the self-styled 'Supreme Leader', Jock Ross, had begun enforcing a military-style discipline that included weekly combat training for members in readiness for conflict with other clubs.

The trouble began when the Comancheros forcibly patched over a small club, the Loners, transforming it into a feeder club called the Bandileros. Resentments mounted as Ross's megalomania grew out of all proportion. The Comancheros' constitution gave the Supreme

Leader ultimate authority to wield power and make decisions. Any sense of democracy was lost as Ross played member against member to divide and rule the group. The Bandileros began to feel less like outlaws and more like privates in Ross's personal army. All the protocols and disciplines negated their reasons for joining a bike club.

First the Comancheros split into two chapters, a city chapter and a western suburbs chapter. Relations gradually deteriorated until members of the City chapter went to California to seek permission to become the first Australian chapter of the Bandidos. According to Arthur Veno, bloodshed over this desertion might have been avoided if a single set of colours had been returned to Ross. The former Comos of the City chapter had handed over their colours to Ross, but one member had sent his to the US. To the tyrannical Ross, this act of disrespect was intolerable, said Veno.

It was only a matter of time before the conflict blew open. Sadly, when it did, seven people were killed, including a 14-year-old girl, in the car park of a suburban hotel. At stake was nothing more than the ego and prestige of the Supreme Leader. The Comancheros had surrendered their role in running their club in favour of being told what to do.

'The whole thing, looking back on it, was so fucking petty. Politics, rules and power struggles—that's what started the feud. But we were actually, in the main, still mates with all the guys who decided to leave and eventually become Bandidos,' a former Comanchero told Veno in 2001.

Long before Russell Oldham killed Hook Monk, there were signs the Bandidos were following the Comos down the same path, police sources say. By 2006, the leadership of the Sydney chapter of the Bandidos was said to be isolated from many members, issuing edicts from a high-rise apartment in the city's eastern suburbs. Riding rules had been relaxed and leaders were fast-tracking certain nominees into the club, causing resentment among members who had put up with long probation periods.

Among the disaffected, there was a sense that crime rather than brotherhood was driving the recruitment process. Monk had reportedly forged links with a major crime group that was dominating the local cocaine market. They were now rubbing shoulders with Sydney's A-list celebrities.

Still Monk and his faction continued to lord it over the membership. In 2002, Monk had helped depose and expel former president Felix Lyle, after a dispute over the club's finances and the bashing of a club member. To make matters worse, Lyle's 24-year-old son was kidnapped by unknown persons and ransomed for $2 million. Suspicion fell on Monk's faction and a poisonous rancour spread through the club.

Russell Oldham had aligned himself with Lyle, believing his expulsion from the Bandidos was unjust. The official reason for expelling Lyle was discrediting the club colours, but the dispute was more personal than that.

Matters came to a head when Oldham met Monk in a popular restaurant, Bar Reggio, in Sydney's Little Italy district in April 2006. Monk had summoned Oldham to tell him he was out of the club. His affair with Lee Smith was an intolerable transgression, Monk told him.

There was no dignity for Oldham. Such a decision is normally carried out in the clubhouse with other members present, but Monk apparently broke the news as he dined with his glamorous girlfriend, plus his bodyguard and his wife. Then Monk made the mistake of inquiring after Lee's health. A loud argument broke out between the two men. In an effort to keep up appearances with the trendy diners, Monk suggested they take their dispute outside.

He made a second fatal mistake in leaving his bodyguard inside. Oldham produced a semi-automatic from a small black bag and shot his president twice in the head. It was an unmistakable declaration of independence.

The internal struggles that had led to Oldham's fateful decision continued to weaken and divide the Bandidos after his death. Some say Monk's murder was the beginning of the end for the Fat Mexican's dominance in Sydney. In February 2010, Felix Lyle signed up to become a Hells Angel and a year later a further fifty to sixty Bandidos quit the club to join the Big Red Machine.

The very public battles that destroyed the harmony of clubs like the Bandidos were a powerful incentive to the old guard of Australian bikers to work together. They knew they were fighting for the true brotherhood and freedom that had underpinned the formation of the clubs in the 1960s and 70s. This was their last chance to re-assert their authority, or else the movement would be left to the drug dealers and the Nike Bikers.

For Hells Angel elder Derek Wainohu, the trip to Melbourne on 22 March 2009 had been a part of that mission. The trip, which had involved meetings with other senior members of Victorian clubs, had gone very well. He was entitled to think the flight home to Sydney on Qantas flight 430 might be a pleasant ride, a time to reflect on progress made.

There was, of course, still a long way to go. While he had been playing diplomat in the south, in Sydney his club was embroiled in an ugly feud with the Comanchero MC. In fact, he had been part of a mediation that had recently gone sour.

Fresh from jail in June 2008, Hells Angels sergeant-at-arms Peter Zervas had opened a tattoo parlour called Angel's Cosmetic Tattoo in Brighton-le-Sands, smack in the middle of Comanchero territory. It was reported that a meeting between the Angels and the Comos to discuss the dispute had disintegrated into violence when Peter's brother Anthony, a club associate, had burst in brandishing a sawn-off shotgun. *The Sydney Morning Herald* reported that in the ensuing scuffle one of the Comancheros was hit on the head with the gun.

This story was later denied by the Angels but, even if the shotgun was a figment of a fertile mind, there was a very public escalation of tension between the clubs immediately afterwards. The *Herald* reported that the Zervas tattoo parlour was sprayed with bullets the day after the meeting. A few weeks later a masked motorcyclist fired more shots into the building.

In October, the parlour was closed after three men smashed the front window and set fire to the interior. Prior to that, half a dozen Comancheros had been reportedly circling the block during the day while a contingent of Hells Angels in colours had stood guard over the parlour.

This disagreement was the latest in a series of violent clashes across Sydney over the past three years between Sydney's leading clubs. The press and the cops were calling it a war, but anything more than a bar-room brawl got that treatment. It was always expected that any tensions would inevitably explode into open conflict. In reality, this was not a war yet—more a series of skirmishes, drive-by shootings, the bombing of clubhouses and businesses. But make no mistake, the battlelines were drawn. If this thing got going, the bikers had enough soldiers to mount an operation worthy of al-Qaeda, police believed.

Derek Wainohu was one of a substantial group of leaders who believed that further bloodshed could be averted. Wainohu's Guildford-based chapter in Sydney could do little on its own, but he was forging links with clubs prepared to back a national network that could defuse the tension before it erupted into public violence. 'So pissed-fights don't become gunfights,' as one veteran biker put it. Things had gone well for him in Melbourne, the Australian stronghold of the Big Red Machine.

In 2005, a Victorian chapter of one club had sent out Christmas cards with photos of its members fooling around with .45 calibre automatic handguns and a sawn-off shot gun. One happy snap featured the club president and a member grinning and holding the unregistered .45s to each other's heads. That indiscretion brought a dawn raid by Victoria Police's Special Operations Group. There were probably just as many guns in Victorian clubs as interstate, but there was a greater level of discipline operating.

The only significant blue in recent years in Victoria had been between the Rebels and Bandidos, but that had ultimately been smoothed over with quiet diplomacy. In October 2008, a senior Bandido member, Ross Brand, had been shot dead outside the club's Geelong headquarters. Police initially feared that the Rebels had been directly responsible for the shooting, part of a long-running hatred between the clubs. The police and the media were gearing for a Sydney-style biker war. However, Brand's death and the wounding of a Bandido associate, Paul Szerwinski, had more mundane origins.

Earlier in the day, members of a local Geelong biker club Death Before Dishonour (DBD), a feeder club to the Rebels, had suffered a mild physical confrontation with members of the Bandidos at the Geelong Cup race meeting. Punches were thrown, but the combatants were quickly ejected from the racecourse.

As payback, John Bedson, described as the 27-year-old founder of DBD, took it upon himself to open fire on four Bandidos as they stood outside their clubhouse later that evening. Brand took one .22 slug in the forehead, while Szerwinksi was hit in the thigh and the wrist. Remarkably, there was no public retaliation from the Bandidos, even though Bedson was the stepson of a senior Rebels officebearer.

Compared with New South Wales, Victoria was a haven of peace and restraint. This was largely because the old school still ruled the Melbourne scene, unlike in Sydney, where it was getting harder to distinguish biker from gangster by this time.

Wainohu had found Victoria's outlaw biker clubs were more than willing to sit down and work together. An informal network was already operating, and now plans were being drawn up for a

United Motorcycle Council branch in Victoria. For the first time, there would be a forum to discuss and resolve disputes between Victoria's nineteen outlaw clubs without violence. A Victorian UMC might also be used as a neutral chamber where disputes between interstate clubs could be adjudicated upon.

Around Australia, biker leaders had been surprised at the cordial atmosphere that had prevailed at UMC meetings, both formal and informal. Bikers are known for their ethos of freedom, but in reality their lives inside and out of the club are governed by a tight set of rules. Give him a set of rules and a clear direction, and he and his mates can achieve extraordinary things, both good and evil.

By 22 March 2009, a mysterious calm had descended over club-land in Australia. It was only in Sydney that the armed skirmishes continued; everywhere else, the guns had fallen silent. Even in Sydney members of clubs steeped in hatred were sitting across the table from one another. For the first time in thirty years, they were 'allowed' to fraternise with the enemy. And they had discovered that he was much like them.

The triggers behind the bloody feuds were not forgotten, but now seemed dated and irrelevant when the outlaw movement was facing a common enemy. State governments across the country were drafting laws that would see the clubs deemed criminal organisations. Under these laws, it would soon be an offence in some states, punishable with five years' jail, for Wainohu to associate with the men he had met in Melbourne. But Wainohu had found that the prospect of laws designed to divide the bikers had in fact united them.

The police had been astonished when the bikers began meeting in the conference rooms of local hotels. It was concluded there was an ulterior motive. This police logic ran that, if the clubs were banned, their criminal enterprises would be in jeopardy. Therefore, the bikers would be forced to carve up their drug territories in the major cities under the new laws. Law enforcement had the implacable view that the club was the central unit of crime in the biker world. Therefore, a unified set of 'gangs' presented an even more heinous prospect than individual clubs fighting each other and running amok.

But to Wainohu and the other leaders, the UMC movement was not about crime but about the survival of their fraternal way of life. It also recognised the fact that no single club, not even the Hells Angels could keep the peace anymore. It was a crisis, but at the same time, an opportunity. The dialogue was now well under way.

There was a buzz around the UMC meetings that the delegates were bringing back to their individual clubhouses. For the first time, the outlaw biker scene in Australia was organising around a positive goal. For most of their thirty years, biker clubs had built their reputation on fear and mistrust. Now, they were acting completely out of character in building bridges of trust.

The UMC leadership feared that without some public support and engagement the clubs could become what many critics suspected they already were: dedicated crime gangs, existing only for the pursuit of evil. The UMC movement provided an alternative future, a chance to redefine a subculture that had in some senses lost its way. Some individual chapters of clubs were now re-assessing their internal values, deciding whether their culture, associated in the public's mind with revenge and violence, could be sustainable in a new world order.

But all that momentum and goodwill was virtually destroyed in twenty minutes of mayhem in Sydney Airport.

The tension reportedly began to build as soon as Wainohu noticed that he was sharing the flight with five Comancheros. Witnesses said later that a Comanchero had been growling at Wainohu and there were words exchanged between the men on the flight.

As the plane taxied towards the terminal in Sydney just after 1.35 p.m., text messages were being sent summoning up reinforcements. By the time Wainohu emerged from the aerobridge into the terminal, there were five Hells Angels and associates waiting, including the Zervas brothers.

But seven Comancheros and friends had answered the call, taking their total number to twelve, which meant the Hells Angels were seriously undermanned.

Wainohu reportedly shouldered a Comanchero, who belted the Angels' boss in the face. Another Como also punched Wainohu and he dropped to the ground. Witnesses told police that, as the Hells Angels retreated, a Como called out to Wainohu: 'Next time we see you, you're going to have a bullet through you. You're a dead man walking.'

At this point, airport security men were ushering passengers away from the brawling bikers. They were seen talking into their radios and it was assumed that they were summoning the Australian Federal Police stationed at the airport for back-up. In reality, the guards had no authority to do that. They would have to radio their headquarters, who in turn would call the state police, like any other citizen.

An international airport in the First World feels like one of the most secure places on the globe. For all the potential dangers of air travel, every aspect of the terminal seems designed to confer safety and calmness. It has limited exits and entrances, a closed road system and a network of traffic control systems from speed humps to road spikes. There's an array of security technology, closed-circuit television cameras, facial recognition software, metal detectors, full-body scanners, detectors for body heat and explosive traces and at some airports fibre-optic perimeter intrusion detection systems.

There's a one in 10.4 million chance that your flight will end up a ball of flames. You're five times more likely to win the national lottery, but still a lot of effort goes into making passengers feel that their time in the air is nothing more than being transported from terminal to terminal.

When you land at your destination having cleared all the security hurdles you have a right to feel confident. You've handed over your nail scissors, the bottle of cologne or even plain water. You have been tested for TNT and half-undressed for the metal detector. You've eaten with ridiculous plastic knives and forks. You have traded a range of freedoms for the warm glow of security you feel now. The air in the arrivals hall feels like a casino, an over-rich mix of oxygen to enhance those good feelings.

Even in this environment, dangers remain. There still remains a statistical one in 250 million chance of being killed by a falling coconut. But the possibility of being caught up in a vicious and brutal biker brawl seems more remote than death by coconut. Even an asteroid strike seems more likely.

But there it was on 22 March 2009, a great roiling mass of mayhem coming towards shocked passengers and staff.

After the initial fracas, the bikers had dispersed. But just minutes later, in the departures area, the conflict reached its terrifying climax. One witness told police the bikers were 'crazy, like raging bulls' with 'fists smashing into each other's bodies'.

The Comancheros alleged that Anthony Zervas caused the second brawl after he stabbed a Como in the neck with a pair of scissors. Other bikies were then attacking each other with heavy bollards used to organise the passenger check-in queues. One was heard to cry in Arabic: 'Your mother is a slut.'

Soon Anthony Zervas was on the ground copping a horrible hiding from at least two Comos. At the horrifying climax to the scene, a bollard was smashed down on the back of Zervas's head and 'a loud crunching noise' was heard. Three other men were also attacking Zervas on the ground.

Zervas died from both blunt-force trauma to his head and three stab wounds to his chest and abdomen. He had been stabbed with his own scissors, found with broken handles inside his clothing, while the other two wounds came from another blade. Little wonder that no-one came to try to break up the fight. You couldn't pay a cop or a security guard enough to wade into a crowd of bikers intent on beating the daylights out of each other. Still, the attitude from the AFP and airport security had been timid to say the least. The officers on duty in Sydney were nowhere to be seen as the bikers were left to battle it out to the death.

When it was over, most of the bikers fled from the terminal, some jumping the taxi queue to hail cabs ahead of startled travellers. Peter Zervas was left to cradle his dying brother on the floor of the terminal.

This was the moment when Australia's outlaw bikers seemed to confirm every allegation ever made against them. Here was a tribe who would not submit to the rules of society. They put their own secret society ahead of all else. In beating a man to death in front of nearly 300 witnesses, these men had shown their only allegiance was to their outlaw colours and their credo. The criminal law, the moral good, common decency and civic respect—none of that meant anything. They were prepared to do whatever it took to assert their authority over their rivals.

Now every myth and legend ever told about the outlaws was suddenly credible. There were no shades of grey any longer. If a subculture like this would condone the brutal murder of a rival in public, it was capable of virtually anything. The body of Anthony Zervas lying on the terminal floor represented the sum of all fears in the public's mind. This crime was evidence of the guilt of all bikers. This was an attack not only on a hated enemy, but also on Australian society itself. Soon the headlines and images would be beamed around the world.

The floundering New South Wales Labor Government, with a crushing electoral defeat already looming, had seen its law and order credentials shredded in a matter of minutes. Now there was good reason to be very afraid on Sydney's streets, no matter what New South Wales Premier Nathan Rees said. At a press conference the next day, Rees announced his intention to punish all outlaw bikies for what the Hells Angels and Comancheros had done. By fighting at Sydney Airport, the bikers had strayed onto his turf. Now they would all be banned.

'This is a new low in the activities of these criminal gangs,' Mr Rees said. 'Once, they kept these things between themselves. This has now overlapped into the public domain. That's why we're taking it so seriously; that's why we've moved very swiftly today.'

There would be a total of 121 people murdered in New South Wales over that year; 1270 people would be charged with assault. But no violent incident would generate anything like the reaction that followed the slaying of Anthony Zervas at Sydney Airport.

In the political mind, Sydney Airport had transformed the bikers from a disorganised, opportunistic crime outfit to something far more sinister: a highly coordinated and disciplined paramilitary force, whose agenda went far beyond crime. The Police Commissioner, Andrew Scipione, spoke as if the bikers had become a threat to national security. 'If these people want to act like terrorists, we'll deal with them like they're terrorists,' he said.

Beating people to death in airport terminals was hardly a popular terrorist tactic at that time, but the extra resources deployed were worthy of a counter-insurgency operation. According to New South Wales Assistant Commissioner Dave Hudson, the rules had changed inside the gangs since 2006. They now operated with a powerful hierarchy commanding and controlling members, just like the Mafia. The clubs were no longer egalitarian organisations run on a flat democratic model of one member, one vote, but an autocracy based around commanders and soldiers.

Premier Rees announced that the New South Wales Gang

Squad would be expanded from fifty-five to 125 officers. The extra seventy-five officers would work in a new elite squad, Strike Force Raptor, which was formed to 'address bikie gang violence'. He pledged to introduce legislation by the end of June that 'would mean certain motorcycle gangs would be "proscribed"—as occurs with terrorist organisations—with bikies able to be jailed for their membership'.

But if the show of force intimidated the bikers, it didn't last long. A week after the airport affray, Peter Zervas was visiting his grieving mother at her home in Lakemba. He had buried his brother Anthony two days earlier. Perhaps he was not expecting trouble—after all, a senior Comanchero had called for peace with the Angels. Zervas pulled up in the driveway and was getting out of the car when a gunman pumped half a dozen shots into him.

Zervas survived but the shooting was yet more evidence that the New South Wales Government ran no electoral risk whatsoever in cracking down on the bikies. On 2 April, Premier Rees fast-tracked his new bikie legislation through the Lower House of the state parliament, with only one dissenting vote. It allowed police to seek a court order to make membership of a declared biker gang illegal. Members who continued to associate with each other faced jail terms of two to five years.

In a rare moment of bipartisanship, Opposition Leader Barry O'Farrell could only criticise the government for not acting sooner. 'I would have no problem if you put all the motorcycle gang members in two rooms and allowed them to shoot themselves to death,' he said.

But the legislation in New South Wales and other states went much further than just 'all the motorcycle gang members'. The proposed laws cast a much wider net, making it an offence for family and friends with criminal records to associate with the members of declared organisations.

By now South Australia had enacted its own version of these laws. Western Australia and Queensland were not far behind. In the panic over biker violence, few commentators made much of the fact that state governments were creating a new class of power for themselves. With this power they could determine which citizens were legally allowed to associate with each other. Government would also ban the wearing of club patches and symbols in public, it was said. South Australia would have a dress code.

Bikers and the people around them had long felt like misfits in society, but now their status was going to be made official. The 1 per cent nation was being written into law across Australia.

16

OUTLAWED MOTORCYCLE CLUB

On 14 May 2009, South Australian Attorney-General Michael Atkinson declared the Finks MC to be a criminal organisation under the SOCCA.

On 25 May, an Adelaide magistrate granted a control order sought by police against a Finks member. On 4 June, police sought another control order against a second Fink. Under the new law, neither member could be present in the court, nor test the secret intelligence on which the application had been made. The magistrates did not have the power to review the evidence either. The judiciary had been reduced to acting as a rubber stamp for the state government and the police.

The members quickly sought a declaration from the Supreme Court of South Australia that the SOCCA legislation was invalid, but the Attorney-General had always expected that the bikies' high-priced lawyers would challenge the laws. He fully expected this to go all the way to the High Court. Nonetheless, in an interview with me back in mid-2008, Atkinson had been contemptuous of the High Court and its role of safeguarding the Australian constitution. 'Fortunately for the people of South Australia, they are not governed by the unelected judges of the High Court. The judges have a judicial role; they don't have a legislative function, thank God,' he had told me.

Assistant Commissioner Anthony Harrison had worked towards this declaration for years. There would be other clubs declared soon. It was gratifying to Harrison that other states, riding a wave of media support, were following his approach. There was a real prospect that each state's laws would be harmonised and a national dragnet would be established. This would put sleepy old South Australia back on the policing map.

Some spoke of Harrison as a future chief commissioner, such was the power of the SOCCA. South Australian Federal MP Christopher Pyne called it 'an Exocet missile' that would smash the outlaw menace once and for all. Harrison modestly deflected such talk, calling the SOCCA just another 'tool in the toolbox' against organised crime. But privately, he knew the SOCCA gave police enormous leverage. No longer would his police officers have to wait until a crime was actually committed to swoop—the act of association had been criminalised.

To his critics in the force, the SOCCA was nothing more than the old consorting laws warmed over, but Harrison would show them all. He would get further powers, and use telephone intercepts and listening devices to monitor the activities of bikers under control orders. He would use liquor licensing laws to have them banned from every pub and club in the state. There would be weekly raids on homes and businesses; employers would be alerted to the risks of employing bikers. There would be tax audits of companies alleged to be front companies for the criminal activities. And at every turn, the criminal intelligence obtained would be kept secret from its targets. It would only be scrutinised once a year by a judge.

He would draw the noose so tight that the bikies would leave South Australia in droves. Jailhouse informers had told police that the outlaws were already feeling the strain. The relentless pressure would break the weak links in the chain. Self-survival would kick in and it would be every man for himself. The crooks would take the easy option and pack up their meth labs, bombs and guns and get the hell out of Dodge City. Those that remained would open up like ripe juicy melons falling off a truck.

It was mildly puzzling to Harrison that this was not happening as fast as he had predicted. A handful had quit clubs or moved interstate but, surprisingly, a lot of them seemed to be digging in. Since January, representatives of more than a dozen clubs had been turning up in colours to meet at rival clubhouses once a fortnight. They were calling themselves the United Motorcycle Club of South Australia. Most surprisingly of all, the Finks, Gypsy Jokers and Descendants, who had always been seen as the most aloof and remote of the outlaws, seemed to be leading this détente.

Meanwhile, the FREE AUSTRALIA Party was thriving. People were rallying to the outlaw cause. This was slightly disconcerting to Harrison, but it was really of little consequence. Once his matrix of declarations and control orders was in place, he would have the power to break up these little gatherings too. An outbreak of unity was the last thing he needed.

To borrow a phrase from Arthur Veno, Harrison was regarded among police as a 'moral entrepreneur', an officer who used fears of social disorder as an opportunity to gather new powers and resources. And this was a once-in-a-generation chance on offer, a sure-fire route to promotion. The bikies and their associates had handed Harrison this precious gift.

The statistics showed criminals were running amok. In June 2007, gunmen had shot four members of the Rebels inside Tonic, a downtown nightclub, after an earlier dispute. In the past year alone, there had been twenty-two incidents where guns had been produced or fired. In May 2008 there had been a running fire-fight between the New Boys and associates of the Hells Angels on Gouger Street, a popular restaurant precinct. Fifteen shots had been fired: one man had been wounded and a female bystander narrowly escaped death as a bullet whizzed through a restaurant window. In the past three years, offences of extortion and black-mail had tripled.

When asked about the extent of bikers' involvement in crime, Harrison was always equivocal: there was no easy answer. However, he would assert that most of the individuals and crime networks that police had targeted in the past two years almost invariably had links to the clubs, however loose or tenuous. It wasn't the same thing as saying the clubs were behind all of Adelaide's crime, but that's how it ran in the media. With a taskforce focusing on the bikers 24/7, Harrison could produce any stats he wanted.

The old Avatar squad had been re-named the Crime Gangs Task Force and now boasted fifty-four officers and seventeen spe-cialist staff, including forensic accountants, criminal intelligence experts and high-level analysts. As more control orders were made, it was certain Harrison would win even more staff and resources. In its first year, the squad had racked up arrests of ninety-six bikers and 187 associates and issued 104 section 21 barring orders under liquor licensing laws.

What Harrison did not reveal was that an estimated 80 per cent of the arrests were for summary offences, unpaid traffic fines and minor warrants. A large proportion of these stats had been gathered at massive roadblocks set up on the routes of out-law club runs and these were costing the state up to $5 million a year. Somewhat perversely, SAPOL claimed this was money well spent because the heavy police presence had cut numbers at massed runs dramatically. This was a hollow boast as the club run was not only the major source of Harrison's crime stats, but also the best opportunity police had to gather intel on who was who in the clubs.

Harrison had a deep visceral loathing not just for the bikers but for the whole subculture that clustered around them. Unlike Sam Bass, who had had a grudging admiration for the bikers, Harrison wanted to eradicate them from society. Once, in a telephone conversation with me, Harrison said he had been genuinely outraged at what went on inside outlaw clubhouses, including the bikies' scandalous treatment of women. He wouldn't elaborate, simply saying that if I knew what he knew (presumably from telephone intercepts and hidden listening devices) I would not be arguing in favour of the bikers. For four years I had been trying to find out what Harrison knew, but I'd been consistently rebuffed.

When declaring the Finks, Attorney-General Atkinson told parliament he did not have to reveal his reasons, but had made 'a sporting decision' to do so. With information supplied by the police, he painted a picture of an organisation that was now more powerful than the state.

In the accompanying 54-page declaration, Assistant Commissioner Harrison had the chance to put forward his evidence. Yet, despite the gravity of the situation and the investigative resources at his disposal, Harrison's facts were strangely contradictory.

Firstly, it was asserted that the Finks 'first came to the attention of SAPOL in 1991', when the club applied for incorporation as an association aimed at 'establishing, carrying on, improving a community meeting place and promoting the interests of motorcycle enthusiasts within the local community'.

However, the *Advertiser* newspaper had nominated the Finks MC as one of 'the six true biker clubs in SA' as far back as January 1977. The reporters had confirmed this by knocking on the doors of clubhouses and residences and actually speaking to the members. There had been Finks in Adelaide since about 1970.

Somehow, the Finks' activities had been overlooked by the police for more than twenty years. This weakened the argument for their serious sustained criminality from the outset, but Harrison pressed on manfully.

Harrison then posited that club recruitment was a centralised process where a nominee, once inducted by the club, was 'allocated to a full member who is responsible for him and sponsors him through the process. It is believed that this policy was developed to prevent law enforcement agencies from infiltrating the organisation through undercover agents.'

The truth was in fact the exact opposite. As in the very best of gentlemen's clubs, full members brought friends before the membership for scrutiny. If they passed muster, they were allowed in as noms. The proposing patch member was responsible for the nom, not because the club ordered him to be, but because of his close connection to the new boy.

In certain circumstances, a club might place a wayward member under the wing of a senior man, but the idea of centralised recruitment was risible to anyone who had spent more than five minutes in an outlaw club. The system was in fact designed to weed out people who would cave in to police pressure and inform on the club. The prestige of the proposing member was always on the line, so he chose carefully. It might take five years for an undercover agent to be nommed by one of the tightly knit Adelaide clubs. Not impossible, but far beyond the budget and concentration span of most agencies.

But the most glaring flaw in Harrison's thinking was buried deep in the declaration: on page eighteen he attempted to come to grips with the nature of the Finks' alleged conduct:

> The criminal activities engaged in by asserted members include
> but are not limited to, theft, drug manufacture and distribu-
> tion, offences of violence, firearms offences and blackmail. The

direction and control of the various criminal activities are left for the discretion and control of the individual members unless sanctioned as an organisation activity.

The first time I read this, I thought it must have been a misprint. It was astounding to me that the police were in furious agreement with me and the bikers. Crime was not centralised, but left to the *discretion and control of the individual members*.

Premier Rann, flanked by senior police, had previously warned ad nauseam: 'We are not just dealing with meatheads on motorbikes, we are dealing with basically the *foot soldiers* of *organised crime.*' Now, Harrison had contradicted his Premier, performing an amazing somersault in the process. In effect, he now said the 'foot soldiers' were left to run a system of disorganised crime.

Of course, nearly all credible analysts of organised crime were saying the same thing. The Queensland Police State Crime Operations Command had recently concluded in a confidential briefing document:

> . . . members now operate small, autonomous criminal networks within the gang, many of which frequently operate without the full knowledge of other gang members. The level of external cooperative ventures is suspected of including members of other OMCG gangs and legitimate business operators within the region.

A year earlier, at a federal parliamentary inquiry into outlawing serious and organised crime groups, Harrison and his SAPOL colleagues were among the few witnesses arguing that bikies ran a highly organised operation that only anti-association laws could address. He told the Inquiry:

The anti-association aspect of really getting to the root of the problem—which is people coming together to plan, organise and allocate tasks in respect to who is going to conduct the crimes and participate in the crimes—is all about trying to prevent those associations occurring.

Yet witness after witness at the federal inquiry had reinforced the view that bikie crime was decentralised and opportunistic, rarely following an outdated hierarchical structure. A cop from Victoria, Detective Superintendent Paul Hollowood, had openly scoffed at the idea of bikie Mr Bigs. The *Underbelly* state had 'bigger fish to fry', he said. 'The whole OMCG argument can be an unhealthy distraction. I do not think it is just law enforcement agencies that talk about it; there seems to be a real preoccupation in the media with the subject as well.'

Hollowood claimed that Victoria had gained a more accurate picture of organised crime through its 1997 Confiscation Act, targeting unexplained wealth rather than tallying the number of acts of associations between notorious characters:

> I think we have regained something like $77 million in assets from Tony Mokbel. That is serious organised crime. I do not see those types of assets with guys riding bikes—nowhere near that. It is where the money is and where it is being derived that is the best indicator for us as to where organised crime is sitting.

But South Australia had now made a decision to follow the patch instead of the money, and they would continue that strategy into the future. It wasn't until October 2009 that South Australia updated its own proceeds of crime legislation, to force the disclosure of the sources of unexplained wealth, but by early 2011 these new provisions had yet to come into force.

Harrison had advanced little evidence to support the political rhetoric that motorcycle clubs had morphed into a mafia on wheels.
The only specific allegations of club-sanctioned activity were centred on blackmail and extortion. Harrison alleged that bikers were
involved in standover tactics and debt collection, and that they
paid the club a percentage of the revenue they collected for the
use of its trademarks and fearsome reputation. This was the clubs'
principal source of revenue, he asserted.

Victims would sometimes report cases to police, but then back
away from making statements or appearing in court, fearful of
reprisals, Harrison told the federal inquiry. It seemed that people
tested what the criminal justice system had to offer them, but then
opted to resolve their issues in other ways, he said.

The problem for police trying to keep law and order in the
badlands is that often the 'victims' have their own criminality to
conceal. Identifying the victim is no easy task for police when
no-one is lily-white. An officer with the New South Wales Crime
Gangs Task Force told me in 2011 that dealing with these 'law and
order shoppers' was a difficult and frustrating exercise: 'They will
come to the police with half a story, to see if they can use us to get
a bikie off their backs. But when they are told we won't make deals
to conceal their crimes, they lose interest quickly.'

Police suggested there was a remarkably efficient parallel
system of justice operating where the bikies and their associates
mixed; here bikies acted as mediators and enforcers of judgements
that seemed as binding as any delivered in the courts.

In the latter half of the 'noughties', state governments across
Australia trumpeted their success in bringing down recorded
crime. Politicians on the campaign trail talked up these numbers
as if it was their policies and actions that were driving the crims
out of business. The reality was that governments had only a limited role in this. Two factors weighed heavily on reported crime
numbers in the major cities. First, a prolonged heroin drought had

reduced street-level crime significantly, as it always does. Second, a growing mistrust of the criminal justice system meant people on the fringes sought other forms of justice. And that's where the bikies came in.

A biker club constantly fields inquiries from associates and friends asking for assistance with myriad problems. It might be an abusive husband who terrorises his wife and kids, a neighbourhood dispute or unpaid business debts, but the common denominator is a feeling that the state cannot deliver a satisfactory outcome.

Ask yourself this: will the law step in when a drunken crazed husband on bail returns to attack his wife in the middle of the night? Will a court-issued apprehended violence order stop him from breaking down the door and carving her up with a kitchen knife? What happens when a child molester gets off on a technicality or receives a light sentence?

What happens when a small business facing ruin receives civil judgement against a debtor who pleads penury only to rise like a phoenix from the ashes with a new company? Where does a single mum turn to when the landlord or the bank is threatening to turf her family onto the street?

In these situations, the biker represents a more compelling form of justice than the state. And people are prepared to pay for the service. The remedies can be harsh—'fines' or 'donations', as they are called. The situation is rarely straightforward and can often beget a world of drama for everyone concerned.

Police only ever see the tip of this iceberg, and they label it extortion or blackmail. In reality, this informal system is an intolerable threat to the rule of law, but, to those who seek its protection, the only consideration is that it works.

This is quite distinct from the kind of standover tactics in which callous thugs extract money from hard-working 'squareheads' by terrorising them. That is actually relatively rare, because victims with nothing to hide are usually quick to report it.

But not all assistance comes with a price tag. Quite often the biker sees himself as an instrument of justice for the underdog. If it comes with a little adventure, that's even better.

Here's a good example of that in action. In the summer of 2009, I received a call from a South Australian bikie representing a group that had been investigating allegations of child sex abuse and murder based on the confessions of a man in custody. The inmate had given the bikies a map that led them to a remote outback location where a paedophile ring had allegedly been operating. They had driven six hours to a spooky old abandoned pub in the middle of the desert. A dilapidated Mr Whippy ice-cream van parked outside added to the horror movie feel.

In the heavy silence the bikies could almost feel the weight of foul deeds. Inside they had found butcher's boning knives, saws and hatchets. Strewn about the floor were surgical textbooks, and notebooks scrawled with mad ravings and indecipherable symbols. In a shed there were drums half-filled with a malodorous sludge that reminded them of congealed blood. There was an ominous trail of the sludge that led into a tunnel dug into an embankment.

Finally, to their horror, they found what they believed were human remains half-buried in a gully near the house. Snatching up some of the bones, they high-tailed it back to town in a state of high anxiety. 'A medical person' had examined one of the bones and concluded it was part of a human finger, the biker told me. And there were hundreds more bones in the gully. They believed they had discovered the lair of The Family, the infamous Adelaide paedophile ring. Here was the place where The Family had disposed of dozens of victims. Here was a chance to solve a string of cold cases previously written off by the South Australian police. And in the process they would show that bikies weren't the only bad guys in town.

I suggested they ring the police immediately and arrange a handover of the evidence. Just having it in their possession was an offence, I warned. They would not hear of that. How could they trust the very authorities who had allowed The Family to flourish? Cooperation with police just wasn't in their DNA, particularly as the Crime Gangs Task Force had been hassling them non-stop. No, they would hand their grisly find to me, and, through publicity, I would force the police to act.

However, taking delivery of human remains was deeply unappealing to me. Finally, after several telephone calls, we reached a compromise. A neutral party would meet another neutral party, to hand over the evidence and details of the alleged crime scene.

The next day, officers from SAPOL's Major Crime Squad were despatched to the far-flung location by charter flight. The local cops were kept out of the loop, in case they were part of the conspiracy, as the bikies feared. It was a tense moment when the investigators and their bikie counterparts met in that lonely landscape.

The bikies expected not to be taken seriously, or even to be arrested for their trouble, but the officers behaved in an exemplary fashion. Here for a brief moment a bikie gang and the Blue Gang put aside their rivalry to work to a common goal. The evidence was bagged and tagged and all parties left with their dignity intact.

A few days later, the results of forensic tests on the bones came back. They weren't human—probably a sheep or a kangaroo—but that wasn't the point. The bikers had shown they could act in a pro-social manner. And the police had demonstrated they could show respect for the bikers, putting aside the politics that surrounded Rann's fatwa on the clubs.

The bikers vowed to continue their investigations. They strongly believed in the information they had been given, and they returned again and again to the creepy pub. If they stumbled upon the paedophile who allegedly operated there, heaven help him. I doubt that the lads would have been willing so quickly to share their prize with the cops a second time.

'We believe that families need to know the truth about the fate of their loved ones,' said the biker. 'But don't expect us to fall in love with police. We just recognise that they have the resources to bring these criminals in. That is, if the government doesn't interfere to protect their mates as they have in the past.'

None of this would have impressed Assistant Commissioner Tony Harrison as he plotted the demise of the outlaw nation. This didn't fit the script of a ruthless crime gang motivated only by profit. Soon clubland would be in chaos, the crooks would be flushed out from their minions, who for years had done their dirty work. All the bikies' chest-beating about camaraderie and brotherhood would be exposed for the sham that it was. When the pressure was on, he believed, they would all cut and run.

But Tony Harrison's expectations were doomed to failure because of something else that was happening in South Australia, which had taken even the bikies by surprise. Despite all the dramas and past hatreds, a truce was holding between the clubs and it had now been more than a year since they had made headlines in the Adelaide papers.

Behind the scenes, clubs were enforcing discipline, telling members that one selfish indiscretion in a bar would affect every club. But even more remarkable was the fact that Adelaide clubs had begun to realise that they weren't so different after all. And they could say it without losing face.

In 2005, I had written to the Adelaide clubs asking for their cooperation for the research I was conducting for the *Bulletin* and the *Sunday* program, but only one club had raised their heads above the parapet. But now others were stepping up. Even the Gypsy Jokers began to emerge from their self-imposed exile.

After Steve Williams' demise, the Jokers had all but disappeared off the radar. They didn't want the world to know their business, even if it wasn't crime and mayhem. They were no longer seen downtown. They stuck to their clubhouse and avoided contact with other clubs. The walls had gone up again. They wanted to be old-school bikers: thousands of kilometres in the saddle each year, on state and national runs, camping out in tents rather than booking into motels like other clubs did. They wanted to be a race apart, they just wanted to be left alone. The Battle of Beachport and its aftermath had been a bummer full-stop, which would not be repeated.

But in early 2008, club president Wayne 'Chilla' McGrath had persuaded his fellow Jokers that the time had come for them to support the greater cause. A club-sponsored poker run had recently been hit with the full force of SAPOL's disrupt and dismantle policy. In a television interview at that time, Chilla had told me the cops had assembled a huge roadblock: fifty cars, twenty-six motorcycles, booze buses, a dog squad and at least two helicopters. A contingent from the STAR Group had stood by in their black four-wheel drives ready to pounce at the slightest sign of rebellion. The Jokers had not seen such heat assembled since Beachport.

Less than half the riders had been club members, but this show of force had been designed to drive the civilian bikers away from the outlaws, Chilla claimed. But the opposite had happened. 'The cops expected some sort of carry-on, but instead of getting riled up, we were all laughing about it. It was actually a joke,' he said. The public needed to know that the government was spending $5 million a year on a pointless war on bikies. His club was made up of workers, taxpayers, family men and, yes, a few criminals too.

'It's mostly crap—we are just busted-arse bikies, if you want to get down to it. [The members] struggle to pay their mortgage, pay their dues each week, so a criminal organisation, I don't think so,' Chilla said. Worse still, his membership of the club was being used to punish his family. His daughter had been refused a permit to work in gaming because her father was president of the Gypsy Jokers.

The Gypsy Jokers decision to speak out was one more step towards unity. However, a few months later Chilla died of a massive heart attack while exercising at home on a treadmill. It was a most un-bikie way to go, but it underlined how mundane and ordinary the lives of most bikies really were. He was just forty-four, a tattoo shop owner, a family man who worried about his weight, a busted-arse bikie in his own terms.

I attended his funeral with a member of another club, who wanted to make public recognition of Chilla's contribution to the common cause. He wanted to blend into the background, but in his club colours that wasn't so easy. As the hearse left the church to the strains of 'Ghost Riders in the Sky', the pair of us, sharing his Harley, joined the rear of the Jokers' motorcade for the ride to the cemetery.

We stood a respectable distance away from the Jokers who had come from all over Australia laid Chilla's coffin into the grave. We watched as the members one by one took turns on the shovel to bury their president.

I nudged the biker and said, 'Go on, mate.' He looked at me, surprised that I knew what he was thinking.

'Go on, you know you want to. So just do it,' I urged.

Without another word, he stepped among the Jokers and was handed the shovel, like it was the most natural thing in the world. There was a sharp intake of breath from some onlookers. This was an intensely private club ritual, but the Jokers understood the vibe completely. In conflict and disharmony, the state had taken its chance to destroy them all. It was time to respect what unified them, rather than what divided them.

When Chilla was properly buried, the Jokers, plus the other biker, stood over the grave swigging from a bottle of brandy and passing it on, backwash and all. Talk of this mark of respect would quickly spread across Adelaide's bikie scene. As I watched him standing among the Jokers, I had a strong premonition that the outlaws were going to win this war, but there was a long struggle still ahead.

On 25 September 2009, the full bench of the Supreme Court of South Australia ruled, two to one, that the control orders made against the Finks members were invalid under the Australian constitution. Justice David Bleby said the majority judgement had been made 'in the belief and expectation that this case is not stopping here'.

The state government had no choice but to take its fight to Canberra, where Attorney-General Atkinson's 'unelected judges of the High Court' would have the final say on his legislation.

17

NUTS TO YOU ALL

From 2003 to 2011, as the political heat was turned up on the clubs around the country, the leadership of most clubs was able to enforce discipline effectively. With a few notable exceptions, such as the confrontation between the Hells Angels and Comancheros at Sydney Airport and the Bandidos power struggle, inter-club rivalries were kept relatively quiet. Through the United Motorcycle Councils, outlaw bikers had a means of resolving disputes on neutral ground for the first time.

But Sydney was still a problem. Independent criminal cells within the clubs continued to clash over their private business interests. It was the nature of that business that no club leadership could control. But members of the rival MCs could still sit down together at UMC meetings. Despite the popular belief that the clubs were now private armies, leaders were highly reluctant to mobilise 'the troops' to support members whose criminal enterprises had gone wrong.

The press, fed by mischievous police, tried to wish every issue into a headline heralding the start of yet another bikie war. Google the search terms 'bikie war' and 'Australia' and 107,000 entries come up, mostly newspaper articles predicting every kind of conflict possible, short of thermonuclear war. The promised match-ups were almost endless: in Adelaide they included Finks versus Hells Angels, Finks versus Rebels, Rebels versus Hells Angels, Hells Angels versus New Boys. In Sydney, it was Hells Angels versus Comancheros, Hells Angels versus Notorious, Comancheros versus Notorious, Notorious versus Nomads, Notorious versus Bandidos, Rebels versus Bandidos, and even the Bra Boys surf gang was allegedly simultaneously doing battle with the Comancheros and the Bandidos. In Melbourne, an island of calm, it was only Rebels versus Bandidos. In Perth it was Coffin Cheaters versus Finks and Rebels versus Rock Machine and Coffin Cheaters versus Club Deroes.

It was like following a few seasons of the World Wrestling Federation. Eventually everyone got a chance to declare war on everyone else. Yet unlike the WWF, few of the promised feuds amounted to very much. At the precise time, most of these clubs were supposed to be gearing up for war they were in fact sitting around meeting tables at their local UMCs ironing out differences and getting to know each other.

My personal favourite was from the *Sydney Morning Herald* of 16 February 2009, which managed to combine the primal fear of Muslims and outlaw bikers in one screaming headline: 'Religious Divide Drives Bikie War'. The reporter warned that an 'ancient religious enmity' was at the centre of a new conflict between the Sunni Muslims of Notorious and Shiite Muslim members of the Comancheros. Meanwhile, Notorious had put a fatwa on the Hells Angels too, allegedly bombing their Crystal Street clubhouse in inner-city Petersham. The religious angle gave the looming conflict a new frightening edge, drawing not on fact but ancient stereotypes about Muslims: 'Neither police nor the Hells Angels have established why Notorious may have attacked the club, though the senior police source offered a simple answer: "They're just bloody crazy,"' opined the *SMH*.

From the comfort of distance, other reporters wrote of clubs 'flying in reinforcements from overseas' and 'stockpiling weapons' for the looming 'explosion of violence'. Apparently, the overseas contingent had ordered local minions to steal large numbers of cars to be used in a campaign of drive-by shootings. It was going to be World War III on the streets of Sydney.

How large numbers of notorious criminals from overseas were getting past immigration officials and law enforcement into Australia was never quite explained. It had already happened, a senior bikie told the ABC in early 2009. The credibility of this particular anonymous 'senior bikie' was based on nothing more than the fact that he travelled 'with six bodyguards in two cars'.

Following the deadly Sydney Airport battle between the Hells Angels and the Comancheros, Sonny Barger's Big Red Machine was apparently very displeased with its local soldiers. The *Daily Telegraph* ran a highly dubious story, claiming that 'shamed Hells Angels leaders' had banned Australian chapters from taking part in the club's 2009 world run, because they had failed to retaliate against the Comancheros.

The anonymous Angels 'insider' told the reporter the US had ordered local members to 'shoot on sight' any Comancheros they came across. This was essential if the Angels 'brand' were to be restored. Putting aside the fact that the Angels were a leading force in UMC-led peace talks, the club apparently had no choice but to follow this completely mad and illogical edict: 'It leaves Sydney's bikie world on edge, with little doubt the war is set to escalate once again,' the reporter claimed, without a shred of evidence.

Unfortunately for the breathless urgers, almost all the predictions of war amounted to very little indeed. What police and the media failed to acknowledge was that things were changing inside the bikie world—they had begun talking to each other again. The UMC had brought the players together and a new form of solidarity was developing between the clubs. Through discussion and negotiation, communication lines had been opened up and numerous disputes had been nipped in the bud.

But more than that, the UMC was a mirror in which clubs were able to better recognise their part in creating their own image. Once there had only been walls protecting the fortress, but now gates were opening. Clubs that remained inflexible and indifferent to public opinion would almost certainly perish. As members of rival clubs mingled at UMC meetings, they saw each other in a new light. They were exposed to how other clubs did business, and naturally compared it with their own club. Slowly, new attitudes and values were being communicated.

Police continued to scoff at the UMC, describing it as a PR sham. But those involved saw something quite profound was taking place. This had become a battle—not to protect criminals, but to preserve the rights of all outcasts.

Anti-association legislation struck at a basic human right. People didn't have to like bikies. Indeed, bikies didn't have much time for the public either. But if nice people stood idle as the state removed the freedoms of the outlaw, who could say where it might end? Who would be next? If the state had the power to decide with whom individuals could associate or not associate, then they were denied what French philosopher Emile Durkheim has called the 'free horizon of expectation': someone else would be making the critical decisions about how they would live their lives.

While the citizenry generally accepted this absence of decision making as part of modern life, the bikies railed against it. The more the state tried to enforce rules and regulations, the greater their spirit of rebellion would be. While crime was certainly a part of this, at its foundation was a desire to be in control of their own lives, or at least to have a say in the critical issues. While their critics suggested they saw themselves as above the law, the club philosophers argued that society had been cowed into submission by a system that created worker ants, not free-thinking human beings. To allow the government to choose with whom people could associate was simply intolerable.

At this nadir in their public popularity, the bikies and their mates had only the law on their side. With Media Mike and his ministers appealing to the High Court against the recent decision of the Full Court of the South Australian Supreme Court, bikers were going to Canberra.

As the Adelaide clubs prepared for their showdown in the High Court, another kind of outlaw was waiting for his date with justice in a Victorian maximum-security jail. While many bikers were at pains to distance themselves from organised crime, Geoffrey 'Nuts' Armour had tried by all means to become a part of it.

On 15 June 2009, Armour, forty-five, executed Desmond 'Tuppence' Moran in his favourite cafe on Union Road, Ascot Vale in Melbourne's north-west. Armour was described in the media as a former Rebels MC president, but on that day he was taking orders from Judith Moran, his 'Big Mama' as he called her.

Judy believed that Des, her former brother-in-law, was holding out on her. She believed that her former husband Lewis had hidden millions in drug money before he was murdered in March 2004 on the orders of rival drug boss Carl Williams, and that 'Tuppy' knew where it was.

Since Lewis's death, Tuppence had been paying Judy a few thousand dollars a month, but this was not enough for her. Tuppence had refused to cough up any more and eventually he gave her a beating to boot. He then threatened to change his will, to leave all of the family assets to charity rather than Judy's grandchildren.

Judy decided that Tuppence had to die before he could change his will, and Nuts had seen to that. Broke and desperate, Armour had hoped that the killing of Des Moran would provide a new start for him. He would head back to Queensland, leaving behind his erstwhile girlfriend, Suzanne Kane. His six-year association with her had been one shit fight after another.

Suzanne Kane had an impeccable criminal pedigree. She was the daughter of Melbourne gangster Leslie Kane, who was murdered in his Wantirna home in October 1978 by rival Ray 'Chuck' Bennett and members of his crew who pulled off the Great Bookie Robbery in 1976. Sue's sister Trish had married Jason Moran, the scion of Melbourne's leading crime dynasty, which had its roots in the notorious Painters and Dockers Union.

To the Moran patriarch, Lewis, Suzanne was the daughter he had never had. She had lived in the Moran household off and on since her teen years while the family built its criminal empire. But she had a tempestuous relationship with Lewis's wife Judy, which was punctuated by spectacular feuds.

Geoff Armour was a 'squarehead' by comparison, growing up in a working-class family in Airport West. 'Peanuts', as he was known to his friends, was a tearaway, but not a criminal. He had no criminal record apart from some minor assault convictions in his youth. Some of his friends ended up in jail, but the majority ended up as workers—tradesmen or small business owners.

'Peanuts' was a bit of a joke among his friends for his hell-raising ways, but some sensed there was a darker edge to him. 'He was always a bit dangerous,' remembered one childhood friend in 2011. 'You had to be careful not to wind him up too much. If he got it into his head that someone was a shit man and they'd done a crappy thing, he was onto them, and it didn't take much.'

Though he wasn't a big drinker or a drug taker, Nuts was always the life of the party. He would burst into people's homes unannounced, shouting, 'Let the games begin'—a signal that debauchery and adventure were just ahead. He would sign off letters to his friends with a humorous: 'Nuts to you all!'

Nuts had a reputation for courage and loyalty, but he also had a fatal weakness for women, which landed him in trouble and scandal all his life. For instance, in the early 1990s, he was running an earthmoving and construction business in Melbourne's west. When a close mate was crushed to death by a bulldozer on a building site, Nuts moved in with the dead man's wife just weeks later. Apparently, he hoped to share in the million-dollar compensation payout she was due.

By 1996, Nuts had left most of his old friends behind and had begun knocking around with the Rebels, earning a patch in quick time as the club rapidly expanded. At the same time, he was also trying to curry favour with Melbourne's top career criminals, hanging around the Hollyford Hotel in Melbourne's CBD. The Hollyford was owned by notorious underworld figure Dennis 'Fatty' Smith, who was running a multimillion-dollar heroin ring out of the pub. Here Nuts was introduced to some of Melbourne's best crooks, including veterans of the Great Bookie Robbery and former members of the Painters and Dockers Union, which had controlled organised crime in Victoria for a generation.

It was through this crowd that Nuts met Judy Moran's sons, Jason and Mark, and later Suzanne Kane. 'He always wanted to be in our company,' one of the Hollyford crowd told me in 2011. 'We didn't take him too seriously. He was always talking about getting guns for us, offering to do this and that. But he was a squarehead to us.' Friends remembered Armour as a handy fighter, though he had spent little time in the gym. For a big man, he was nimble and fluid in his movements, often surprising rivals with better credentials.

Nuts had become an officebearer in the Rebels' new Sunshine chapter.

During this period, the Rebels were the fastest-growing 1 per cent club in the country; they reached 2000 members in seventy chapters Australia-wide by 2011. It had been one of the first clubs in the nation, having been founded in Queensland in 1969. However, its recruitment rules were relaxed in the 1990s. Older members became concerned that a new breed of 'plastic gangstas' was beginning to dominate some chapters, and Nuts was the kind of biker guaranteed to raise the hackles of the purists.

On Thursday evenings, Nuts would invite the Hollyford crowd to the clubhouse as he tried to rapidly build the numbers. He would supply prostitutes, alcohol and drugs as inducements to join up. A who's who of Melbourne crime was asked to join, including accused cop killer Victor George Peirce, Dennis 'Fatty' Smith, Jason Moran and his brother Mark. The entry requirements were loose indeed.

There is no suggestion that the club sanctioned any of this. Contrary to popular belief, once a chapter is authorised, recruiting is left to the local leadership. There are very rarely edicts on who can be brought in. Though of course, if a chapter goes off-track generally, the club hierarchy may well step in.

'Nuts told us that all we had to do was turn up four Thursday nights in a row and we would get our colours. But it wasn't our cup of tea at all,' one potential nominee told me. 'There was a big wig down from Sydney one time and Jason Moran grabbed his [colours] jacket and put it on. He said: "What? You have to suck up to this bloke to get your colours, do ya?" We thought the whole thing was a joke.' Apparently Nuts would rent his string of Harleys out to nominees for $100 a week each. The money was non-refundable if the nominee failed to make the grade.

Later, in a humorous dig at Nuts and the bikers, some of the Hollyford crew let people know they were forming their own bikie club, the Mockingbirds MC. They printed up bumper stickers, stubby holders and T-shirts bearing the club logo and soon word spread of the new club seeking to muscle into the outlaw action. But there was no club, it was just a hoax—Mockingbird is rhyming slang for turd.

By 2003, Nuts's life was becoming complicated. He had begun a secret affair with Suzanne Kane. The problem was that Kane already had a partner, a one-time Hells Angels prospect named Lee Pascu, who was also a loyal Moran associate. They were living together and Suzanne had given birth to Lee's son in 2000.

Complicating matters further, Pascu had been a childhood friend of Carl Williams. Growing up in Broadmeadows, Pascu had attended the same high school. He had even helped Carl choose a coffin when his elder brother Shane died from a heroin overdose in 1997. For a time, Lee and Carl had both been working inside the Moran drug operation. But that was not to last.

In October 1999, Jason Moran shot Carl in the stomach as punishment for undercutting him on sales of ecstasy. Williams immediately suspected Pascu of being a double agent who had led him into the Moran ambush. Pascu visited Williams in hospital to deny any involvement and he offered to mediate the dispute. Williams said he accepted his old friend's explanation, but declined the offer.

Just a month later, Pascu was wounded in the shoulder in an ambush as he got into his car outside his West Meadows home. Unbeknown to him, Sue Kane was also sleeping with Williams, now his archenemy. Eventually, Pascu began to suspect that Carl was in the background, a fear confirmed when a second attempt was made on his life in 2001. Life was quiet for a while as Pascu and Sue set up house in Melbourne's west, but Pascu was always on guard.

Early in 2003, Pascu's worst fears were realised. Coming home unexpectedly, Pascu heard Sue talking on the telephone as he walked down the side of the house. She was slagging him off to the other party on the line. Pascu stayed outside and listened intently.

The other party to the call was Nuts and it emerged in the conversation that he had taken a contract on behalf of Carl to kill Pascu. Carl, flush with drug money, was offering contracts of more than $100,000 per hit as he began an orgy of reprisals against the Morans. The money had apparently assuaged any bitterness that Nuts may have felt about sharing Sue with Carl.

Pascu never let on that he had overheard Sue and Nuts discussing the plot. Nuts then enjoyed a reputation for being mercurial—he was liable to pop up anywhere, any time. He was a frightening proposition for Pascu, who wasn't a killer and wasn't even much of a tough guy. He had found the rigours of life as an Angel prospect too taxing and had failed to make the cut.

Anyway, the Moran fold had been less demanding and more lucrative than life with the Angels. Pascu certainly didn't want to tangle with Nuts so, at the first opportunity, he packed his stuff and took off on his bike, leaving his baby son with Sue Kane.

Throughout 2003, Nuts was determined to make good on his contract for Carl Williams. With an accomplice, Nuts hunted for Pascu, demanding mutual friends reveal his whereabouts. After hiding out for months, Pascu decided it was better to get out of town, heading to Darwin, where he remains to this day.

Former close friends found they no longer knew Nuts. Around this time, he had an argument over nothing with a close friend in a country pub and ended up shooting him non-fatally. Nuts went on the run to Queensland before being arrested and extradited. But the case collapsed after the friend decided he wouldn't give evidence against his mate.

From 2003, Nuts became increasingly violent and unhinged. It was later revealed he was the prime suspect in the 2005 disappearance of Melbourne carpet layer George Templeton. Templeton was last seen leaving the house he shared with his fiancée, a stripper named Robyn Lindholm, at 1.30 a.m. on 3 May 2005. Police believed Nuts had threatened to kill Templeton for beating up Lindholm, with whom the biker was said to be having an affair. According to media reports in 2011, Nuts's name was also being mentioned in regard to two other murder investigations.

In 2005, Armour fell out with the Rebels, reportedly leaving the club in bad standing. The exact reason is not known, but it was certainly true that his adventures were attracting plenty of unwanted attention to the club. Like many men who joined a motorcycle club, Nuts's personality had changed when he got his patch, friends said. The power had gone to his head. Without the club, his life went downhill at a rapid rate. He was drawn into the madness and greed of the Morans' crumbling empire.

When Lewis Moran was executed on the orders of Carl Williams in March 2004, Suzanne Kane lost her closest ally. Lewis had reportedly given her two BMWs and a Mercedes-Benz when he was flying high in the drug trade. Now she had no means of support. Grief briefly united Judy and Kane, but not for long. Judy gave Suzanne a small scoop of Lewis's ashes, but she wasn't going to be satisfied with that.

Des Moran knew that his brother Lewis had stashed away $200,000 worth of pseudoephedrine (a precursor ingredient for speed manufacture) but, when he checked its hiding place, it was gone. Des immediately accused Suzanne Kane and Nuts of stealing the stash. By this time, Judy and Sue had also resumed their bickering and arguing.

With their popularity at a low ebb, Kane and Nuts headed for Perth. Nuts set up a two-truck transport operation and a building company, the indiscreetly named Outlaw Constructions. But by 2009, Nuts's ventures had gone belly-up, while Sue had racked up huge personal debts. Owing a total of $200,000, they had little choice but to return to Melbourne when Judy Moran offered Nuts a contract to kill Des Moran.

His first attempt, in March 2009, was an almost comical

failure. Nuts hid outside Moran's Ascot Vale home and waited for Des to get into his car. But Moran handed the keys to his mate Mick Lindsell because he had been drinking. In the darkness, the would-be assassin mistook Lindsell for his target. Donning an ill-fitting balaclava, Armour stepped up with a .38 calibre handgun and fired one shot through the windscreen at the driver.

Miraculously, the round lodged in the steering wheel. Lindsell's luck held when the gun jammed as Nuts tried to fire again. He ran away, stopping to pick up the gun he had dropped in his flight. His next blunder was to discard the balaclava and gun, covered in his fingerprints and DNA, in a nearby front yard.

Nuts returned to Perth to ponder his next move. When Des mistakenly accused someone else of the attack, Nuts must have thought he was in the clear. Maybe he was just too broke, or stupid, to care. Soon the police were tracking every move Nuts and his accomplices made.

In May 2009, Judy made a six-day visit to Perth. Before long Nuts, Sue Kane and her nine-year-old son were all headed back to Melbourne. Judy mortgaged her Ascot Vale house for $400,000 and bought herself and Sue a pair of Chrysler Sebring convertibles for $110,000. Nuts got a Land Rover Discovery four-wheel drive for $72,000. It was enough incentive for the hapless gunman to step up to the plate a second time, before Des could change his will.

Nuts's life had become a nightmare. The once-feared outlaw bikie was reduced to living off the charity of Judy Moran. It was a ghastly domestic scene in Judy's house. Nuts and Sue were having screaming arguments while Judy treated her contract killer like the hired help. In the days leading up to Des Moran's murder, police listened on telephone taps as Judy and Sue Kane tried to alert Nuts to the whereabouts of his target.

Judy left one message on Nuts's phone saying: 'Where are you, dickhead? I ring you four million times. We're going shopping and I'll have a look at a maroon jumper for you, okay? Give us a ring. Ciao.' Police said 'maroon jumper' was code for Des Moran.

On the day of his death, Des Moran had been easy to find in his local cafe. Wearing a novelty wig tied in a ponytail, Nuts pointed his Glock semi-automatic at Moran through the plastic fly strips of the cafe's front door. Moran's last words were 'Oh shit!' before he was shot three times in the upper body. Nuts wasn't going to mess this up a second time, so he pumped a further four shots into Moran as he lay dying on the floor.

Any slight possibility that Nuts and Judy would get away with this was destroyed soon after. They foolishly brought the getaway car back to Judy's house and hid the murder weapon, other fire-arms, ammunition, plus Nuts's wig and clothing, in a wall safe. Judy Moran still pleaded not guilty and at her trial the whole sordid story of her association with Suzanne and Nuts became public property. From the prisoner's dock, in a motorised wheelchair, she stoutly denied any part in the plot even though every piece of evidence screamed to the contrary.

Witness after witness painted a picture of Nuts as a desperate individual who had failed utterly in life—as a businessman, bikie and gangster. Sparing himself the shame of the same ordeal as Judy, Nuts pleaded guilty to murder and was later sentenced to 26 years in jail. Sue Kane pleaded guilty to being an accessory to murder after the fact and was sentenced to two years' jail, but she was released immediately. The judge suspended all but seven months and seventeen days of the sentence. With time already served, she was able to walk free.

To the public, Nuts was a dangerous lunatic who would think nothing of shooting a man he barely knew in a busy suburban cafe. But club men took a more sympathetic view. This was a moral tale that showed the vulnerability of bone-headed men. It showed how scheming, conniving women could lay a gullible brother low. There were quite a few men like Nuts in outlaw clubs: scroungers and wannabes desperate to make a quick buck. They could sometimes be saved from their own stupidity by the intervention of their clubs, but just as many drifted out to an uncertain fate.

Suzanne Kane had brought Nuts into the orbit of Judy Moran and he had been reduced to doing the dirty work. Once, he had once been associated with the toughest guys on the highway. Now, as he served life in jail, Nuts would be forever linked to a murderous old woman in a motorised wheelchair.

18

THE GOOD, THE BAD AND THE UGLY

If there was ever a moment to show how little control club elders exercised over their admirers and imitators, this was it. Just after 5 a.m. on 11 February 2010, two men were travelling in a rented Commodore sedan through Adelaide's northern suburbs with a special delivery for New Boys boss, Vincenzo Focarelli.

Focarelli and his group had become a major irritant for the local Hells Angels. From their base in Focarelli's Hindley Street tattoo parlour, the New Boys were gaining numbers and strength. Police said the club was a growing force in street drug sales, having graduated from the northern suburbs to the CBD.

When Focarelli left the Hells Angels' North Crew, reportedly after a dispute with a member over money, he took a couple of other prospects with him and created the New Boys. He and his followers threatened to wipe the Big Red Machine off the map. However, most of their attention had been directed at Angels associates and hangers-on, rather than patch members.

According to police, New Boys and Angels associates had squared off in a blazing gun battle on Gouger Street in May 2008, which had left two bystanders slightly injured from flying glass and shrapnel.

This time, courtesy of the special delivery, Focarelli would be finished once and for all. Without Focarelli and a few other hard men, they were just a bunch of kids hanging around shopping centres, it was said by police and rivals.

Of course, the two men in the Commodore had their own links to drugs. One was a 23-year-old Hells Angels hang-around, Barzan Palani, who had been charged with methamphetamine possession, while the other man, Vahe Hacopian, thirty-one, had done time for cannabis trafficking. But murder was a big step up in class for the pair.

The centre console of a moving vehicle is no place to carry a bomb. Less than a hundred metres from Focarelli's house, the driver, Hacopian, pulled over just after negotiating a sharpish bend. It's not clear exactly what happened next, but perhaps the bombers needed to prime their device.

After the ensuing terrific explosion, Hacopian's shattered body came to rest in the gutter 6 metres from the car. The blast wave had ripped the roof and doors off the car, leaving Palani, the Angels associate, dead in the passenger seat, still in his seat belt. Smoking debris was strewn 50 metres away.

The attempted bombing was manna from heaven for the South Australian Government in the fight to save its SOCCA legislation in the High Court. Police Minister Michael Wright said the bombing showed the 'true nature of outlaw motorcycle gangs': 'These tough anti-bikie laws, the toughest in the nation, will be applied to all bikie groups,' he warned.

UMC delegates had some hard questions for the Hells Angels. If they had sanctioned this attack, they had betrayed the rest of the clubs who had put aside personal disputes for 'the good of the

UMC'. But the Angels quickly moved to reassure delegates that the club had not sanctioned the operation.

That was an assessment senior police agreed with. Detective Superintendent John Venditto, officer in charge of the Major Crime Squad, was not even sure this venture was bikie-related. Whatever one thought of bikies, they were blessed with more intelligence than this. 'When people drive around with bombs in their car as blatantly as this, I don't know that they're actually that smart,' he said.

Within hours, police had tracked down the bombmakers' workshop, where they found a second device, some cannabis and a firearm. A third plotter was arrested. No evidence was found linking patch members to the planning or execution of the bungled mission.

The Enfield bombing underscored a new dilemma for club leaders: the nationwide campaign against bikies had made them fashionable again. Through the 1990s, the movement had been slowly withering; it had started to become the preserve of paunchy, ageing men with grey beards. But politicians like Rann and the moral entrepreneurs of the police force had made being a bikie cool again.

As the moral panic took hold, there were thousands of disaffected, damaged youth clamouring to get in. The clubs needed new younger members if they were to survive, so all sorts of kids were allowed to hang around. If they showed something useful, they might get a chance to nom, but most would be filtered out. Some were given a kick in the pants on their way out the door.

Each club had an outer circle of followers who believed if they could show some 'class' they might finally get a patch. They were besotted with the club, or a particular member, and so they doggedly persisted, as if getting in would be the crowning achievement of their lives.

But only drug-addled delusion would lead anyone to believe

that blowing up Focarelli would make their patch dreams come true. This was the very last thing the Angels wanted added to their record. Ultimately police were never able to establish the incident was directly linked to the club and the UMC tried to focus on the task ahead as if nothing had ever happened.

As they waited for judgement day in the High Court, Adelaide's bikers stayed 'on message'. The full bench of the South Australian Supreme Court had found two to one against the State Government in the Finks' case, but there was no certainty they would win in Canberra. Like a political party on the hustings, the UMC had let all clubs know that there should be no selfish acts of stupidity, because all members would wear the cost.

Despite all the pressure from police, the nucleus of the clubs had remained surprisingly resilient. The challenges they had faced had if anything made them more cohesive. But the way things were run was quite different now.

Recently one veteran biker, after carefully considering the matter, told me that if I kept hanging around the scene for another five years I had a chance of gaining acceptance in his world. Sadly, my editor wouldn't wait till 2016.

There had been a reason for clubs to fast-track me in the beginning, despite the risks. They had wanted the public to know there was more to them than crime and violence. But by late 2009, it was time to close the door, the message having been broadcast. The UMC would now be my point of contact and access would be through a public relations firm. To meet the outlaws at first, I had hung around in Stormy's brothel; now I was submitting proposals for consideration to the PR flak, along with the other hacks.

For a considerable time I had enjoyed carte blanche to speak to whoever would put up with my questions. There had been numerous opportunities to meet families and work mates, and hang out in clubhouses, tattoo shops, pubs and nightclubs. In order to dispel the myths, clubs had extended me a privilege that no other reporter had ever enjoyed. I had seen how bikers ran their lives, how they juggled work and family with club duties, how they perceived themselves. On one level, I felt I had been asked to show the members how the public might view them, if the true facts were known. If I was going to write that the members were 'The Good, the Bad and the Ugly' it would have to be from close-up. With some grimacing and flinching, they had provided the access.

In fact, I had been criticised by other reporters for being too close to the bikers, to which I would always reply, 'Well, you're too far away.'

Don't get me wrong: I was very relieved that a third party like this PR firm, which wasn't part of the biker scene, would now be involved. Trying to interpret the shifting sands of club politics was difficult and sometimes terrifying. As a non-member, you never felt like you were really in, even at the best of times. No matter what assurances were given, this always ended up as a one-to-one proposition. My access was in fact dependent on nothing more solid than the good humour and caprice of each and every member. One silly comment to the wrong person was enough to earn you a bollocking.

I happily accepted that risk, knowing that each biker was his own man, not a foot soldier for the bosses. He was not scenery for some theatre piece any club might have wanted to stage. It was demeaning to him to be cast like that. He demanded respect as an individual. I would only earn some back by doing 'the righty' by every one of them. I can't begin to explain how exhausting and nerve-racking that was.

At the same time, I had to convince my sceptical media bosses that bikies were not running the world's greatest criminal enterprise. Let's face it, the story I was offering was not nearly as sexy as the familiar one they had, that bikies were taking over the world.

That cliche was easy to write: you could do 90 per cent of it without leaving the office, which made it the perfect story for the desk-bound modern reporter. The police would supply most of the anecdotes, carefully filtered to create whatever impression they believed suited their agendas. The problem was that I knew that much of that story was wrong or wildly exaggerated. And I believed that pursuing the truth, not the myth, was still my job. Stoking fear and discontent seemed a dismally shameful perversion of that.

Nonetheless, I got the distinct impression that I could easily finish up pissing everyone off, just as Art Veno had. It was odds-on that no-one—the bikies, the politicians, the cops and maybe even potential employers—might be speaking to me by the end.

In October 2009, bikies from all over Australia were descending on Perth. Finks from all over Australia were in town for the opening of their new clubhouse in Balga. Meanwhile, other clubs were pouring in for the Westdale rock concert and motorcycle races staged by the local chapter of the Gypsy Jokers near Beverley, two hours east into the desert. The Perth-based Coffin Cheaters MC was also reportedly holding an anniversary party at their clubhouse in Bayswater.

Tom Mackie, with a group of the Descendants, had flown in from Adelaide for Westdale and he couldn't remember the last time he had seen so many different club patches in such close proximity. It was a sign of the times. There was still tension between some clubs, but with their members sitting across from each other at UMC meetings there was an outlet for any grievances. The Descendants were actually looking forward to catching up with old mates in other clubs. Meanwhile, through the UMC, the club had established firm new friendships with other clubs. Perth had been a battleground for different clubs a few years earlier but there was no sense of foreboding at all as the Descendants saw other bikers mingling with each at the airport and in town.

The WA police did not share that view. They turned on the full circus for the bikers. More than 400 officers were reportedly rostered on that weekend. Groups of bikers riding across from the eastern states were hit with massive roadblocks at the WA border crossings. The Western Australian government was planning its own version of South Australia's SOCCA laws and this was a chance to give the bikers a taste of the future, when such gatherings of clubs would be illegal.

The arrivals terminal at Perth Airport was just teeming with police: plainclothes, uniform, state, federal. I counted at least thirty-five inside the terminal, not counting half a dozen sniffer dogs.

I had picked up two bikers at the airport and we were gathered in by the dragnet as we drove out. Undercover officers had followed the two bikies out of the domestic terminal to the pick-up zone, where they got into my vehicle. A few hundred metres up the road, we were directed by police to a side street, where an extraordinary security operation took place.

'Welcome to Western Australia,' said one, with an ironic laugh.

'If you fuck up this weekend, there will be no bail,' said another.

For the next twenty minutes, eighteen officers went through their routine under a blazing portable spotlight. The rental car was thoroughly searched. Luggage was opened. Clothes were carefully sifted through, wallets and bum bags turned inside out. Two officers with stills cameras snapped our pictures, while a third on a video camera filmed the entire process. An officer took our mobile phones and went through our call lists and private text messages.

We were all body-searched. One of the bikers was asked to drop his pants and lift his genitals so police could check for hidden contraband. It was my turn next, but just then officers realised they had a reporter in the net and they backed off.

For the two club members, this was nothing new. But for ordinary citizens who regard free association as a right, this was a challenging moment. In this age of terrorism, we expect our police to be tough and proactive, but when the system is turned on you, it's a different matter.

Even the bikers were surprised at the intensity. 'This is ten notches up from what we have experienced elsewhere,' said one. But it was all taken in good stride. The weekend turned out to be a mild and pleasant affair, despite the dire predictions of police. WA Assistant Commissioner Nick Anticich had warned the public that bikers were coming to Perth 'to make a statement and potentially to commit offences' despite repeated denials by all concerned, this furphy blared across the weekend's media. To me, this was just a cover story from the police to justify the extraordinary waste of taxpayers' money. It seemed laughable that anyone coming to Perth to 'potentially commit offences' would do it quite so publicly.

As I caught up with members in the Balga clubhouse that evening, it was clear the Finks, like the rest of the bikers, were indeed in town to party and meet girls, as disappointing as that must have been to the media bosses who had sniffed blood in the air.

The big black gates of the Fink clubhouse closed behind me. In the street, the television crews were milling about self-importantly, preparing their live crosses to the 6 p.m. news. Ferret, who was the sargeant-at-arms of the club's Blacktown chapter in New South Wales, was helping them set up a clever sequence with his motorcycle. In a couple of minutes of airtime, the viewers would get a bite-sized version of the story I had been trying to tell for four years. Then the crews would take down their lights, roll up their cables and move on to the next story because there was nothing more to see there.

Articulate and confident men like Ferret, who was now the chairman of the NSW United Motorcycle Council, were more than able to tell their own story and were stepping up to challenge the myths and legends in the media.

It occurred to me that the bikers could get more out of a few snappy quotes on the evening news than from all the serious analysis I had tried to force into the 'quality' media.

The bikers had also found their own voice. Back in 2005, there were no bikers stepping up to tell their stories in public. A few experts like Arthur Veno and reporters like me had been left to interpret this arcane world. We probably got a lot of it wrong, but it was rarely challenged or corrected, such was the distrust of media.

Now UMC spokespeople and club members were regularly giving their side of the story, responding to the untruths and exaggerations in the media. Reporters were furnished with contact details of spokespeople so they could check the facts for the first time. (Many reporters still didn't bother.) There were bikers giving talks to university students about the reality of their lives and what these new laws would mean for all citizens. And if the media still wouldn't report the facts, the clubs and state UMCs could go direct to the audience via social media sites like Facebook and YouTube. The days of never complaining and never explaining were over.

The FREE Australia Party was granted registration in South Australia in March 2009, despite close scrutiny of its members by the electoral commission. A number of the bikers were excluded for submitting invalid address details, but Bear estimated that more than 100 of FREE's 150 members had come from the clubs. Membership of a political party had offered an exemption under the new SOCCA laws, but many bikers had taken to politics with great zeal, he said.

Rann's onslaught had led some bikers to read up on the history of human rights back to the Magna Carta. 'It just opened my eyes to what rights I had—rights I had taken for granted or didn't really know existed. It made me want to get involved to put my point of view [across]. I never would have done this before,' said one in 2011.

'I felt that the underlying beliefs and values in the world had gone out the window. In the club, we have rules that are based on morals and ethics. In our world, you have to speak the truth,' he said.

Bikers who had dropped off the political grid years before could see universal principles in the law that did endure, principles that the SOCCA law flouted. These were matters not just for bikers, but for everyone in society.

On 1 May 2009, the Rebels diverted their national run to Adelaide and, with hundreds of other outlaw club members, they rode to the South Australian parliament to deliver the petition calling for the overturning of Rann's new laws. An Australian Democrat MP, David Winderlich, accepted the petition on the steps of parliament, telling the crowd that he had been advised it was political suicide. But other politicians were beginning to sense a change in the wind too.

The UMC in South Australia had organised a Protest Poker Run for the same month to promote supporter T-shirt sales and a fundraising raffle of two motorcycles. The idea of the poker run is that participants are dealt a card at each stop on the route and the best poker hand at the end wins the prize.

The first stop on the route was the Adelaide Hills town of Macclesfield. Arrangements were made with the publicans along the route to ensure they had adequate staff for the expected numbers. Local sporting clubs and charity groups were advised as well, so they could set up sausage sizzles and soft-drink stalls in the towns to aid their own fundraising. This was going to be a true community event.

However, South Australian police decided to drag the various hoteliers before the state licensing commission and applied for the pubs' licences to be revoked for the day, citing 'public safety' and 'overcrowding' as likely problems. Despite these kinds of runs never having had any problems over the decades, the licensing commission upheld the police application. Suspiciously, the Classic Adelaide Car Rally had passed through the same town a few weeks earlier and patrons had spilled out of the pubs onto the streets watching the passing cars without any hint of licensing problems. Apparently, the 'four-wheel crowd' was okay, but the 'two-wheel gang' was a threat to public safety.

The UMC run still proceeded to Macclesfield and the committee decided to purchase all the local charities and food outlets goods to acknowledge the people's efforts to accommodate the run. The other hotels visited on the run were changed at the last minute to avoid the issue of overcrowding in their venues. The UMC vowed to return to Macclesfield in numbers to compensate the hotels for the loss of trade that day, and on Australia Day 2010, two months later, 200 club members rode to Macclesfield and spent the day there, this time with no interference from the South Australian police.

It seemed to the bikers that, after years of self-imposed isolation, the police and government wanted to keep them separate from the rest of society. It suited their agenda to emphasise the differences between the 1 per cent world and the rest. Other institutions were following this lead, assuming that all outlaw clubs were soon to be banned. Banks were quietly dropping clubs as customers and calling in loans from businesses known to be associated with bikers.

In November 2009, when two UMC members wearing club colours went along to see Queensland's anti-association laws debated in the state parliament, an attendant asked them to leave the public gallery because they were intimidating the groups of school children. They refused, saying they were only exercising their rights as citizens in a democracy. The government refused to meet them, but the Shadow Attorney-General Lawrence Springborg gave them fifteen minutes, which turned into an hour and a quarter. On the strength of what Springborg was told, the Queensland Liberal/National Party Opposition voted against the bill, the first time a major political party had sided with the bikies. The bill still passed, but these small wins gave the movement confidence to keep working together.

In August that year, when Ferret rose to speak at the National Press Club in Canberra, he was speaking for the movement. Here was a measure of how far the bikers had come. As the chairman of the New South Wales UMC, Ferret represented the vast majority of bikers who did not see their club membership as a licence for crime but as a legitimate lifestyle choice.

'Good afternoon, my name is Ferret,' he began memorably. 'I work in a tattoo parlour in the western suburbs of Sydney. I'm a father of two, a grandfather of five. I've been a member of the Finks Motorcycle Club for twenty-two years and it's as much a part of who I am as being a father or a grandfather. It's where I met my best friends, spent some of the milestones of my life and found people who share my lifelong interest in motorcycles,' he said.

'Contrary to what you may hear from government press releases, being a Fink doesn't mean that I must be involved in drug trafficking, violence, intimidation or any other form of crime, organising it, participating in it or condoning it, but that's me. I'm not here to tell you that members of motorcycle clubs are all saints. There may be people amongst our members who have been in trouble and what happened at Sydney Airport was a tragedy.'

His simple message was that the scrutiny applied to bikers should be extended to all, especially the organs and functionaries of authority. 'Not all politicians or police are squeaky clean. But I would say that there is more organised criminal activity every day in Australia's governments and police services than you would ever find at your local biker clubhouse,' he said.

And as implausible as that seemed, Ferret was probably right. The media reporting of the extent of biker crime had been wildly disproportionate to reality, when compared with reliable published data. Crime statistics showed that gang-related violence in Australia made up just 0.6 per cent of all crime, and the bikers were responsible for less than 0.3 per cent of that. Respected criminologist Paul Wilson of Queensland's Bond University, who also spoke at the Press Club, backed that up. He went on to say that the laws proposed in New South Wales and South Australia were the most repugnant that Australia had seen since then Prime Minister Robert Menzies had tried to ban the Communist Party in 1950.

Breaking up biker clubs would do little to address crime. The anti-association laws being promoted by state governments would strip all citizens of fundamental rights without making them the least bit safer, said Wilson.

Ferret asked the media to understand just what was at stake with the new laws. 'I might be just one person, I'm just a dad from western Sydney, but I'm telling you today it's not just about me or even about people who ride motorcycles; it's an issue about human rights,' he said.

'It's an issue for every person listening to me here in the press gallery and at home across Australia. Don't just believe me, find out for yourself, read the legislation. You'll soon see what our governments are doing to us is a lot more scary than a few guys with tattoos and leather jackets,' he concluded.

It was an entertaining and insightful address, but just how many of the media went off and actually followed Ferret's advice and read the legislation is hard to say.

But the judges of the High Court were certainly reading it line by line as they prepared to deliver their verdict on the South

Australian legislation. The future of the outlaw nation was no longer in the hands of public opinion, politicians and the media. Finally the Australian constitution would play its part.

19

SOMEWHAT LESS THAN ZERO

On 11 November 2010, the High Court ruled that the control orders under South Australia's SOCCA legislation offended the separation of powers under the Australian Constitution. The provision forcing judges and magistrates to rubber-stamp control orders on the say-so of the Attorney-General was the stumbling block. The executive was attempting to usurp the functions of the judiciary. In other words, a politician was trying to tell a judge what to do.

It's such a basic principle it's amazing the Rann Government believed it could get away with it. The final verdict wasn't even close; the beaks of the High Court voted six to one to dismiss the appeal and award costs against South Australia.

The Premier continued to talk tough, promising new legislation 'within weeks'. In August 2011, the government finally came up with a new package that was strikingly similar to SOCCA but for the important difference that it was predicated on approaching crime based on what a person did, not who they were. The new legislation still shared much of the same hysterical overkill as the earlier version and legal experts remained dubious about its future.

Despite the loss of the control orders, SAPOL's gangbuster Assistant Commissioner Anthony Harrison continued to use the SOCCA. Police were still dutifully counting the associations of members and warning of dire consequences if they kept meeting. But without the control orders, the association notices had less force than a parking ticket. In fact, they had no force at all. The SOCCA still enabled police to declare any group they wished but there was no longer a mechanism to do anything about it.

The High Court ruling was the high tide mark, from which this latest moral panic soon began to recede. Even though the anti-association laws that had been introduced in New South Wales, Queensland and Western Australia were still to be tested in higher courts, the defeat of the South Australian legislation seemed to spread despondency and inertia among the politicians.

Very simply, state politicians around Australia had other issues on their minds. Labor was swept from office in Victoria in 2010 and in New South Wales in 2011, and the tough talk from the former opposition parties in Sydney seemed to end when they took the Treasury benches. The Liberal National Party opposition in Queensland had already committed to opposing anti-association legislation after lobbying by the UMCQ.

In mid 2011, the new Victorian Government under Premier Ted Baillieu was talking of drafting new anti-biker laws. This had followed a concerted campaign by sections of the media and the powerful Victorian Police Association.

Then chief commissioner of Victoria Police, Simon Overland, before taking office, had long believed that specialist bikie squads were unnecessary to address the bikie issue in his state. In 2005, Overland told me that it was a waste of scarce resources to have a squad targeting one group in society. The Purana taskforce, which had brought the Melbourne gangland war to a close, had the skills and expertise to go after bikers who graduated to serious organised crime but there had been little evidence of that so far.

However, in May 2011, under increasing pressure from the media, Overland caved in, announcing that gang squad Echo Taskforce would now focus solely on the biker clubs.

Facing a storm over allegations Victoria Police had provided favourable and incomplete crime statistics to the government before the 2011 state election, the bikie taskforce must have been a welcome diversion. Here was a squad that could produce crime statistics almost at will, just as Avatar and its successor the Crime Gangs Taskforce had in South Australia.

News of this move was accompanied by a dire warning in the *Sunday Herald Sun* newspaper, presumably leaked by police, that the Victorian biker population had exploded to 4000. This was clearly false. Most agencies agreed that there were no more than 3500 living in the entire country. But it served to heighten the fear and alarm, drowning out any credible arguments for restraint. As had happened all around Australia, the erroneous figure would be repeated ad nauseam. As the media beat-ups became ever more shrill, polls showed that Victorians were eager to see membership of outlaw motorcycle clubs made a criminal offence.

Meanwhile, in South Australia, where it had all begun, the war on bikies was a political loser now. Despite all his huffing and puffing, Rann's campaign on bikers had ended with a massive slide in his own popularity. After being the most loved state premier in 2003, he was now the most reviled. His party decided to move him on before the next state election. The architect of the SOCCA, Attorney-General Michael Atkinson, had already fallen on his sword.

Then there was also a startling admission by the SAPOL Chief Commissioner Mal Hyde in January 2011. In an interview with Monash University Professor David Baker, Hyde appeared to scuttle every claim South Australian authorities had previously made with regard to the bikies' role in organised crime: 'In terms of bikies, we actually don't have a major problem here in the sense that it exceeds the problem in other states and territories,' he said, without any prompting from the interviewer. 'When you count the number of bikies, South Australia only has about 6 per cent of the national figure and we have 8 per cent of the population of Australia, so we are actually under-represented in bikies. There is a great deal of public concern that may not necessarily match the serious crime that they are committing.'

So bikies weren't so bad after all. This was the same police commissioner who had stood nodding alongside his Premier as Rann told the media the bikies were 'terrorists' and 'the foot soldiers of organised crime'. Rann had said he had only given the police the laws they had requested.

Hyde had let the cat out of the bag: he hadn't really needed the contentious anti-association laws after all. Meanwhile, South Australia had squandered the chance to put more effective proceeds of crime legislation in place and that, all experts agreed, was the most effective means of combating organised crime. Of course, having the forensic accountants deal the bikies a death by a thousand paper cuts was boring compared with sending the STAR Group crashing into clubhouses to stop members associating. They must have known that most of the bikies were broke anyway.

To the Descendants' Tom Mackie this all looked a lot like 1981, when the bikie cop Sam Bass and his squad had been pulled into line. The panic over bikies was replaced with indignation about police methods. Judicial inquiries were held into allegations that some police were heavily involved in the drug trade, but no charges were ever laid. Still, the stink of their bikie squad days followed them. None of their careers prospered. It was an era best consigned to the past for SAPOL.

Mackie reasoned that the High Court decision would not be kind to Harrison's career, even though he was squeaky-clean. In early 2011, a Greens MP had introduced a motion to allow parliament to review all the secret evidence that SAPOL had gathered to support its plans for control orders over key clubs. As in 1981, the focus was switching back to the police.

After 1981, the clubs expanded and consolidated, building the clubhouses that still stood today. The same would happen again now, in Mackie's view. The UMC had raised more than $200,000 for the High Court defence from clubs and supporters. They now had a war chest to fight the next legal attack that came along.

For Premier Mike Rann, the plan to drive the bikies out of his state had failed dismally. In fact, if better-crafted laws in other states got up, the traffic would all be headed for Adelaide. Rann had effectively succeeded in legalising outlaw bikies in South Australia. As punishment for thumbing his nose at the constitution, the High Court had bitch-slapped him with a leather-bound precedent that would stand for years to come. Mackie was going to enjoy the cops' exquisite agony when the interstate hordes came roaring in from the desert.

Any hope of salvaging the SOCCA was dashed in June 2011 when the High Court also knocked out the New South Wales laws, after an application by Derek Wainohu of the Hells Angels. In a majority ruling, the High Court declared the New South Wales laws invalid because they undermined the institutional integrity of the state's Supreme Court.

It was an even bigger win than the South Australians had managed. The court also found that the laws were outside the legislative powers of the New South Wales Parliament. There was virtually no room to move to redraft the South Australian laws.

The two High Court rulings represented an extraordinary achievement. Though Finks and Hells Angels had been the applicants, this was essentially a class action by all bikers against the state governments. And they had won a comprehensive victory. Sonny Barger's Hells Angels had managed to survive the attack under the RICO anti-racketeering laws in the US in the 1970s, but they had never demolished a law the way the Australian bikers had. But being made legal presented its own challenges. The former outlaws had won the right to regulate their own affairs. They had preserved their free horizon of expectation, but what would happen when the conflict was behind them? Some feared that keeping the peace would be much harder (and less exciting) than waging the war.

Perhaps, without a common enemy to fight, the clubs would tire of scoffing party pies and being nice to each other at UMC meetings and eventually fall back into their old ways. Conflict is too ingrained in the psyche of the biker to simply wish it away. No law or police squad could ever stop them fighting.

There was a sense that things were returning to normal in Adelaide. I recently heard my favourite bordello madam was out of bank-ruptcy and entertaining prospective investors for a new Stormy's.

'Adelaide should kiss my arse!' she said, with a burst of cack-ling laughter. 'I'm the best damn brothel keeper this town has ever seen!' She always knew she would be back. 'Sweetheart, in my business, where there's a willy, there's a way,' she said.

In November 2010 the Millennium Drought finally broke, flushing out the dry riverbeds and stagnant lakes of South Aus-tralia. There were good times ahead for farmers. There would be new jobs and business investment across the state.

Australia had avoided the worst of the global financial cri-sis of 2007–08. With better economic times ahead for all, crime would continue to fall naturally, regardless of any get-tough law-and-order policy. And while state governments made magic from statistics to shock and amaze, the other system of rough justice would carry on as best it could in the outlaw nation.

There were many people who could never accept that the bikers had won a victory on behalf of all Australians. That was too much of a U-turn for most. Even the outlaw celebrations at the High Court decisions were fairly low-key. This was just the beginning of the fight, many said. They expected that politicians would counterattack once more with new laws and new squads of cops. There would be more confrontations, more attacks in the media. That's just how the world is for the outlaws. No-one could argue with the fact that the bikers had put aside their differences to work together. In so doing, they had seen that all their club patches were cut from the same cloth.

The FREE Australia Party that Bear from the Gypsy Jokers had created purely to dodge Rann's laws had now taken on a life of its own. It was planned that by the end of 2011, the party would be registered federally and contest national elections. When I started my research into the clubs, I was flat out getting to speak to bikies. Some day in the near future, there might conceivably be one in a parliament somewhere.

And even if the UMCs did not survive long, key members now had each other's phone numbers. They had looked each other in the eye across the table. Pissed fights would not need to become gunfights. But of course, the public would never know anything of this diplomacy, unless of course it all went wrong.

And as one biker told me, outlaws expect nothing more or less than that. 'When we do wrong, no-one forgets. When we do good, no-one remembers,' he said.

On 11 August 2011, a jury found that Mark Standen, the former assistant commissioner of the NSW Crime Commission, had conspired with others to import 300 kilograms of pseudoephedrine and to pervert the course of justice. At the time of writing, Standen was under investigation for further drug importations.

This was 'just the tip of the iceberg', law enforcement sources told the *Sydney Morning Herald*.

This seemed an ideal moment to match the rhetoric of the past six years with the reality.

Politicians and senior police had consistently warned that, if they were to beat the so-called bikie menace, law enforcement needed sweeping new powers. They reassured the doubters that these powers would not be abused. Standen's fall from grace showed the dangerous flaws in such an approach. Standen had used the cover of the secretive and largely unaccountable NSW Crime Commission to involve himself in a transaction that simply dwarfed anything the bikies had been accused of, let alone convicted of. Politicians like Mike Rann had maintained steadfastly that bikies were the ones selling drugs to kids. After the Standen verdict, the scoreboard suggested something quite different.

One pundit suggested to me that, compared with what Standen had been up to, bikie crime was 'four-fifths of fuck-all'. It wasn't exactly quantitative analysis but, at the time of writing, I was still waiting for anything to contradict it.

ACKNOWLEDGEMENTS

I want to express gratitude that my family and I live in Australia where a book such as this can be published. We are blessed with fundamental rights such as freedom of speech and association that other countries can only dream of. These rights should never be traded away for political ends or spurious notions of security. You don't know what you've got until it's gone.

Nonetheless, this has been a difficult book to write. After so much sensationalised media coverage, there is an understandable mistrust of journalists and writers within Australia's 1 per cent community. Motorcycle clubs around the world have rarely explained or complained about their portrayal but there came a time in this country where to remain silent was no longer an option. It has been inspiring to see men of integrity emerge as leaders from their ranks.

I'd like to thank all the motorcycle clubs who have hosted me and put up with my vast ignorance and annoying questions.

The United Motorcycle Councils of South Australia and Queensland and their member clubs have been generous in their support. I thank each and every one for their input to my education. It's ironic that self-regulation through the state and national UMCs has been much more successful at keeping the peace than any new laws or police squads over this period.

There is a long list of members, nominees, associates, families and friends of motorcycle clubs who also deserve thanks for their hospitality and friendship but I respect their wish to remain anonymous. They know who they are.

I owe a debt of gratitude to my friend Richard Walsh who understood the idea of a book that did not stereotype members of motorcycle clubs. Thanks also to my publisher at Allen & Unwin Sue Hines and editor Siobhán Cantrill for their eternal patience and support.

Love and heartfelt thanks to all my family including Noliwe and Jack Shand, their mother Sekai Nzenza-Shand, my parents Dr John and Robin Shand. I'd like to also acknowledge the contribution of my uncle Alec Shand QC who sadly passed away in July 2011 as this work was coming to completion. He helped to shape my view that anti-association laws are bad laws.